Trade Justice

Trade Justice

James Christensen

OXFORD
UNIVERSITY PRESS

OXFORD
UNIVERSITY PRESS

Great Clarendon Street, Oxford, OX2 6DP,
United Kingdom

Oxford University Press is a department of the University of Oxford.
It furthers the University's objective of excellence in research, scholarship,
and education by publishing worldwide. Oxford is a registered trade mark of
Oxford University Press in the UK and in certain other countries

Published in the United States of America by Oxford University Press
198 Madison Avenue, New York, NY 10016, United States of America

British Library Cataloguing in Publication Data
Data available

Library of Congress Control Number: 2017939155

ISBN 978–0–19–881035–3

For my parents,
Angela and William Christensen

Acknowledgements

While writing this book I have accumulated a number of debts. My largest debt is to Simon Caney, who supervised the doctoral thesis upon which the book is closely based. Discussing political philosophy with Simon at Magdalen College—surrounded by books, and with deer grazing in the meadow outside—was a recurrent highlight of my time at Oxford, and the book has benefitted considerably from Simon's input. I am also grateful to Simon for the encouragement he offered. In the early stages of my doctoral research—prior to the publication of Aaron James's path-breaking text on trade justice—I was occasionally tempted to abandon the subject in favour of a more established alternative. Simon persuaded me to stay the course, and I am glad that he did.

I would also like to extend my gratitude to my two thesis examiners, Chris Armstrong and Zosia Stemplowska, both of whom provided valuable feedback, and ensured that my viva was a stimulating and enjoyable experience. In addition, Chris was on hand to offer advice when it came to revising the thesis for publication.

I have received helpful comments from a number of other friends and colleagues, and, with apologies to anyone whom I have accidentally omitted, I would like to thank: Alex Barker, Paul Billingham, Clare Burgum, Ian Carrol, Cecile Fabre, Iason Gabriel, Christine Hobden, Pietro Intropi, Bruno Leipold, Pietro Maffettone, David Miller, Margaret Moore, Tom Parr, Mathias Risse, Zak Taylor, Jesse Tomalty, Katy Wells, Stuart White, and Caleb Yong. I would also like to thank the anonymous OUP reviewers, each of whom offered both encouragement and constructive criticism that enabled me to improve the final draft.

Early drafts of several chapters were presented at the Nuffield Political Theory Workshop and Oxford's Graduate Political Theory Workshop. I am grateful to participants for their feedback. The index was compiled by Kim Stringer, who has done a fine job.

My research was funded by the Arts and Humanities Research Council, Oxford's Department of Politics and International Relations, and Merton College.

Finally, I would like to thank my parents, Angela and William Christensen. I dedicate this book to them.

* * *

In chapters 2 and 5 I make use of material that originally appeared in the following articles, and I am grateful to the publishers for allowing me to do so:

'Weapons, Security, and Oppression: A Normative Study of International Arms Transfers', *The Journal of Political Philosophy*, Vol. 23, No. 1, 2015, pp. 23–39. DOI: 10.1111/jopp.12045.

'Fair Trade, Formal Equality, and Preferential Treatment', *Social Theory and Practice*, Vol. 41, No. 3, 2015, pp. 505–26. DOI: 10.5840/soctheorpract201541326.

Contents

1

Introduction

I

Trade Justice

The global economy encircles us all. It contracts distances and bridges cultures, its workforce occupying sleek offices in New York and Tokyo and airless sweatshops in Jakarta and Manila. It finds expression in the glittering corporate towers of multinational business enterprises and in the desperate struggle of a peasants' revolt. At the heart of the global economy is the international trading system, a complex institutional edifice constructed in the aftermath of the Second World War, its founders anxious to replace volatile, nationalist antagonisms with a commercial, cosmopolitan peace. These lofty ambitions notwithstanding, the trade system remains a locus of fierce social conflict. The protesters who besiege gatherings of its managers—most famously on the streets of Seattle at the turn of the millennium—regard it with suspicion and hostility, as a threat to their livelihoods, an enemy of global justice, and their grievances are exploited by populist statesmen peddling their own mercantilist agendas. If we are to support the trade system, we must first assure ourselves that it can withstand moral scrutiny. We must ensure that it works for and not against those whom it envelops; that it serves to emancipate, not ensnare.

Progress in this domain has been hobbled by theoretical neglect. While international trade has received considerable attention from economists and legal scholars, it has been largely ignored by those trained in normative modes of analytic thought, at least until very recently. This is despite the prominent position assumed in contemporary philosophic discourse by more general questions about the ethics of economic globalization. This neglect is perhaps attributable to scholarly modesty, to an understandable reluctance to wade into an interdisciplinary debate the intellectual boundaries of which lie beyond the limits of one's own expertise.[1] But this explanation for neglect does not constitute a justification. On the contrary, there can be no justification for leaving the subject in the hands of those who—however proficient in their own fields—are ill-equipped to deal with the distinctively normative concerns that lend the subject its particular urgency.

To be sure, answers to pressing normative questions will sometimes hinge on the resolution of economic debates. As suggested a moment ago, the academic contribution to the movement for trade justice must be interdisciplinary in nature. For that reason it will sometimes be necessary for those engaged in normative research to defer to the literature developed by economists. But, as I hope this book will make clear, economics cannot tell us everything that we need to know. Philosophical analysis will prove to be indispensable.

While questions about trade justice have been neglected, some thinkers have ascribed to the trade regime an important role in their treatment of the more general subject of *global* justice. Indeed, the existence of the trade regime played a crucial part in the argumentative strategy of the first major work on this subject—Charles Beitz's *Political Theory and International Relations*.[2] Beitz regarded the trade regime as a central pillar of a larger, international scheme of social cooperation, and argued that such cooperation gives rise to demanding, egalitarian principles of distributive justice. But the principles Beitz identified were not themselves explicitly trade-related. Beitz's principles undoubtedly had implications for the trade regime, but these were not explored. We might say that Beitz was interested in the trade regime only as a *trigger* of justice-based concern, and not as a *subject* of justice-based evaluation, in and of itself. This book addresses the questions that Beitz and his followers disregarded.

II

The Benefits and Burdens of Trade

Some people benefit from trade, while others lose out. Trade exposes identifiable individuals (both human and non-human) to certain *harms*. These range from serious threats to physical safety (created, for example, by international arms transfers) to various socio-economic harms such as the destruction of jobs and the suppression of wages. If we take seriously the demands of justice,

---

[1] The same explanation has been offered for the initial reluctance of philosophers to write about climate change. See Stephen M. Gardiner, 'Ethics and Global Climate Change', *Ethics*, Vol. 114, No. 3, 2004, pp. 555–600, at p. 556.

[2] Charles R. Beitz, *Political Theory and International Relations* (Princeton, NJ: Princeton University Press, 1979).

we must either prevent these harms, or ensure that they can be justified. Our everyday moral judgements suggest that some harms can be inflicted permissibly, while others cannot. A romantic partner might be thought to harm me—in the general sense of setting back my interests—by ending our relationship, but we do not infer from this that she has wronged me in any way. By contrast, when a thief harms me—again in the sense of setting back my interests—by stealing my wallet, we do believe that I have been wronged. We must try to establish whether the various harms created by trade wrong those upon whom they are inflicted, or whether their imposition can be justified. This task is taken up in chapters 2, 3, and 4.

Countries continue to trade, in spite of the harms it inflicts, because of the benefits it promises. The standard case for trade appeals to the economic gains it makes possible.[3] The primary set of economic gains created by trade is revealed by the theory of 'comparative advantage' (or comparative costs), which tells us that trade between two countries can be mutually beneficial even if one country is better than the other at producing all goods and services (that is, even if one country has an 'absolute advantage' in the production of all goods and services). Both countries can benefit by specializing in the production of the goods that they are relatively good at producing (that is, by specializing according to comparative advantage) and exchanging those goods for (or using the income generated by the sale of those goods to import) the goods that they are relatively bad at producing. To put the point differently, trade is beneficial because the opportunity cost of importing a good from abroad can be lower than the opportunity cost associated with producing that good domestically. When a country produces a good that it is relatively bad at producing, instead of purchasing it from elsewhere, it uses resources that could be used more efficiently in alternative lines of production.

Trade has a number of additional economic benefits. For example, trade enables each country to acquire a higher quantity, and a more diverse range, of goods than it could if it were economically isolated (or 'autarkic'). Most importantly, trade can stimulate economic growth. (The gains associated with economic growth are usually referred to as 'dynamic', as opposed to 'static', gains.) Trade can promote growth through a variety of channels. For example, trade exposes domestic firms to foreign competition, which gives them a strong incentive to become more efficient; if they do not, they may not survive. Trade can also encourage growth by facilitating the transfer of technology and

---

[3] Helpful, non-technical statements of the case for free trade are presented in Joseph E. Stiglitz and Andrew Charlton, *Fair Trade for All: How Trade Can Promote Development* (Oxford: Oxford University Press, 2005), Ch. 2, and Douglas A. Irwin, *Free Trade Under Fire: Third Edition* (Princeton, NJ: Princeton University Press, 2009), Ch. 2.

knowledge. Firms in one country are made aware of novel production processes and business methods used by firms in other countries, and are thus able to become more efficient. And, to take one final example, by expanding the size of the market, trade enables firms to take advantage of economies of scale.

While the benefits of trade, and of participation in the trade regime, are widely acknowledged, we may nevertheless ask whether those benefits are distributed in an equitable fashion. In order to answer that question, we need to know what an equitable distribution would look like. What would constitute a 'fair share'? These questions are addressed in chapters 5 and 6.

III

Trade Justice in a Non-Ideal World

I have sketched, with broad brush strokes, the issues that this book addresses, and at the end of the chapter I will outline its contents in more detail. First, however, I should describe the book's methodological approach. My aim here is not to provide a comprehensive theory of perfect justice in trade. Rather, I start with pressing concerns about international trade as we know it, and consider how those concerns can and should be addressed in the short- to medium-term. To use the terminology introduced by John Rawls, much of this book's contents fall on the *non-ideal* side of the ideal/non-ideal divide in political theory. Whereas ideal theory 'presents a conception of a just society that we are to achieve if we can',[4] non-ideal theory 'asks how this long-term goal might be achieved, or worked toward, usually in gradual steps. It looks for courses of action that are morally permissible and politically possible as well as likely to be effective.'[5]

Much contemporary work in political theory is ideal in character, and this focus can be disappointing, even disorienting, for those who come to political theory looking for insights into our present predicament. It is natural to expect political theory to provide assistance in navigating our deeply flawed world, and not simply to map out the contours of some utopian future. Making progress from where we are now is the primary social task, yet it is one that is often neglected in contemporary political thought. In order to ascertain which principles would regulate a perfectly just society, political thinkers engaged in ideal theorizing enquire about the effects that different principles would produce in a world where everyone complied with them; the

---

[4] John Rawls, *A Theory of Justice* (Cambridge, Mass.: Harvard University Press, 1971), p. 246.
[5] John Rawls, *The Law of Peoples* (Cambridge, Mass.: Harvard University Press, 1999), p. 89.

fact that, in our world, many people do not—and sometimes cannot—comply with requirements of justice is set aside. In the universe envisioned by ideal theorists, there are no 'burdened societies' in which 'historical, social, and economic circumstances' make the achievement of justice 'difficult if not impossible',[6] and no 'outlaw states' oppressing their subjects or aggressing against their neighbours.[7]

The approach adopted here, which takes these constraints more seriously, might make my book more accessible to politically engaged readers alive to the problems that blight the world we know. On the other hand, those readers may regard some of my conclusions as disappointingly conservative. I defend the international arms trade, the sale of drugs for use in the administration of the death penalty (under very specific conditions), and the toleration of sweatshop labour. Moreover, while I support restrictions on trade aimed at reducing harms to non-human animals, I do not directly challenge the broader practices of animal exploitation in which those harms are inflicted. It is important to emphasize, then, that these commitments reflect the non-ideal level at which much of the book operates. For political thinkers engaged primarily or exclusively in ideal theory, a number of the questions I address simply do not arise, for the problems that generate them are assumed away. In a world in which everyone understands and complies with the demands of justice, there would be no need for arms, and thus no need for an arms trade; no one would commit crimes that anyone could believe should be punishable by death; no human being would be so desperately poor as to countenance working gruelling shifts in appalling conditions for rapacious multinational corporations; and the remarkable creatures with whom we share the planet would not be ruthlessly exploited and abused by human chauvinists.

Those who focus on ideal theorizing recognize that an account of what is required of us in the here and now may appear considerably less attractive than a theory of perfect justice. Rawls, who placed so much emphasis on the importance of liberty, acknowledged that the 'denial of the equal liberties can be defended . . . when it is essential to change the conditions of civilization',[8] and G. A. Cohen, who placed so much emphasis on the importance of equality, acknowledged that the 'demand [for egalitarian justice] can seem shrill, and even dangerous' when implementing equality might counteract a process that is improving the condition of the worst-off.[9] But, given their focus on ideal theory, these acknowledgements appear at the periphery of their respective works, and they are not concessions with which either

---

[6] Rawls, *Law of Peoples*, p. 5.   [7] Rawls, *Law of Peoples*, p. 90, fn. 1.
[8] Rawls, *Theory of Justice*, p. 132.
[9] G. A. Cohen, *Self-Ownership, Freedom, and Equality* (Cambridge: Cambridge University Press, 1995), p. 10.

philosopher is readily associated. The more conservative measures that I defend here are proposed in the same spirit as those countenanced by Rawls and Cohen: as temporary, transitional measures to be tolerated only until civilization arrives.

While this book makes a number of concessions to the non-ideal circumstances in which we find ourselves, it also advances some bolder proposals. In the final chapter, for example, I argue that the trade regime should be regulated by demanding, egalitarian principles of distributive justice. My hope is that the book's relatively conservative elements will be balanced by those that are more radical.

IV

A Partially Integrated Approach

In addition to distinguishing between ideal and non-ideal theory, we should recognize that an approach to trade justice can be either 'isolationist' or 'integrationist'.[10] According to isolationist approaches, we should conceive of justice in trade as a discrete subject, and not as one part of a larger theory of global justice. While accounts of, say, global distributive justice and global environmental justice will advance various principles applicable in the international domain, those principles should be set aside or bracketed when attempting to establish the requirements of just trade. In other words, questions about trade justice should be treated in isolation. Integrationist accounts, by contrast, insist that our account of just trade must be conceived as one part of a larger theory of global justice. When deciding which trade policies can be demanded as a matter of justice, we should take into consideration principles vindicated by accounts of, *inter alia*, global distributive justice and global environmental justice. Our accounts of the various strands of global justice should be integrated into a comprehensive whole.

Both approaches have advantages and disadvantages. One virtue of the isolationist approach is that it makes our task more manageable. By bracketing various aspects of the global justice debate, isolationism allows us to focus our attention on the subject at hand. By contrast, integrationism can seem excessively demanding. Indeed, a fully integrationist approach would yield not merely an account of just trade, but rather a general account of global

---

[10] The terms 'isolationism' and 'integrationism' are borrowed from Simon Caney. See his 'Global Justice, Climate Change, and Human Rights', in Douglas A. Hicks and Thad Williamson (eds.) *Leadership and Global Justice* (Basingstoke: Palgrave Macmillan, 2012), and 'Just Emissions', *Philosophy & Public Affairs*, Vol. 40, No. 4, 2012, pp. 255–300.

justice that includes, as one constitutive element, an account of just trade, but that also comprises accounts of global distributive justice, global environmental justice, and so forth. On the other hand, a fully isolationist approach to trade can seem overly narrow, and fatally insensitive to other relevant aspects of global justice.

As the above references to 'fully' integrationist and isolationist approaches suggest, integrationism and isolationism are best seen as two extremes appearing at opposite ends of a spectrum—rather than as two views that exhaust all possible options—with the best approach perhaps lying somewhere in between. Such an 'intermediate' path is sought in this book. Sometimes I defend a particular trade-related view by invoking more general principles of global justice, but the principles to which I appeal are minimally controversial, and can be endorsed by a wide variety of perspectives. For example, in chapter 5 I appeal to the notion that there is a duty to alleviate severe poverty, and consider some trade-related implications of this duty. By doing this I pursue an approach that is, in one relevant respect, integrationist—I derive trade-related conclusions by appealing to a general principle of global distributive justice—without burdening my account with the task of justifying a controversial distributive principle. Elsewhere I show that a variety of different general views can converge upon the same or similar trade-related conclusions. I do this in discussions of compensatory transfer payments (chapter 4), special and differential treatment (chapter 5), and distributive equality (chapter 6). Again, this allows me to avoid the narrowness of isolationist approaches without assuming the demanding responsibilities of an approach that is fully integrationist. When it can be shown that a particular conclusion is defensible from a variety of competing perspectives, offering a robust defence of any single perspective becomes less essential.

V

Duty Bearers

A final methodological question that needs to be considered concerns the addressees of an account of trade justice. A conception of justice should be action-guiding, but whose actions should it aim to guide? Upon whom do duties of justice fall? In the context of trade, there are a number of candidate duty bearers. Duty bearers have been variously identified as states, the World Trade Organization (WTO), consumers, and private firms. Let us consider each of these potential duty bearers in turn.

(i) States have a number of trade-based duties of justice. The deliberations of states, both within the WTO and elsewhere, determine the content of trade-related agreements. In other words, states choose the rules that are to govern international trade. Thus, states have a duty to negotiate toward just agreements. In addition to this, states also have a duty to comply with trade-related agreements, at least when those agreements are adequately just. By virtue of their role in formulating rules for trade, states are regarded here as the *primary* bearers of trade-related duties of justice.

(ii) Those who take to the streets to protest in the name of trade justice often direct their complaints at the WTO itself. While there undoubtedly *are* principles of justice that should regulate the WTO, these principles are likely to be fairly minimal. In addition to providing a forum for deliberation, one of the primary functions of the WTO is to monitor the trade policies of member states and to ensure that WTO agreements are being implemented. The WTO is also required to resolve disputes that arise between members.[11] Thus, the duties of justice borne by the WTO can be regarded as obligations of *formal* justice. An institution is formally just when its rules are enforced consistently and impartially. As Rawls puts it: 'If we think of justice as always expressing a kind of equality, then formal justice requires that in their administration laws and institutions should apply equally (that is, in the same way) to those belonging to the classes defined by them.' He adds: 'Formal justice is adherence to principle, or as some have said, obedience to system.'[12]

(iii) Much popular normative discourse about trade has focused on the putative obligations of individual consumers. The Fair Trade movement, for example, implores consumers to purchase goods produced by firms that pay adequate wages, provide acceptable working conditions, and so forth. Questions regarding the trade-related duties of consumers are bracketed here on account of the relatively small role that consumers can play in realizing trade justice. Consumers cannot determine the incidence of tariff barriers, or the level of domestic subsidies; they cannot offer compensation to displaced workers, or redistribute the gains from trade; they cannot prevent the exportation of weapons to oppressive regimes, or exempt poor countries from certain rules; and so forth. The major decisions that affect the justness of trade are made by states.[13]

---

[11] The nature of the dispute settlement procedure is determined by negotiations between states. A just procedure is one of the things that states are obligated to negotiate towards.
[12] Rawls, *Theory of Justice*, p. 51.
[13] On the duties of consumers, see Andrew Walton, 'The Common Arguments for Fair Trade', *Political Studies*, Vol. 61, No. 3, 2013, pp. 691–706.

(iv) A number of trade-related duties of justice are borne by private firms, though I will not have much to say about these here. First, private firms are required to comply with the rules agreed by states, at least when those rules are adequately just. Second, given the influence many large firms can exert over legislative processes, such firms must refrain from using that influence to lobby for unjust legislation. Finally, firms may be required to refrain from engaging in certain types of commercial activity—e.g. selling arms to oppressive regimes—even if such activity is not legally proscribed.

VI

Outline of the Book

Let me conclude this introduction by outlining the content of the chapters to follow. Chapter 2 begins our enquiry into the harms of trade. More specifically, it considers various ways in which trade poses serious threats to physical safety, and thus appears to stand in tension with basic rights to life and limb ('security rights'). The largest part of the chapter is given over to an examination of the arms trade, a topic that political philosophers have virtually ignored. I argue that an ethically defensible arms trade is possible, but that we must refrain from selling certain kinds of weapons, and that selling weapons to certain kinds of government will rarely be justifiable. I also consider the practice of arming revolutionary groups, and argue that the relative merits of this way of supporting such groups should be reassessed. The next part of the chapter considers the permissibility of selling drugs to states that are likely to use them to administer the death penalty. I argue for the counter-intuitive conclusion that states that oppose the death penalty on the grounds that it violates security rights may sometimes be permitted, and even required, to export drugs commonly used to execute convicts. The final part of the chapter considers the practice of transferring hazardous waste to developing countries. I argue that, unless certain demanding conditions are satisfied, such transfers violate security rights.

Whereas chapter 2 argues that trade must be restricted in order to protect humans from serious physical harms, chapter 3 contends that trade must be restricted in order to protect the physical integrity of non-human animals. For strategic reasons, I aim to defend animal-protecting trade restrictions without appealing to the claim that animals have rights, or that animal interests carry as much weight as human interests. The first part of the chapter identifies the aims of animal-protecting trade restrictions, the values they are intended to serve, and the nature of the harms they are used to prevent or reduce. The second part of the chapter examines a variety of objections to animal-protecting trade restrictions, and argues that those objections can be answered.

Chapter 4 concludes our enquiry into the harms of trade. It addresses the ethical implications of the fact that trade can harm individuals by destroying jobs, suppressing wages, and undermining cultural distinctiveness. I argue that, under certain circumstances, concerns about socio-economic losses and cultural degradation can justify trade restrictions. However, I also argue that developed countries may restrict trade only on the condition that the restrictions they impose do not reduce the development prospects of poor countries. Toward the end of the chapter I defend the right of developing countries to restrict trade with developed countries.

At this stage in the book, the focus shifts from the burdens of trade to its benefits. The trade regime provides its members with opportunities to access the markets of others, and chapter 5 considers the claim that these opportunities must be allocated in a particular way. More specifically, it considers the claim that the distribution of these opportunities must conform to an ideal of 'formal equality', according to which all states are to receive and offer equal, or uniform, treatment (e.g. by matching the market liberalization efforts of others). The first section of the chapter explicates the idea of formal equality and its rationales, identifies a number of positive arguments for departing from formal equality, and rebuts several objections to granting 'special and differential treatment' to developing countries. The second section analyses one specific element of formal equality in the trade regime, namely, the principle of reciprocity, and argues that that principle should not be regarded as a requirement of fairness. The next section considers the claim that without the 'harmonization' of domestic laws and policies, market access will be impeded by a slanted playing field that unfairly weakens the competitiveness of some countries and firms. This fairness-based argument for harmonization is rejected.

Chapter 6 focuses on the income gains made possible by trade and asks how these should be distributed. I argue that these gains should be distributed in a globally egalitarian fashion, and contend that this conclusion is supported by a wide range of diverse views. The majority of the chapter criticizes the 'statist' claim that principles of distributive equality apply only within states and not among them. I argue that statists cannot draw a sharp normative distinction between states and the trade regime because the normatively relevant relationships they identify within the former also exist among members of the latter.

2

The Harms of Trade I

Weapons, Drugs, and Hazardous Waste

In September 2015, eight protesters were arrested during a demonstration outside a Defence & Security Equipment International (DSEI) event in London. The protesters, who claimed they were trying to prevent the unlawful sale of weapons that would be used to commit human rights violations abroad, were subsequently acquitted on the grounds that 'clear' and 'credible' evidence of illegal weapons sales had not been challenged by the prosecution.[1] This incident highlights perhaps the most serious concern about international trade: that it facilitates the infliction of severe physical harm and thereby undermines basic rights to life and bodily integrity ('security rights'). And arms transfers do not constitute the only form of international trade that appears to threaten these rights. The sale of drugs to regimes that are likely to use them to administer the death penalty also stands in tension with rights to security, as do transfers of hazardous waste to the developing world. Weapons, lethal drugs, and hazardous waste all have in common a capacity to cause serious physical harm. Furthermore, arms and lethal drugs are purchased *because* they have that capacity.

This chapter considers whether—and under what conditions—these trades can be justified. The largest part of the chapter is devoted to a discussion of the arms trade. Despite its controversy, the arms trade has been virtually ignored by political philosophers, and thus merits considerable attention. In the first section, I introduce the right to security, and show how that right can play a central role in justifying an arms trade. I then move on to show that the right

---

[1] Jon Stone, 'Protesters who blockaded London arms trade fair acquitted after judge sees evidence of illegal weapons on sale', *The Independent*, 15 April 2016 (available at: http://www.independent.co.uk/news/uk/politics/dsei-protesters-acquitted-london-arms-fair-illegal-weapons-sales-a6985766.html).

to security can also ground a *pro tanto* case for restricting the arms trade in certain ways. More specifically, I argue that the right to security grounds a *pro tanto* case for the claim that states are duty-bound to refrain from trading certain types of weapons, and to refrain from selling weapons to regimes that exhibit an oppressive character. Section II explicates, and responds to, an argument commonly used to defend the sale of arms to oppressive regimes. According to this argument, states have a special duty to protect the security of their citizens, and discharging that duty sometimes involves providing weapons to those oppressive regimes that are well placed to suppress terrorist threats. In section III, I consider and rebut two further objections to the claim that states must refrain from selling weapons to oppressive regimes. In section IV, I consider the permissibility of supplying weapons to rebel groups engaged in revolutionary war against an oppressive regime. I argue that while supporting such groups may be permissible, or even required, supporting them by providing arms is, from a moral perspective, highly problematic.

When I use phrases like 'states are duty-bound to refrain from selling weapons to X', I shall mean both that states are themselves duty-bound to refrain from selling weapons to X, and that states are duty-bound to prevent their citizens (e.g. their arms companies) from selling weapons to X. While it is plausible to think that states are required to refrain from doing certain things that their citizens are permitted to do, I take it that the reasons I adduce in support of the claim that states are duty-bound to refrain from making certain arms transfers also support the claim that citizens are duty-bound to refrain from making those transfers. I also take it that the duties borne by citizens can permissibly be enforced by the state. The duties I identify are conceived as duties of justice, and, more specifically, as duties to refrain from engaging in activities that violate the (security) rights of others. I endorse the common view that such duties may be coercively enforced.

In sections V and VI, I consider the permissibility of exporting certain products that, while not weapons, have weapon-like qualities, viz. have the capacity to inflict serious physical harm. Section V considers the exportation of drugs to states that are likely to use those drugs to administer the death penalty. I note certain similarities between this trade and the sale of arms to oppressive regimes. But I reach the perhaps unexpected conclusion that it can be permissible, and, in some cases, obligatory, for a state to export execution drugs, even if that state believes that capital punishment violates security rights. Finally, in section VI, I examine the morality of transferring hazardous waste to developing countries. I argue that, if such transfers are to be permissible, a number of very demanding conditions must be satisfied. Unless those conditions are met, waste transfers to developing countries violate rights to security.

I

Arms Sales and Security

It is natural to feel instinctively uneasy about the existence of markets in weapons, and some activists call for the arms trade to be completely abolished.[2] While this stance is, perhaps, understandable, it is, I think, ultimately misguided: an ethically defensible arms trade is possible. The first step in my argument for this claim is to note that all persons have a right to security, or, perhaps more accurately, that all persons have a cluster of security *rights*: rights not to be assaulted, tortured, raped, poisoned, killed, and so forth. In short, all persons have a right to *physical safety*.[3] As Henry Shue has observed, there are not many people who would be willing to deny that all persons possess this minimal right.[4] The right to security generates a variety of correlative duties. For now, notice that it puts states under a duty to protect the security of their citizens. The next important step in the argument is to point out that, in order to discharge this duty, states need weapons (or at least that in all realistically imaginable scenarios they need weapons). Without weapons, states would be unable to protect their citizens from armed aggressors (armed criminals, terrorist groups, belligerent regimes, etc.). Weapons enable states to both deter and repel such threats, and thus to protect their citizens' security.

It might be said that, in theory, states could protect their citizens' right to security not by acquiring weapons with which to deter and repel armed aggressors, but rather by bringing about the worldwide abolition of weapons. There are multiple reasons for dismissing this claim. First, and most obviously, bringing about the worldwide abolition of weapons is not an option that is realistically available to states. Second, even if states agreed to mutual disarmament, there would always be the very real possibility that certain states would secretly retain their arsenals. And, third, even if mutual disarmament was achieved at time T, there would always be the very real possibility that certain states would (perhaps secretly) rearm at time T + n. When a state disarms, it leaves itself and its citizens vulnerable, even if other states have also agreed to disarm.

Now, some states lack the capacity to produce their own weapons, or at least to produce weapons of adequate quality and in sufficient quantities.

---

[2] This position is taken by the Campaign Against the Arms Trade (CAAT). See CAAT, 'About CAAT: Ending the Arms Trade' (available at: http://www.caat.org.uk/).

[3] For this conception of the right to security see Henry Shue, *Basic Rights: Subsistence, Affluence, and US Foreign Policy (Second Edition)* (Princeton, NJ: Princeton University Press), pp. 20–2. For a more expansive conception of the right see Jeremy Waldron, *Torture, Terror, and Trade-Offs: Philosophy for the White House* (Oxford: Oxford University Press, 2010), Ch. 5. I will add some depth to the notion of security as I proceed.

[4] Shue, *Basic Rights*, p. 21.

Consequently, in order to acquire weapons of adequate quality and in sufficient quantities, and to discharge their duty to protect the safety of their citizens, such states must import weapons from abroad. If these states were unable to import weapons—if no international trade in weapons were permitted—they would not be able to ensure the security of their citizens. Blocking all international arms transfers would penalize states that lack the capacity to produce their own weapons, and unjustifiably jeopardize the security of the people who live in those states.[5]

The argument presented in the previous paragraph establishes that international trade in (at least certain kinds of) weapons can be morally permissible when it consists in transfers to states that lack the capacity to produce weapons (of adequate quality and in sufficient quantities), and that import weapons in order to discharge their duty to protect their citizens' security. But a great many international arms transfers are not of this kind. For most of the twentieth century, the largest arms exporters mainly sold weapons to other economically developed countries,[6] most of which, by virtue of being economically developed, presumably either possessed or could acquire the capacity to produce weapons of adequate quality and in sufficient quantities. The argument presented above does not explicitly vindicate these kinds of transfers. But it does provide the resources needed to do so. It establishes that weapons have a legitimate function, viz. they enable states to discharge their duty to protect the security of their citizens. And if weapons have a legitimate function, it is hard to see why trade in weapons would be morally permissible only when it consists in transfers to states that lack the capacity to produce weapons of their own. If a state possesses the capacity to produce its own weapons, but has a comparative disadvantage in weapons manufacturing, it makes sense for that state to purchase weapons from abroad and to devote the resources it would have otherwise used to manufacture weapons to alternative lines of production. If weapons have a legitimate function, then it is at least *pro tanto* acceptable for a state to produce weapons, and if it is acceptable for a state to produce weapons, it is acceptable for a state to eschew weapons production and purchase weapons from abroad, which a state has a good reason to do when it lacks a comparative advantage in weapons production.

---

[5] It might be argued that a state can protect the security of its citizens without possessing weapons of its own. It could do this by entering into an agreement whereby its citizens are protected by the security forces of another state. But few people would be willing to surrender responsibility for their security to another sovereign state—many people are unwilling to surrender responsibility for their security to *their own* state—for a situation could arise in which that state is no longer able or willing to fulfil its obligations. This is not to deny that states are often dependent to some degree upon their allies for protection, but simply to point out that states are typically eager to avoid *complete* dependence.

[6] Rachel Stohl and Suzette Grillot, *The International Arms Trade* (Cambridge, Polity Press: 2009), p. 22.

The arms trade, then, can be justified by appeal to the right to security. States are permitted to purchase weapons either because doing so is (i) necessary to protect their citizens' security, or (ii) the most efficient way of protecting their citizens' security. And in order for a state to be able to purchase weapons, others must be permitted to sell weapons. (A state is able to purchase weapons provided that there is at least one supplier, and irrespective of whether private firms are permitted to sell weapons in addition to state-owned firms, but the advantages associated with allowing multiple suppliers to compete in a market at least ground a presumption against denying private firms permission to offer their services.)[7]

So far, I have defended the moral permissibility of (a form of) the arms trade by appealing to the value of security. But that same value can be used to identify moral limits to the arms trade. More specifically, the value of security can be used to discern limits on the range of weapon-types that may permissibly be traded, and on the range of appropriate recipients of arms transfers. There is much to say about the latter issue, but, first, let us briefly address the former. All weapons are designed to incapacitate, injure, or kill, and so all weapons pose a threat to individuals' physical safety. But some weapons pose an unacceptably large threat to individuals who have not made themselves liable to attack, and who are thus not permissible targets. Paradigmatic examples of such weapons include landmines and nerve gas, both of which kill and maim indiscriminately. These weapons pose a threat that is either spatially or temporally extended to an unusual and excessive degree. Nerve gas generates harms that are highly diffuse; it can travel large distances and kill non-combatants far from the battlefield. The threat posed by landmines has a shorter range, but extends far into the future: people continue to be killed and dismembered by unexploded mines long after hostilities have ceased. Ammunition containing depleted uranium, which was used extensively by British and US forces in Iraq and the Balkans, also potentially falls into this category. Upon impact, depleted uranium shells release radioactive particles that are potentially cancer-causing, persist in the environment for decades, and can travel far from the site where they were originally released.[8]

---

[7] It might be argued that arms markets can be criticized on the grounds that they enable firms to profit from injustice: arms companies profit when states purchase weapons from them in order to protect themselves against unjust aggressors. But notice that this is by no means a distinctive feature of arms markets. Insurance markets also enable private firms to profit from injustice; as do markets in locks and intruder alarms: firms operating in these markets profit because some people refuse to respect the property rights of others. Yet no one proposes abolishing these markets. This is because we believe that concerns about profiting from injustice are outweighed by countervailing considerations. My sense is that the same is true for arms markets. In any case, my aim here will be to identify restrictions on the scope of arms markets that can be grounded in the same value that justifies arms transfers in the first place, namely, the value of security.

[8] Sandra S. Wise et al., 'Particulate Depleted Uranium Is Cytotoxic and Clastogenic to Human Lung Cells', *Chemical Research in Toxicology*, Vol. 20, No. 5, 2007, pp. 815–20; Randall R. Parrish et al.,

It is not my intention to discuss this issue in any depth, for the primary question regarding weapons in this category is whether it is ever permissible to *use* such weapons, and thus whether they should be manufactured in the first place. But, given that these weapons exist, and that states possess them, it is worth at least acknowledging that if their use is impermissible, their sale is too. If, for agent-neutral reasons, it is impermissible to use a particular item, it is also impermissible to enable, and benefit from enabling, the use of that item by others.[9]

Let us now consider limits imposed by the right to security on the range of appropriate recipients of arms transfers. I noted earlier that the right to security imposes upon states a duty to protect the security of their own citizens. In addition to this duty, the right to security puts states under a duty to refrain from depriving any person, wherever she resides, of the substance of that right. Indeed, 'the core of the right [to security] is a right that others not act in certain ways',[10] and, given their capacity to inflict great harm, states are certainly included among those others. Some states fail to honour this duty with respect to individuals living beyond their jurisdiction. They behave in a wrongfully aggressive and provocative manner, waging unjust wars, arming militant groups attempting to overthrow legitimate governments, and supplying weapons to terrorist organizations. Sometimes they engage in terroristic activity themselves.[11]

Some states violate the security rights of their own citizens. Some fail to provide an adequate degree of security, while others actively deprive their citizens of their security. Their police and military forces kill unarmed protesters, torture dissidents, beat prisoners, rape civilians, and engage in various other violent crimes. For many individuals, the very agent that is duty-bound to protect them represents the primary threat to their security. Indeed, acknowledgement of the threat states pose to their own citizens has recently prompted

---

'Depleted uranium contamination by inhalation exposure and its detection after $\sim$ 20 years: Implications for human health assessment', *Science of the Total Environment*, Vol. 390, No. 1, 2008, pp. 58–68.

[9] One complication arises from the fact that it might be permissible to possess and threaten to use certain weapons, even if it would be impermissible to follow through with that threat. This might well be true of nuclear weapons, which represent a special category of weapons. Given the spatially and temporally extended nature of the threat posed by nuclear weapons, and the severity of the harm they can inflict, the use of nuclear weapons is surely impermissible. But threatening to use nuclear weapons might be permissible precisely because such threats render the use of nuclear weapons less likely. Perhaps what we should say is that it is impermissible to sell (and thus enable others to use) weapons that it is impermissible to use unless one can be reasonably sure that the states to which one sells those weapons will not actually use them. Or at least we should say this about nuclear weapons, which occupy a special category all of their own.

[10] Shue, *Basic Rights*, p. 39.

[11] On terrorist states see Robert E. Goodin, *What's Wrong with Terrorism?* (Cambridge: Polity Press, 2006), Ch. 4.

a shift of focus among scholars and international institutions from the security of states (state security) to the security of individuals (human security).[12]

While it is clear that duties generated by the right to security are violated by regimes that kill and injure innocent members of their own citizenry, or wrongfully aggress against foreign countries, there is good reason to think that those duties are also often violated by states that provide arms to regimes that kill and injure their own innocent citizens or wrongfully aggress against foreign countries. When a state arms such regimes it facilitates, and thus becomes complicit in, those regimes' crimes. States therefore have a *pro tanto* duty to refrain from arming such regimes.[13] In the following two sections, I will defend this claim against several objections. I will focus on the claim that states must refrain from selling (and must prevent their citizens from selling) weapons to regimes that oppress their own citizens, but most of what I say also applies to states that wrongfully aggress against other countries.

II

Arming Oppressive Regimes

The claim that states must refrain from arming oppressive regimes can be resisted in the following manner. One might argue that the duties generated by the right to security sometimes conflict, in the sense that situations sometimes arise in which a state must choose between discharging its security-related duties to its own citizens and discharging its security-related duties to citizens of other states. In such cases, the argument claims, states may permissibly opt to discharge their duties to their own citizens, at the expense of the fulfilment of their duties to the citizens of other states. Or, put more modestly,

---

[12] Ved P. Nanda, 'Preemptive and Preventive Use of Force, Collective Security, and Human Security', *Denver Journal of International Law and Policy*, Vol. 33, 2004, pp. 7–15, at p. 10. The idea of human security is usually thought to possess multiple dimensions. We can endorse some aspects of the human security approach while rejecting others. For example, we can agree that security should refer, in the first instance, to the safety of individuals, and only derivatively to the integrity of state institutions, without signing up to the idea that security refers to protection from all kinds of threats, including threats from poverty.

[13] An especially difficult question concerns the provision of weapons to states that are legitimate (and that a fortiori, discharge their security-related duties to the degree that they are able to do so) but are also unstable (i.e. are liable to being overthrown by (unjust) internal or external aggressors). On the one hand, unstable states may have an especially strong claim to weapons transfers by virtue of the fact that they may urgently need weapons in order to protect their vulnerable position. But, on the other hand, there is a strong risk that any weapons transferred to unstable states will fall into the hands of unjust agents if and when those states are overthrown. A state may be legitimate at time T, when weapons transfers are made, but illegitimate at T + n, after the machinery of government has been taken over by militants. A related concern is discussed in more detail in section IV, which considers the permissibility of transferring weapons to rebel groups seeking to overthrow oppressive regimes.

states may permissibly opt to discharge certain duties to their own citizens, at the expense of the fulfilment of certain duties to the citizens of other states. The argument continues: states can sometimes enhance the security of their citizens by providing weapons to oppressive regimes, because such regimes are sometimes willing to contribute to the suppression of terrorist threats. When states can enhance the security of their citizens in this way, they are duty-bound to transfer arms to oppressive regimes.

This argument might be used in an attempt to defend recent US foreign policy decisions. Since the terrorist attacks of 11 September 2001, the US has increased arms supplies to a variety of oppressive regimes on the grounds that those regimes, if well equipped, can play a valuable role in the 'war on terror', and thereby positively contribute to the security of US citizens. As Rachel Stohl and Suzette Grillot observe, recent US arms export policy has put commitments to refrain from arming oppressive regimes

> on the backburner in order to give highest priority to countries which are supporting US efforts in Iraq and Afghanistan and which assist in the eradication of international terrorist networks... An analysis of twenty-five countries that play strategic roles in the United States' global anti-terror operations finds that the events of 11 September 2001 have dramatically increased US arms sales to countries that have been repeatedly criticized by the US State Department for human rights violations... In 2006, the US State Department reported that 'serious', 'grave,' or 'significant' abuses were committed by the government or state security forces in more than half of these twenty-five countries.[14]

It is tempting to reply to the claim that sates have a duty to arm oppressive regimes when, by doing so, they can enhance the security of their own citizens by arguing as follows: a state's duty to enhance the security of its own citizens is a *positive* duty, whereas a state's duty to refrain from undermining the security of others is a *negative* duty, and that, other things being equal, honouring negative duties takes priority over discharging positive duties. This strategy has two weaknesses. First, some people will deny that the distinction between positive and negative duties carries much (if any) weight. And, second, it is not obvious that a state's duty to enhance the security of its citizens is best conceived of as a positive duty. One might maintain that there is a negative duty not to assume a particular role and then fail to perform the functions associated with that role,[15] that providing security is a primary function of the state, and that state officials therefore violate a negative duty when they decline to take measures necessary to enhance the security of their citizens. Given these weaknesses, I will criticize

---

[14] Stohl and Grillot, *International Arms Trade*, pp. 34–5 (footnote omitted).
[15] Thomas Pogge, 'Are We Violating the Human Rights of the World's Poor?', *Yale Human Rights and Development Law Journal*, Vol. 14, No. 2, 2011, pp. 1–33, at p. 11.

the claim that states must arm oppressive regimes when doing so conduces to their citizens' security without appealing to the distinction between positive and negative duties. I will identify four problems that the claim faces.

The first problem the argument encounters concerns its empirical claim that states can enhance the security of their citizens—and, more specifically, reduce the threat they face from terrorism—by arming certain oppressive regimes. In his discussion of trade-offs between security and liberty, Jeremy Waldron argues that those who recommend curtailing civil liberties in order to reduce the threat to security posed by terrorist organizations must show that the curtailments they propose will actually have a positive impact upon security.[16] An analogous argument applies here. Those who advocate arming oppressive regimes on the grounds that doing so will enhance domestic security must be able to demonstrate convincingly that the security gains they envisage will actually be forthcoming. They must, in particular, be able to counter the common claim that arming a regime that a terrorist group opposes will actually increase that group's hostility towards us, swell its ranks, and strengthen its resolve. This will not be easy.

A second problem concerns the argument's normative claim that states have a duty to arm oppressive regimes when doing so enhances the security of their citizens. This claim is problematic because the right to security is not plausibly conceived of as a right to be *maximally* secure. This is not just because, specified in such a way, the right to security could not be adequately reconciled with other rights (such as the right to privacy), or because, specified in such a way, it would generate duties that are, in an absolute sense, overly demanding. It is also because the interest in being maximally, as opposed to *reasonably*, secure is not weighty enough to place others under a duty. To illustrate this point, consider the duties imposed upon a mother by her child's right to security. The mother may be able to enhance her child's security by hiring a guard to patrol the perimeter of their house; hiring a security guard might reduce the probability that a dangerous intruder will break in and pose a threat to the child. Moreover, hiring a security guard might not be financially burdensome (suppose the mother is quite wealthy), and we can stipulate that hiring a security guard would not violate anyone's rights (or wrong anyone in any other way). Still, provided that the probability of a house invasion is already low—suppose the mother and child live in a reasonably safe neighbourhood—it does not seem plausible to claim that the child's right imposes upon her mother a *duty* to hire a security guard. By hiring a security guard the mother goes *beyond* the call of duty; she provides her child with more than the *adequate* degree of security to which her child is entitled. The

---

[16] Waldron, *Torture, Terror, and Trade-Offs*, pp. 44–5.

upshot of these considerations is this: in order to show that the right to security imposes upon states a duty to transfer arms to oppressive regimes it is not sufficient to show that such transfers will have a positive impact on security; rather, what must be shown is that arming oppressive regimes will contribute to providing the adequate degree of security that the right to security is a right to.

Suppose that the previous two problems can be surmounted. Suppose we have good reason to think that by arming oppressive regimes a state can increase, and not diminish, the amount of security enjoyed by its citizens, and that the extra security it can provide is owed as a matter of right. A third problem is that, in order to vindicate the provision of weapons to oppressive regimes, it must be shown that there are not acceptable alternative methods for generating the extra security that such provision offers. Citizens may currently enjoy less security than they are entitled to, but if the state can make up for the shortfall using one of several different available methods, they do not have a duty to use one method in particular.

States have at their disposal a wide variety of strategies for protecting their citizens from terrorist attack,[17] many of which appear less morally problematic than arming oppressive regimes (which is not to say that they are all entirely unproblematic from a moral perspective). These strategies include: measures that block terrorist financing; various kinds of psychological operations ('psyops') including those that counter terrorist propaganda (by, for example, 'amplifying the voices of Islamic scholars who explicitly reject or contradict radical Islamist dogma'[18]), and disinformation campaigns aimed at sowing discord within terrorist organizations; surveillance programmes that make use of advanced technology (e.g. CCTV cameras equipped with face recognition capabilities); target hardening; and critical infrastructure protection. States can also pursue more long-term policies aimed at eliminating the conditions that facilitate terrorist radicalization and recruitment. These can include foreign aid programmes, development projects, and debt cancellation. Those who advocate arming oppressive regimes as a means of enhancing security must demonstrate that (some combination of) these measures, and others like them, are either (i) insufficiently effective, or (ii) unacceptable for non-efficacy-based reasons. Given the strong *pro tanto* reasons we have to refrain from transferring weapons to oppressive regimes, the burden of proof must lie with those who support such transfers.

The final problem is also the most serious. Suppose that our interest in a certain quantity of security is sufficiently weighty to impose upon our state a duty to provide us with that quantity of security. Suppose, too, that our state

---

[17] Ronald D. Crelinsten, *Counterterrorism* (Cambridge: Polity Press, 2009).
[18] Crelinsten, *Counterterrorism*, p. 142.

can provide that quantity of security only by supplying weapons to an oppressive regime. Even if these conditions hold, it does not follow that our state is under a duty to supply the weapons. This becomes clear when we notice that the duty that our interest in a particular quantity of security imposes upon our state has not yet been adequately specified. This duty is not plausibly conceived of as a duty to provide the relevant quantity of security *whatever it takes*, but rather as a duty to provide that quantity of security if and when it can be provided through morally permissible means.

Consider an analogy. Suppose I am expected to attend a close friend's wedding, and that, on the way to the ceremony, I get caught in a traffic jam. As a result of the delay, I can get to the wedding on time only by driving at dangerously high speeds and running red lights. Clearly, I am not permitted to drive at dangerously high speeds and run red lights. The set of options morally available to me is not expanded by the fact that the normal option-set is too restrictive to enable me to get to the wedding on time. Moreover, provided that I allowed myself a reasonable amount of time to travel to the wedding, and that the traffic jam could not have reasonably been foreseen, we should deny that by arriving late to the wedding I have violated a duty to my friend. If I had a duty to be on time, then clearly my late arrival would constitute a violation of that duty. But we should deny that I had such a duty, and say instead that I had a duty to pursue a morally permissible course of action that could reasonably be expected to get me to the wedding on time. (When we say that one has a duty to be on time to a friend's wedding it is this more nuanced duty that we actually have in mind. The shorter phrase is convenient shorthand.) I would violate that duty if I carelessly failed to leave myself enough time to travel to the wedding, or if I chose to take a circuitous scenic route, and was late as a result. But I would also violate that duty if, after being innocently delayed by a traffic jam that I could not have reasonably anticipated, I proceeded to drive at dangerously high speeds and run red lights, thereby recklessly endangering other motorists and pedestrians. Similarly, by arming oppressive regimes, a state violates its duty to provide a particular quantity of security if and when that quantity can be provided through morally permissible means. Arming an oppressive regime is not a morally permissible means as it inflicts undue harms on those who are vulnerable to its oppression, just as driving at dangerously high speeds inflicts undue harms on other motorists and pedestrians.

Now, it might be objected that, in the case I described, driving dangerously fast and running red lights is impermissible because the harms it inflicts (including risks) are disproportionate to the gains I was trying to secure by not disappointing my friend. But, it might be argued, dangerous driving would be permissible in a case in which the harms (including risks) it inflicts were proportional to the gains the driver sought to obtain. Suppose there is a man in my car who will die unless he receives immediate medical attention. In such a scenario, it seems that I am morally permitted to drive in a manner that imposes upon other motorists and pedestrians a degree of risk that is higher than that which could permissibly be imposed in less exceptional circumstances. Analogously, it might be argued, (i) it is permissible for a state to inflict the harms associated with arming an oppressive regime when those harms are proportional to the expected gains it seeks to secure, and (ii) the harms the US inflicts, or contributes to inflicting, when it arms oppressive regimes *are* proportional to the expected gains it seeks to secure—namely, the gains associated with not being attacked by terrorists.[19]

In response: the relevant comparison is not between (i) the harms associated with arming an oppressive regime and (ii) the gains associated with not being attacked by terrorists. Rather, the relevant comparison is between (i) the harms associated with arming an oppressive regime and (iii) the reduced probability of being attacked by terrorists that can be attributed to arming that regime. As we have already seen, there is a wide variety of strategies that states can pursue to protect their citizens from terrorist attack. This means that we have good reason to suspect that the marginal gains of *also* supplying weapons to an oppressive regime are likely to be small. It is *those* gains—not all of the benefits associated with not being attacked by terrorists—that have to be weighed against the harms associated with arming an oppressive regime. Proponents of arming oppressive regimes will have to show that the harms their policy will inflict are not disproportionate (excessive in relation) to the gains they hope to achieve. Opponents will have to show that those harms *are* disproportionate.

In order to illustrate how the relevant proportionality calculation could be made, let us consider in greater detail the nature of the harms that can be generated by weapons transfers to oppressive regimes. One country that received large quantities of US weapons in the aftermath of 9/11 is Uzbekistan, a country presided over by an authoritarian regime that is regularly accused of committing serious human rights abuses.[20] Here is a short excerpt from the US State Department's 2006 Human Rights Report for that country.

> The government's human rights record, already poor, continued to worsen during the year. Citizens did not have the right in practice to change their government through peaceful and democratic means. Security forces routinely tortured, beat, and otherwise mistreated detainees under interrogation to obtain confessions or incriminating information. In several cases, authorities subjected human rights

---

[19] I am assuming that the harms that an exporting state contributes to inflicting upon innocent civilians when it transfers weapons to their oppressive government are a foreseen but unintended side effect of the transfer, and not part of the intended outcome.

[20] Stohl and Grillot, *International Arms Trade*, p. 35.

activists and other critics of the regime to forced psychiatric treatment. Human rights activists and journalists who criticized the government were subject to harassment, arbitrary arrest, politically motivated prosecution, and physical attack. The government generally did not take steps to investigate or punish the most egregious cases of abuse . . . The government continued to refuse to authorize an independent international investigation of the alleged killing of numerous unarmed civilians during the violent disturbances of May 2005.[21]

Elaborating, the report notes that 'torture and abuse were systematic', and that methods used by security forces included 'suffocation, electric shock, deprivation of food and water, and sexual abuse . . . ' Security forces were accused of abusing human rights activists by 'dropping them onto concrete floors, forcing needles under their fingernails, suffocating them with gas masks, and burning their skin with lighted cigarettes'.[22]

In line with what was said above, the relevant question for us here is not whether these harms are disproportionate to the marginal gains attributable to arming a regime of this kind, but rather whether the marginal contribution made to the infliction of such harms by providing weapons is disproportionate to those gains. It is important to note, then, that weapons transfers contribute to harms such as those described in at least three ways. First, they provide tools with which security forces coerce, maim, and kill. Second, they increase the power of the regime relative to internal dissidents, and to members of the international community that may wish to intervene to protect basic rights: as a result, the regime is more likely to be able to continue inflicting serious harms upon its citizens. Third, arms transfers constitute a form of international cooperation, and thus demonstrate that such cooperation is not contingent upon respect for basic rights: they counteract any verbal exhortations made by the exporting state, and reveal that opportunities for cooperation will be forthcoming irrespective of whether basic rights are respected. Again, this increases the probability that the regime will continue inflicting serious harms.

It is not possible to say that a proportionality calculation of the kind I have described will *never* recommend arming an oppressive regime. That is, it is not possible to say that the harms associated with arming an oppressive regime will *always* be disproportionate to the gains of doing so. But the case has to be made. And given that the expected gains are likely to be small, making the case on any particular occasion will be a sizeable challenge.

---

[21] US Department of State, *Country Reports on Human Rights Practices: Uzbekistan, 2006* (6 March 2007) (available at: http://www.state.gov/j/drl/rls/hrrpt/2006/78848.htm).

[22] US Department of State, *Country Reports on Human Rights Practices*.

III

Arming Oppressive Regimes: Two Further Defences

In this section I consider two further objections that can be pressed against the claim that states must refrain from selling weapons to oppressive regimes. First, it might be argued that arms sales to oppressive regimes can pave the way to improvements in the human rights practices of those regimes. When a state transfers weapons to an oppressive regime it can win favour with that regime, and request that it reciprocate in certain ways, e.g., by being more respectful of human rights. My sense is that anyone willing to think objectively about these matters will not take this argument very seriously. It might be true that, under certain circumstances, some oppressive regimes will be willing to modify their behaviour in return for weapons, especially if those weapons are provided at a discounted price. But there are a wide variety of incentives that states can offer in an attempt to influence the behaviour of oppressive regimes, and common sense indicates that weapons—tools that increase the ease with which oppressive regimes can violate the rights of their subjects—are among the least appropriate of those incentives.

A second argument runs as follows. Given that oppressive regimes will inevitably acquire weapons from somewhere, they may as well acquire them from us (i.e., liberal democratic states).[23] Indeed, the argument continues, an oppressive regime purchasing arms from us is preferable to an oppressive regime purchasing weapons from another oppressive or illiberal regime. The largest five arms exporters are Britain, France, the US, Russia, and China,[24] and, according to the current argument, it would be better for an oppressive regime like Uzbekistan to enter into an arms agreement with one of the three relatively liberal democracies on that list than to enter into an arms agreement with Russia or China. This is for a variety of reasons. First, as we have just noted, arms exporters may be able to exert some degree of influence over their trading partners, and it would be better for an oppressive regime to be influenced by a liberal democracy than by another oppressive or illiberal regime. Second, the revenues Russia and China derive from arms sales to oppressive regimes will be used, *inter alia*, to augment their own arsenals. If we are concerned to minimize the quantities of weapons acquired by oppressive and illiberal regimes (and minimization is the only realistically achievable goal), we should do our best to deny such regimes access to the funds needed

---

[23] As Jonathan Glover notes, this kind of argument was sometimes used in an attempt to justify arms sales to apartheid-era South Africa. Jonathan Glover, 'It makes no difference whether or not I do it', *Proceedings of the Aristotelian Society Supplementary Volume*, Vol. 49, 1975, pp. 171–209, at p. 171.

[24] Stohl and Grillot, *International Arms Trade*, p. 3.

to buy and produce weapons, even if that means stealing their would-be trading partners in the international arms market—which may well be other oppressive regimes. Third, successful sales boost the profits of our arms industry, irrespective of who those sales are to, and our arms industry can invest those profits back into the production of weapons systems for use by our own armed forces, and thereby enhance our security.

One way to respond to this argument is to reject its consequentialist reasoning, but it can also be challenged on its own consequentialist terms. Three challenges can be made. As we shall see, the first is not decisive, but the second and third have considerable force. The first challenge begins by noting that states will buy weapons from the firm that offers them the best deal. When firms compete for a particular customer they will often drive down their prices in order to match those offered by their counterparts. By permitting our firms to offer weapons to an oppressive regime, we increase the competitiveness of that particular market, and thereby enable the regime in question to acquire weapons at a lower price, and thus a larger quantity of weapons than it would otherwise have been able to acquire.

One weakness of this argument is that, if we permitted our firms to drive down prices, we would also reduce the income that oppressive states can derive from arms sales. We would make it less expensive for oppressive regimes to buy weapons, but also less profitable for them to sell weapons. Whether increasing the competitiveness of a market in which an oppressive regime operates is a good or bad thing depends upon whether the regime in question is a net exporter or a net importer.

The second challenge notes that we may possess certain types of weapons, or weapons of a particularly high quality, that other potential suppliers lack. This is certainly true of the US. Thus, by transferring arms to an oppressive regime, the US enables it to become more effective at oppressing its subjects than it would otherwise have been. The third challenge points out that by trading arms with an oppressive regime we forego any possibility of persuading third parties to refrain from engaging in such trade. If we demonstrate a willingness to surrender the benefits of trading with certain oppressive regimes, we may have a chance of convincing others to surrender those benefits, too. The moment we provide weapons, that chance vanishes.[25] Relatedly, at our disposal are a variety of coercive economic measures that can be used against those who trade arms with particular oppressive regimes. But clearly we could not employ such measures if we were also trading with those regimes.

---

[25] A related point is made in Glover, 'It makes no difference', p. 178.

The two objections considered in this section fail. Selling weapons to oppressive regimes cannot be defended on the grounds that doing so may lead to improvements in the human rights practices of those regimes, or on the grounds that oppressive regimes will inevitably be able to acquire weapons from some source or other.

IV

Arming Rebels

In the previous sections I considered the implications of the right to security for the practice of arming oppressive regimes. In this section I consider the moral permissibility of transferring arms to rebel groups waging revolutionary war against oppressive regimes. A concern for the security rights of those ruled by oppressive regimes gives us a *pro tanto* reason to welcome the overthrow of those regimes, and to support the groups attempting to overthrow them. But that same concern also casts doubt on the strategy of supporting those groups by arming them.

Before I proceed, one clarification should be made. In what follows, I do not distinguish between *trading* and the broader notion of *transferring*. States often simply give, rather than sell, weapons to rebel groups, and if one thinks there is sometimes a moral duty to supply weapons to rebel groups, that duty is surely best conceived as a duty to give weapons free of charge, rather than as a duty to supply weapons in some way, including via the market. But, for present purposes, the distinction between trading and transferring is not germane. The issues I raise concern the provision of weapons to rebel groups per se, not the manner of that provision, and I will tend to speak simply of 'arming' rebel groups.

Given that arming is one form of supporting, determining (i) if and when it is permissible to arm rebel groups involves (ii) determining if and when it is permissible to support rebel groups in some way. My intention is to focus on the distinctive issues that arise in relation to the former concern, but one general point about supporting rebel groups needs to be made first. If supporting a rebel group is to be permissible, it seems clear that several conditions, adapted from just war theory, must be satisfied: the rebel group must have a just cause—the aim of the group cannot be to overthrow one oppressive regime and replace it with another; the harms that will occur if the rebels, with outside assistance, continue to fight must be proportional to the harms that the war effort can be expected to prevent; the war must be necessary— less harmful means of getting rid of the regime must be unavailable; and it must be reasonable to expect that the rebel group, at least if it receives outside help, will not deliberately inflict violence upon non-combatants. These conditions will be relevant in what follows.

When a state transfers arms to a rebel group operating beyond its borders, it intervenes in the internal affairs of another state, and it is worth noting at the outset that this practice is invulnerable to a well-known, and quite general, critique of external intervention. According to this critique, which was originally formulated by John Stuart Mill, interventions motivated by a desire to liberate victims of oppression are almost always misguided. They are almost always misguided because, in order to be able to live as a free individual, one must first learn how to do so—one must acquire certain political virtues—and this can be accomplished only through successful revolutionary struggle. If outside powers intervene in the affairs of an oppressive state, and attempt to hand to the people their freedom on a plate, those people will not know what to do with it. Intervention deprives its intended beneficiaries of the opportunity to develop the very capacities that they will need to live as free individuals.[26] Summarizing Mill's argument, Michael Walzer writes: 'The (internal) freedom of a political community can be won only by the members of that community ... No one can, and no one should, do it for them.'[27]

Whatever merits this argument may have when applied to cases where the armed forces of one country actively prosecute a war intended to depose a foreign tyrant, it cannot plausibly be applied to cases of intervention involving nothing more than the provision of arms. When the members of a political community procure their freedom with weapons supplied by outside sympathizers, it is not the case that their freedom has been secured by others. Outside parties have simply provided the tools with which the community's members have waged a revolutionary war; they have not waged that war on their behalf. If the political virtues needed to live as a free individual are cultivated in revolutionary struggle, there is no reason to think that such virtues will not be possessed by those who fight a revolutionary war with weapons supplied by outsiders. It is hard to see how the contrary claim could be defended. How could it be true that the revolutionaries I have described lack the virtues needed to live freely, but that they would have possessed those virtues had their weapons been provided by one of their fellow citizens?

While the practice of arming rebel groups is not vulnerable to Mill's critique of intervention, the practice exhibits a distinctive shortcoming: while the advantages conferred by other forms of intervention can be terminated at

---

[26] John Stuart Mill, 'A Few Words on Non-Intervention', in John M. Robson (ed.), *The Collected Works of John Stuart Mill, Volume XXI: Essays on Equality, Law, and Education* (London: Routledge and Kegan Paul, 1984).

[27] Michael Walzer, *Just and Unjust Wars* (New York: Basic Books, 1977), p. 88.

any time, the advantages conferred by the provision of weapons cannot. Compare and contrast three states, one of which supports a rebel group by providing arms (state A), one of which supports a rebel group by providing troops to fight alongside the rebels (state B), and one of which supports a rebel group by providing air support (state C). If state B decides at some point that it no longer wishes to support the revolution, it can simply recall its troops. Similarly, if state C decides that it no longer wishes to support the revolution, it can simply recall its jets. State A, by contrast, is in a very different situation. It cannot simply ask for its weapons back. It can refuse to provide additional weapons, of course, but there is little it can do about the weapons it has already sent: it lost control of those the second they entered rebel hands. It is true that the ammunition A provided will eventually run out. But that does not change the fact that the advantages provided by A's policy extend into the future in a way that the advantages provided by B and C do not. And while the ammunition will run out, the weapons themselves can be used again and again. One can imagine a future world in which weapons feature self-destruct mechanisms that can be remotely triggered. In such a world, state A could cease its provision of support for the rebel group as easily and immediately as states B and C. But until such technical innovations come about, states that support rebel groups by providing arms suffer the disadvantage I have described.

Why are these considerations morally salient? It was noted earlier that certain conditions must be met if support for a rebel group is to be permissible. The important point to acknowledge now is that those conditions, or at least some of those conditions, might obtain one day, but not the next. For example, at time T it might be reasonable to believe that the rebel group one is contemplating supporting will not deliberately inflict violence upon non-combatants, but at time T + 1 it might became painfully clear that that belief was unfounded. A rebel group that had hitherto behaved in a morally appropriate manner might suddenly start engaging in attacks on civilians. Such a scenario is not at all improbable. As Allen Buchanan has recently explained, rebel groups often face strong pressures to engage in immoral conduct, and those pressures can intensify over time. This can happen if, for example, the regime the rebels are trying to overthrow attempts to dissuade people from participating in the revolution by increasing the penalties it imposes on those who engage in revolutionary activity. When a regime does this, rebels have a strong incentive to respond by imposing penalties on those who do *not* take part in the revolution: doing so may be their only way of maintaining participation at adequate levels.[28] If the penalties the rebel group decides to impose are excessive—if, say, it decides to execute those who refuse

---

[28] Allen Buchanan, 'The Ethics of Revolution and its Implications for the Ethics of Intervention', *Philosophy & Public Affairs*, Vol. 41, No. 4, 2013, pp. 291–323, at p. 319.

to participate—continuing to support the revolution will be morally unacceptable, and states wishing to honour their moral duties will wish to terminate support. Now, states that have supported the revolution by sending troops or jets will be able to terminate support immediately; by contrast, states that have supported the revolution by providing weapons will not.

It might be objected that the contrast I have drawn between a state that supports a revolution by sending troops or fighter planes, on the one hand, and a state that supports a rebel group by providing weapons, on the other, is not as sharp as I have suggested. It might be pointed out, for example, that a state that sends troops to assist rebel fighters cannot revoke the advantages it has already conferred—it cannot change the fact that its troops have, say, killed numerous regime soldiers—and so its situation is no different to that of a state that sent weapons. This objection misses the point. It is true that a state that sent troops or jets to support a rebel group cannot, at time T, revoke advantages that its policy conferred at time T − 1. But that is also true of a state that sent weapons. The point is that a state that sends weapons has committed itself to continuing to confer *further* advantages well into the future, whether it wants to confer those advantages or not. To put the point crudely, weapons are a gift that keeps on giving.

But there is another reason to suspect that I have exaggerated the differences between the situation faced by a state that intervenes by supplying weapons and a state that intervenes in another way. Recalling troops can be politically damaging, especially if it is done by the same administration that committed to putting 'boots on the ground' in the first place. Performing a potentially humiliating policy U-turn, and thereby admitting that an expensive policy one initiated was misguided, is hardly something that politicians take lightly. Therefore, it might be said, recalling troops can be just as difficult as retrieving weapons.

This objection elides the distinction between difficulty and costliness. As G. A. Cohen observed, ' "difficulty" and "cost" are two widely conflated but importantly distinct ways in that it can be *hard* for a person to do something…At the far end of the difficulty continuum lies the *impossible*, but it is the *unbearable* which occupies that position in the case of costliness.'[29] To illustrate: it is not difficult to speak without thinking and say something insensitive, but doing so may be very costly (if, say, you compromise a valuable relationship as a result). By contrast, studying philosophy can be difficult, but it is not costly for someone who can think of no better way to spend their time. Applying this distinction to the case at hand, we can see that while recalling troops may be costly, it is not nearly as difficult as retrieving

---

[29] G. A. Cohen, 'On the Currency of Egalitarian Justice', *Ethics*, Vol. 99, No. 4, 1989, pp. 906–44, at pp. 918–19 (original emphasis).

weapons. Moreover—and this is the important point to observe—retrieving weapons surely lies closer to the impossible end of the difficulty spectrum than recalling troops does to the unbearable end of the costliness spectrum.[30] In cases where terminating intervention is of paramount importance, a scenario in which one is capable of terminating intervention, albeit at a price, is preferable to a situation in which one will struggle to terminate intervention *at any price*.

I should stress that my aim here has not been to show that supporting rebel groups by sending troops or providing air support is better, all-things-considered, than supporting rebel groups by providing them with weapons. I have described other methods of supporting rebel groups solely for the purpose of illustrating a distinctive problem with arming them, and I have not meant to suggest that these other methods do not have their own distinctive shortcomings: they clearly do. Sending troops, for example, would expose our own combatants to large risks of serious physical harm. It should also be noted that the problem I have identified with transferring weapons also applies, *mutatis mutandis*, to some other methods of support. For example, if a state trains members of a rebel group in combat it cannot then 'untrain' them if it decides it no longer wishes to provide assistance. Intervening in revolutions is fraught with difficulty, and all methods of support have attendant risks. It is, nevertheless, important to emphasize the dangers associated with the provision of arms, for that strategy is often perceived to be superior to more direct forms of military intervention, which tend to be eschewed when possible on the grounds that they put troops in harm's way, upset the electorate, and are extremely expensive.[31] The upshot of the considerations adduced here is that providing arms should not be regarded as an unproblematic way of assisting rebel groups that is necessarily preferable to other available methods. By transferring weapons to a rebel group, an intervening state provides that group with the means

---

[30] It is worth adding that in the kind of case that I have envisioned, in which terminating intervention is of paramount importance, *not* recalling one's troops will also be (very) costly. An administration that has sent troops is thus faced with a choice between two costly options, neither of which is especially difficult to perform, whereas an administration that has supplied weapons has virtually no choice at all.

[31] I have emphasized the fact that arming rebel groups imposes serious risks on innocent civilians who are among the intended beneficiaries of intervention. But it should be noted that, when choosing among different modes of intervention that may otherwise be morally comparable, we are not necessarily required to choose the one that distributes the risks of intervention in the way that is most favourable to the intended beneficiaries. It may sometimes be permissible to choose a form of intervention that imposes greater risks on the beneficiaries, while reducing the degree of risk borne by the interveners. Having said that, we should bear in mind that taking risks for the sake of others is part of a professional combatant's job. For discussion of these points, see Jeff McMahan, 'Humanitarian Intervention, Consent, and Proportionality', in N. Ann Davis, Richard Keshen, and Jeff McMahan (eds.), *Ethics and Humanity: Themes from the Philosophy of Jonathan Glover* (New York: Oxford University Press, 2010), Section 3.4.

to violate the security rights of the very people the intervention is intended to help, and revoking those means will be extremely difficult.

This concludes my discussion of the arms trade. We have seen that that trade has an important role to play in ensuring that the right to security is protected. But we have also seen that the right to security generates duties to restrict the arms trade in significant ways. Weapons that pose an excessively large threat to non-combatants must not be traded, and arguments commonly used to justify arming oppressive regimes will rarely succeed. We also saw that while we may have good reasons to support rebel groups attempting to overthrow oppressive regimes, supporting such groups by arming them is, from a moral perspective, highly problematic.

V

The Death Penalty

One unifying theme of the last four sections has been a concern about the sale of commodities capable of inflicting serious physical harm to agents likely to use those commodities in a morally unacceptable manner. I have focused on the sale of weapons to agents who are likely to use those weapons in a way that straightforwardly violates basic security rights. But there are commodities other than weapons that are capable, and purchased for the express purpose, of inflicting serious physical harm, and some states purchase such commodities for use in practices that, while highly problematic, command support in certain quarters. I have in mind drugs such as sodium thiopental and pentobarbital, and the use of such drugs to execute prisoners on death row. The execution of certain convicts is deemed by some states to be morally permissible on the grounds that the convicts against whom the drugs are used have forfeited their security rights, and, more specifically, the right not to be killed. That claim is, of course, highly contested. In this section I enquire into the morality of trade in execution drugs, and consider whether respect for security rights requires the prohibition of such trade.

Intuitively, one set of states seem to be under a strong duty to refrain from selling drugs to states that are likely to use them to execute convicts, namely, those states that have outlawed the death penalty on the grounds that the execution of convicts constitutes wrongful killing. If a political community holds that its members are duty-bound to refrain from executing convicts, it seems that, in order to be morally consistent, it must also hold that its members are duty-bound to refrain from assisting others to execute convicts. And if selling drugs such as sodium thiopental to a state that is likely to use that drug to execute convicts amounts to assisting that state in the execution of convicts, which seems plausible, sales of the drug to that state must not be allowed. This *pro tanto* reason for prohibiting sales is analogous to the reason identified above for banning the exportation of weapons to oppressive regimes: in both cases the exported product will be used to inflict serious harms that are regarded, at least by the exporting state, as wrongful harms. By selling (or allowing the sale of) the means to inflict wrongful harm, the exporting state becomes complicit in its infliction.

Even political communities that do not oppose the death penalty per se may oppose certain applications of the death penalty, and may therefore seem to be committed to banning the exportation of execution drugs to certain states. For example, the citizens of Arizona may believe that while it is morally acceptable to execute convicted murderers, it is not morally acceptable to execute those convicted of drug trafficking. If Arizonians hold this view, they should also hold that it is morally unacceptable to assist in the execution of drug traffickers, and they therefore seem to be required to refrain from selling execution drugs to states such as China and Indonesia that have been known to execute drug traffickers.

There is, however, a sizeable obstacle preventing us from easily arriving at the conclusion that political communities opposed to the death penalty must prohibit the sale of drugs to states likely to use them to execute convicts, namely, drugs used in lethal injections also serve conventional medical purposes. Sodium thiopental, for example, is commonly used as a general anaesthetic. In November 2010 the British government resisted calls to ban the exportation of sodium thiopental on the grounds that while roughly eighty-five criminals a year would be executed by lethal injection, sodium thiopental might benefit 600,000 medical patients.[32] Note that if sodium thiopental qua anaesthetic was easily substitutable, while sodium thiopental qua execution drug was not, the government's argument would lack force. In order to make an even minimally compelling case against banning exportation of the drug, the government would have had to have shown not only that sodium thiopental could benefit large numbers of patients, but that there were no acceptable alternative means for providing those benefits, and that, consequently, an export ban would result in those benefits being denied. Note also that the kind of argument advanced by the British government would not be able to justify continued exportation of an execution drug unless it could be shown that the medicinal benefits of the drug in question were *significant*. Few people today are willing to accept that trivial gains for many people can outweigh serious harms to a few.

---

[32] Clive Stafford Smith, 'A welcome U-turn from Vince Cable on execution drug', *The Guardian*, 29 November 2010 (available at: http://www.theguardian.com/commentisfree/cifamerica/2010/nov/29/capital-punishment-vincentcable/print).

Suppose that a drug used in lethal injections also serves a conventional medical purpose, is non-substitutable, and can deliver significant benefits to large numbers of people. Should a state such as Britain that is morally opposed to the death penalty continue to allow exportation of that drug to countries where it will be used to execute convicts, or not? Note that what we have here is not obviously a clash of a positive duty (the duty to provide a valuable medicine) and a negative duty (the duty to refrain from participating in the execution of convicts). If the British government prevents its pharmaceutical firms from exporting a drug that will alleviate the suffering of many people, and if, as a result, those people are denied access to that drug, it seems plausible to say that the British government is actively harming those people: it is prolonging their suffering and causing them to endure burdens that they would otherwise not have had to endure.

We are seemingly being pulled toward the conclusion that, in some cases, there will be a clash of two negative duties—the duty not to assist in the killing of convicts and the duty not to prolong the suffering of innocents. In order to try to avoid facing this dilemma, let us reconsider the claim that a state that permits the exportation of execution drugs necessarily assists in the killing of convicts. Perhaps we were too quick to concede that proposition. In the summer of 2011, a Danish pharmaceutical company began requiring that US distributors sign an agreement stating that they would not sell a sedative called pentobarbital to prisons likely to use the drug in lethal injections.[33] This policy demonstrates that it is possible to export drugs used in lethal injections to countries that employ the death penalty without assisting in the imposition of that penalty. Perhaps what we should say, then, is that a country such as Britain that regards capital punishment as a form of wrongful killing is morally required either to prohibit the exportation of drugs to countries where they are likely to be used to kill convicts, *or* to take alternative steps to ensure that the drugs it exports will *not* be used to kill convicts. If the drugs in question, in their capacity as conventional medicines, deliver significant benefits, and would otherwise be unavailable in the importing country, we should say that the latter approach, when available, *must* be taken. If a government can permit the exportation of those drugs while also preventing them from being used to inflict wrongful harm, it cannot justify prohibiting their exportation and blocking access to the benefits they provide.

A principle embodying these requirements looks preferable to an alternative that insists that a country that regards capital punishment as a form of wrongful killing must always prohibit the exportation of drugs to countries

---

[33] Adam Gabbatt and David Batty, 'Danish firm Lundbeck to stop US jails using drug for lethal injections', *The Guardian*, 1 July 2011 (available at: http://www.theguardian.com/world/2011/jul/01/lundbeck-us-pentobarbital-death-row/print).

where they are likely to be used to kill convicts. The latter looks unreasonable given that such drugs often serve legitimate medical purposes, and given that, as we have just seen, it is possible to prevent those drugs from being used to kill convicts without prohibiting their exportation. But the first principle, while preferable to the alternative, is itself put under strain by a further observation: when prisons are denied access to traditional execution drugs they sometimes turn to less effective alternatives that inflict slower and more painful deaths.[34] These alternatives may be other drugs, or older execution methods such as firing squads, electrocutions, or gas chambers, the reintroduction of which has recently been countenanced by a number of US states.[35] These observations reveal a problem with the principle I alluded to, namely, it fails to recognize that, in certain cases, those who think capital punishment constitutes wrongful killing may nevertheless be morally permitted to allow the exportation of effective execution drugs *even when* they cannot prevent those drugs from being used to kill convicts—i.e., when failure to do so would result in the infliction of more painful deaths. They must surely be permitted to allow the exportation of effective execution drugs in such cases because, by doing so, they would simply be reducing the magnitude of a harm the infliction of which they are helpless to stop.[36] We may believe that they are in fact *required* to allow exportation in such circumstances. How might such a conclusion be resisted? It might be said that allowing exportation will threaten the integrity of those involved, for they regard contributing to wrongful killing as anathema to the values by which they define themselves.[37] But allowing one agent to sell the tools that a second agent will use to kill, and doing so in order to minimize the harms that the killing involves, is far removed from the kinds of contribution to wrongful killing that are likely to pose large threats to one's integrity. Moreover, there are constraints on the acts and omissions one can perform in order to preserve one's integrity. The relevant question—the answer to which will presumably depend on the details of the specific situation—is whether the interest in protecting one's integrity from the modest degradation it can be expected to suffer as a result of contributing to wrongful killing in the manner under

---

[34] Tom Dart and Ed Pilkington, 'States subjecting death row inmates to longer deaths amid scramble for drugs', *The Guardian*, 30 January 2014 (available at: http://www.theguardian.com/world/2014/jan/30/death-row-inmates-longer-deaths-scramble-drugs/print).

[35] 'The return of the firing squad? US states reconsider execution methods', *The Guardian*, 28 January 2014 (available at: http://www.theguardian.com/world/2014/jan/28/return-firing-squad-us-states-execution-methods/print).

[36] Such cases mirror the 'Jim and the Indians' scenario described by Bernard Williams in 'A Critique of Utilitarianism', in J. J. C. Smart and Bernard Williams, *Utilitarianism: For and Against* (Cambridge: Cambridge University Press, 1973), pp. 98–9.

[37] Williams, 'A Critique of Utilitarianism', pp. 116–17.

discussion can justifiably be pursued by denying convicts access to a less painful death.[38]

I began this section by noting that political communities that are morally opposed to the death penalty have a *pro tanto* reason to ban the exportation of drugs to states that are likely to use those drugs to execute convicts. That reason is analogous to the reason for banning the exportation of weapons to oppressive regimes. However, we have seen that political communities that are morally opposed to the death penalty do not have a *conclusive* reason to ban the exportation of execution drugs. Somewhat surprisingly, we have seen that allowing the exportation of those drugs can be morally required. Allowing exportation is morally required if (i) the drugs have important medicinal properties, (ii) would otherwise be unavailable in the importing country, and (iii) there are effective ways of ensuring that they will not be used to execute convicts. And allowing exportation is at least morally permissible (and may perhaps sometimes be morally required) in cases where exportation will reduce the harm that will inevitably befall those against whom the drugs are to be used.

VI

Hazardous Waste

Sections I–V considered the permissibility of trade in commodities that are capable of inflicting serious physical harm, and that are purchased for the express purpose of doing so. In this section, I consider the permissibility of a trade that involves the transfer of a commodity that has the capacity to cause serious physical harm, but that is not transferred because it has that capacity, namely, hazardous waste. I focus in particular on transfers of hazardous waste from developed to developing countries. I ask whether respect for security rights requires the prohibition of this trade.

Trade in hazardous waste between the developed and developing world has been driven by a number of factors.[39] Increased production of hazardous waste, rising costs of disposal (triggered by the introduction of more stringent regulations), and vociferous public opposition to the creation of new domestic disposal facilities have prompted rich country firms to look beyond their borders for places to send the wastes they generate, and those firms have often managed

---

[38] For pertinent discussion, see Victor Tadros 'Duress and Duty', in Saba Bazargan and Samuel C. Rickless (eds.), *The Ethics of War: Essays* (New York: Oxford University Press, 2017).

[39] The phrase 'hazardous waste trade' is not strictly accurate, as it is waste disposal services, and not the waste itself, that are bought and sold. But I shall continue to use the phrase for the sake of brevity.

to find takers in the developing world.[40] In recent decades, measures have been taken to reduce transfers of hazardous waste from developed to developing countries, but the practice has not been completely outlawed. A 1995 Amendment to the Basel Convention on the Control of Transboundary Movements of Hazardous Wastes and Their Disposal[41] provides for the prohibition of transfers from OECD to non-OECD countries, but the Amendment has not yet entered into force as it has not been ratified by the required number of countries. Moreover, even if the Amendment enters into force, it will not constrain the US, as the US is not party to the Basel Convention.[42] Should we regret the fact that the Amendment has not yet entered into force? Should transfers of hazardous waste from developed to developing countries be banned? Let us consider the normatively relevant features of those transfers.

Trade in hazardous waste attracts a large amount of attention from international organizations, NGOs, and the media because hazardous waste, by definition, poses a threat to human health and safety.[43] But the fact that hazardous waste is dangerous cannot, by itself, give us a reason to oppose the hazardous waste trade. This is because there are lots of markets in dangerous products and services that are regarded as morally acceptable. For example, skydiving is dangerous, but we do not think that anything morally objectionable occurs when an individual pays for the opportunity to skydive. The reason, of course, is that the risks associated with skydiving typically fall exclusively on the individual who pays for the experience, and, moreover, those risks are typically voluntarily assumed by that individual. If skydivers typically jumped out of planes travelling over crowded urban areas populated by individuals who had not voluntarily assumed the risk of being crushed by a falling body, and if parachute failure were a common occurrence, we would probably be inclined to revise our ethical evaluation of skydiving, and to say that there *is* something morally objectionable about it. Trade in dangerous goods per se is not necessarily morally wrong. But the moral permissibility of trade in dangerous goods is called into question when those goods impose costs (including risks) upon individuals who are not party to the transaction, and thus have not agreed to bear those costs.

To tailor these observations to the subject at hand, we can say that the moral permissibility of trade in hazardous waste is called into question if costs associated with that trade are not borne exclusively by those buying and

[40] Mary Critharis, 'Third World Nations are Down in the Dumps: The Exportation of Hazardous Waste', *Brooklyn Journal of International Law*, Vol. XVI, No. 2, 1990, pp. 311–19, at p. 311.

[41] UNEP, *Basel Convention on the Control of Transboundary Movements of Hazardous Wastes and Their Disposal*.

[42] For discussion, see Patricia Birnie et al., *International Law and the Environment: Third Edition* (New York: Oxford University Press, 2009), pp. 474–475ff.

[43] Hazardous waste also poses a threat to the health and safety of non-human animals, but that is not why it attracts attention.

selling waste disposal services but are instead also imposed upon third parties. The antecedent in the conditional proposition just outlined is undoubtedly true. Risks posed by hazardous waste, like the risks posed by nerve gas and landmines, are spatially and temporally extended. One way in which

> hazardous wastes can affect human health and the environment [is] through leakage of toxins into groundwater, soil, waterways, and the atmosphere. Environmental and health effects can be immediate—such as on-site human exposure to toxic chemicals in the waste—or long-term—contaminated waste can leach into groundwater or soil and then into the food chain.[44]

Moreover, developing countries are often undemocratic; their governments cannot be held accountable for their actions in free and fair elections, and thus have little incentive to refrain from doing things that impose costs upon their subjects.[45] Therefore, the individuals and groups voluntarily acquiring hazardous waste and the individuals and groups exposed to the dangers it produces will not be coterminous.

I said that the moral permissibility of trade in hazardous waste is called into question if costs associated with that trade are imposed upon third parties. But something being called into question is not the same as something being negated, and we cannot say that the moral permissibility of trade in hazardous waste, or any other good, is negated simply by virtue of the fact that the trade imposes costs on third parties. Before we can make that claim we have to enquire about the nature and magnitude of the costs involved, for the imposition of costs upon third parties will not always tell decisively against a trade. The salesman or saleswoman who sells my neighbour a motorcycle imposes costs on me if a consequence of the sale is that I am regularly disturbed by the noise of the motorcycle's engine. But while this noise might be irksome, the burden it constitutes is not serious enough to negate the moral permissibility of the sale.

However, the costs associated with hazardous waste are in a different league. Those exposed to hazardous waste can suffer severe physical harm. Hazardous wastes include substances that are toxic, dangerously reactive, highly corrosive, infectious, and radioactive.[46] Harms associated with exposure to hazardous waste include asthma, pneumonia, liver and kidney damage, heart disease, infertility, spontaneous abortion, developmental disabilities, blindness, paralysis, cardiac

---

[44] Jonathan Krueger, 'The Basel Convention and the International Trade in Hazardous Wastes', in Olav Schram Stokke and Øystein B. Thommessen (eds.), *Yearbook of International Co-operation on Environment and Development 2001/2002* (London: Earthscan Publications, 2002).

[45] Debra Satz, *Why Some Things Should Not be For Sale: The Moral Limits of Markets* (New York: Oxford University Press, 2010), p. 109.

[46] Jang B. Sing and V. C. Lakhan, 'Business Ethics and the International Trade in Hazardous Wastes', *Journal of Business Ethics*, Vol. 8, 1989, pp. 889–99, at p. 894.

arrest, cancer, and death.[47] Moreover, when hazardous waste is sold to poor countries, the risk of exposure is often high. This is because poor countries often lack the infrastructure and expertise necessary to ensure that waste is disposed of in a proper manner.[48] They also lack the resources needed to enforce compliance with regulations, and to minimize the harms that are generated when accidents occur.[49] This is a crucial moral difference between transfers of hazardous waste among developed countries and transfers of hazardous waste from the developed to the developing world.

So far, I have objected to international hazardous waste markets on the grounds that they expose non-consenting individuals to the risk of serious harm. However, a moment's reflection reveals that we sometimes deem it permissible to expose non-consenting individuals to such risks. We permit the use of motor vehicles, for example, despite knowing that many non-motorists (including children) will be killed and maimed by those vehicles. But there is a plausible justification for our tolerance of this practice, a justification that appeals to our knowledge that the incidence of harm to non-motorists will be low, and that non-motorists will also receive many sizeable benefits. They will benefit, for example, from a healthier economy, and more effective emergency services. Now, poor countries do not benefit from the industrial processes that generate the wastes that rich countries seek to export: the lion's share of benefits generated by those processes is captured by the citizens of the developed world. But poor countries can benefit from the large sums of money that corporations are willing to pay to get rid of hazardous waste.[50] However, there is no guarantee that those payments will benefit the citizenry at large; they may accrue to a small number of waste brokers, or to undemocratic governments who have no intention of investing the funds in programmes that will benefit the majority of the population.[51] Indeed, the undemocratic governments of poor countries may use the money they receive from rich-world corporations to buy off opponents and augment their security forces, thereby consolidating their power. Impoverished individuals are then doubly disadvantaged by transfers of hazardous waste: they

---

[47] D. Kofi Asante-Duah and Imre V Nagy, *International Trade in Hazardous Wastes* (New York: Routledge, 1998), pp. 120–4.

[48] Critharis, 'Third World Nations', p. 312; Jeffery D. Williams, 'Trashing Developing Nations: The Global Hazardous Waste Trade', *Buffalo Law Review*, Vol. 39, 1991, pp. 275–80, at p. 277; Roberto Sanchez, 'International Trade in Hazardous Wastes: A Global Problem with Uneven Consequences for the Third World', *The Journal of Environmental Development*, Vol. 3, No. 1, 1994, pp. 139–52, at pp. 140–2.

[49] Sanchez, 'International Trade in Hazardous Wastes', p. 142.

[50] In 1988, a US firm proposed to send a shipment of waste to Guinea-Bissau for a payment that would have amounted to twice that country's GDP. See Williams, 'Trashing Developing Nations', p. 278.

[51] Sing and Lakhan, 'Business Ethics and the International Trade in Hazardous Wastes', p. 898.

are exposed to the risks generated by the waste itself, and are further repressed by their government.

The considerations adduced above do not show that waste transfers to developing countries can never be justified, but they do reveal that, if they are to be justified, certain highly demanding conditions must be satisfied. Either it must be the case that (i) everyone who will be exposed to the risk of harm has consented to be exposed to that risk (satisfaction of this condition is extremely unlikely), or that (ii) the risks to which individuals will be exposed are low (because the country in question possesses adequate disposal facilities, etc.), and the expected benefits will be high (e.g., because the government is committed to poverty eradication, and is likely to use the income it receives from the waste transfer in pursuit of that goal). Unless one of these conditions is satisfied, transfers of hazardous waste from developed to developing countries constitute a violation of security rights. If neither (i) nor (ii) is satisfied, waste transfers contribute to the infliction of serious physical harms to which individuals have a right not to be subjected.

In an infamous memorandum sent to his colleagues while Chief Economist at the World Bank, Lawrence Summers offered the following, startling, defence of waste transfers to poor countries:

> The measurement of the costs of health-impairing pollution depends on the foregone earnings from increased morbidity and mortality. From this point of view a given amount of health-impairing pollution should be done in the country with the lowest cost, which will be the country with the lowest wages. I think the economic logic behind dumping a load of toxic waste in the lowest-wage country is impeccable and we should face up to that.[52]

It is not my intention to discuss Summers's memorandum in any depth, as it has been analysed in detail elsewhere,[53] but several comments are in order. Let us assume that Summers is suggesting that representatives of the developing world should recognize the merits of, and permit, compensated transfers of waste into their countries, and not that transfers should be made irrespective of whether compensation is offered, and irrespective of whether they are sanctioned by poor countries. Let us also add to the argument an additional premise, namely, that one ought to do whatever minimizes costs. (Without this premise the argument is a non-sequitur. The claim that pollution ought to be done where its cost is lowest does not follow from the claim that the cost of pollution is determined by (at least *inter alia*) the lost earnings it precipitates. One can endorse the latter claim while rejecting the former.) In light of the

---

[52] Quoted in Daniel M. Hausman and Michael S. McPherson, *Economic Analysis, Moral Philosophy, and Public Policy: Second Edition* (New York: Cambridge University Press, 2006), p. 12.

[53] Hausman and McPherson, *Economic Analysis, Moral Philosophy, and Public Policy*, pp. 12–23; 259–73.

preceding remarks, the argument can be reformulated as follows: poor countries ought to accept compensated transfers of hazardous waste because (i) such transfers minimize the costs associated with that waste, and (ii) bring certain benefits (i.e., the money that rich countries are willing to pay to get rid of the waste).

Reformulated in this way, the argument's deficiencies are all too apparent. We have already noted that the citizenry of poor countries might not benefit from the money paid for waste transfers, so point (ii) can be set aside. Point (i) clearly gives poor countries no reason to welcome waste transfers. Poor countries can accept that the costs produced by hazardous waste are lower in the developing world, while also believing that it would be unwise to shoulder those costs. It obviously does not follow from the fact that one can bear a particular burden at lesser cost than others that one *ought* to bear that burden; one's decision will depend on the size and nature of the burden, and on one's assessment of the benefits that can be acquired by bearing it. If the burdens associated with hazardous waste are respiratory problems, paralysis, cancer, and so forth, the belief that such burdens will be less costly in poor countries than in rich countries (because the amount of foregone earnings will be lower) hardly provides the former with a compelling reason to shoulder those burdens.

Furthermore, the claim that transferring hazardous waste to developing countries minimizes the costs associated with that waste is highly suspect. As we have already noted, poor countries often lack the infrastructure and expertise needed to ensure proper disposal of waste. This means that harmful exposure to waste—and loss of earnings as a result of exposure—is more likely in developing countries. It might be argued that, given the size of the income disparity between rich and poor countries, infrequent and relatively minor accidents in the former would still result in greater pecuniary losses than frequent and more serious accidents in the latter. But this argument could show that the costs associated with exposure to hazardous waste are lower in developing countries (even when developing countries experience more frequent and serious accidents) only if we hold that those costs are to be measured *exclusively* in terms of foregone earnings; that is, if we hold that physical harms produced by exposure are not, in themselves, relevant to the measurement of those costs. And that is clearly implausible. Any sensible measurement will reveal that the costs associated with frequent and serious accidents are higher than those produced by infrequent and minor accidents simply by virtue of the fact that the former generate a much higher degree of physical harm, and irrespective of whether, due to income disparities between rich and poor countries, the latter happen to cause greater income losses.

So much for Summers's memorandum. I have argued that waste transfers to developing countries are morally problematic because such transfers are likely to seriously harm individuals who have not consented to them. But it can be argued that such transfers can also wrong those who *have* consented. It is often said that market exchanges do not count as truly voluntary when they take place against a backdrop of severe deprivation,[54] and a number of thinkers have appealed to this idea in order to criticize waste transfers to developing countries.[55] Debra Satz, for example, writes:

> Trade in toxic waste holds up a mirror to global inequality. Because of that disparity the rich countries are able to exploit the vulnerabilities of the less developed countries (LDCs). Critics might suspect that, were they not so poor, the LDCs would not consent to the transfer of toxic waste to their lands, or perhaps they would hold out for better terms.[56]

Important as they are, these considerations do not tell decisively against waste transfers to poor countries (and Satz does not claim that they do). If (improbably) the risks associated with importing a particular batch of hazardous waste were restricted to a group of individuals who were fully informed about the nature of those risks, and who decided to import the waste anyway (because they regarded the risks as an acceptable price to pay for the benefits the exchange could generate), it would be unduly paternalistic to block the exchange on the grounds that it would not have been consented to under different conditions. Satz is absolutely right when she says that '[t]rade in toxic waste holds up a mirror to global inequality', and it is surely objectionable that such inequality forces poor countries into such desperate exchanges. But that is a reason to tackle inequality, not to deprive the poor of opportunities to alleviate their plight. While such inequality persists, it would be wrong to deny poor, informed individuals of the freedom to import hazardous waste on the grounds that their consent is not genuine. If we are to restrict waste transfers to poor countries, it must be on the grounds that those transfers impose serious harms on third parties, not for paternalistic reasons.

[54] Michael J. Sandel, 'What Money Can't Buy: The Moral Limits of Markets', *The Tanner Lectures on Human Values*, 1998, pp. 87–122, at p. 94.

[55] We might say that the poor are *coerced* into accepting waste transfers. This claim could be justified with the following argument. The poor have a right to a higher standard of living, a right that imposes duties upon the rich. When the rich propose to transfer hazardous waste to poor countries, they are effectively saying: 'we will provide you with resources that can be used to attain a higher standard of living (thereby going some way toward discharging our duties to you), but only if you agree to take this hazardous waste off our hands. If you do not accept our offer, we will withhold the resources.' The rich thereby coerce the poor by threatening to deny them that to which they have a right if they do not agree to the proposed deal. An argument of this kind is suggested, in a different context, in Alan Wertheimer, 'Two questions about Surrogacy and Exploitation', *Philosophy and Public Affairs*, Vol. 21, No. 3, 1992, pp. 211–39, at p. 227.

[56] Debra Satz, *Why Some Things Should Not Be for Sale: The Moral Limits of Markets* (Oxford: Oxford University Press, 2010), p. 109. Cf. Sing and Lakhan, 'Business Ethics and the International Trade in Hazardous Wastes', p. 895.

VII

Conclusion

In this chapter we have considered whether a number of serious physical harms created by international trade can be justified. In sections I–IV we looked at the international arms trade, a subject that is neglected in the existing literature. We saw that the arms trade has an important role to play in ensuring that people's security rights are protected, but we also saw that those rights generate duties to restrict the arms trade in significant ways. Weapons that pose an excessively large threat to non-combatants must not be traded, and common arguments used to justify arms transfers to oppressive regimes will rarely (if ever) succeed. We also saw that while we may have good reasons to support rebel groups attempting to overthrow oppressive regimes, supporting such groups by arming them is more problematic, morally speaking, than is usually acknowledged. In section V we considered the sale of drugs used to administer the death penalty. We reached the unexpected conclusion that the exportation of those drugs can be morally required of states that believe that the execution of convicts violates the right not to be killed. Finally, in section VI, we examined hazardous waste transfers from developed to developing countries. We saw that such transfers can be justified only if one of two demanding conditions is satisfied. Unless one of those conditions is satisfied, such transfers must be restricted. Otherwise, security rights are violated.

3

The Harms of Trade II

Non-Human Animals

In the previous chapter we saw that trade will sometimes visit upon human beings serious physical harms the infliction of which cannot be justified. In such cases, trade must be restricted. In this chapter, we shall see that humans are not the only ones exposed to serious harms by trade. Trade also harms non-human animals. The harmful practices considered in chapter 1 involve one set of individuals transferring products that inflict harm upon another set of individuals. By contrast, the harmful practices to be considered here involve one set of individuals supporting and incentivizing the infliction of harm by purchasing goods that are produced in an injurious manner. In recent decades, a number of high-profile trade disputes have addressed the use of trade restrictions ostensibly imposed in order to prevent complicity in such practices. For example, in 1991, under the dispute settlement procedure established by the General Agreement on Tariffs and Trade (GATT), Mexico challenged a provision of the US Marine Mammal Protection Act (MMPA) that prohibited the importation of tuna caught using fishing methods and technologies harmful to dolphins. A common method used by fisheries in the Eastern Tropical Pacific involves deliberately setting purse seine nets on schools of dolphin in an attempt to catch the yellowfin tuna that dolphin are known to swim with, and this practice has caused myriad dolphin fatalities. To take another example, in 1998, India, Malaysia, Pakistan, and Thailand objected to a US ban on the importation of shrimp harvested with technologies harmful to sea turtles. In both cases, the GATT dispute panel decided in favour of the complainants, and against the US (but the panels' reports were not adopted).[1] More recently, in May 2014, the WTO Appellate

---

[1] A helpful overview of both cases, commonly known, respectively, as *Tuna–Dolphin* and *Shrimp–Turtle*, is provided in Michael Bowman et al., *Lyster's International Wildlife Law: Second*

Body upheld an EU ban on the importation of seal products that had been challenged by Canada and Norway.

This chapter defends animal-protecting trade restrictions. My aim is to identify the values that can be served by animal-protecting trade restrictions, and to show that proposals to implement such restrictions are not defeated by arguments commonly levelled against them. For strategic reasons, I try to do this without invoking the claim that animals have rights, or that animal interests are as weighty as human interests. Section I looks at the aims of animal-protecting trade restrictions, at the values they are intended to serve, and at the nature of the harms they are used to prevent or reduce. Section II analyses a range of objections to animal-protecting trade restrictions, and demonstrates that those objections are not successful.

I

Animal-Protecting Trade Restrictions

Animal-protecting trade restrictions can have a number of different aims. The aim might be (i) to restrict trade in (products derived from) animals belonging to particular species in order to protect those animals; (ii) to restrict trade in certain goods in order to protect animals that are harmed incidentally by that trade; (iii) to protect an ecosystem or habitat that sustains animals from various species; or (iv) to enforce compliance with a treaty the purpose of which is to protect animals from particular species.

In addition to having different aims, animal-protecting trade restrictions can be motivated by a variety of different considerations. They might be motivated by anthropocentric reasons based on the *instrumental* or *inherent* value of animals to humans, or by altruistic reasons based on animals' *intrinsic* value.[2] Animals are valued instrumentally by those who appreciate them not *as* animals, but rather as sources of, say, food or income, or as biological resources that contribute to the maintenance of ecosystems. Animals are valued inherently by those who appreciate them *as* animals—who enjoy their companionship, marvel at their beauty, or are contented by knowledge of their mere existence. Those who keep pets, encourage birds into their

Edition (New York: Cambridge University Press, 2010), Ch. 19. While the Tuna–Dolphin report was not adopted, it was brought into WTO jurisprudence by a subsequent Appellate Body report. See Steve Charnovitz, 'The WTO's Environmental Progress', *Journal of International Economic Law*, Vol. 10, No. 3, 2007, pp. 685–706, at p. 701.

[2] On the distinction between the instrumental, inherent, and intrinsic value of nature see, for example, Rosemary Rayfuse, 'Biological Resources', in Daniel Bodansky et al. (eds.), *The Oxford Handbook of International Environmental Law* (New York: Oxford University Press, 2007), pp. 367–8.

garden, or visit zoos, for example, recognize the inherent value of animals. By contrast, the intrinsic value of animals refers not to the value they possess for humans, but to the value they possess in, of, and for themselves.

Recognition of the intrinsic value of animals grounds the ascription of moral status to animals. This moral status can be explicated in different ways. We might think that, by virtue of their intrinsic value, animals bear moral rights that impose correlative duties upon human beings. Alternatively, we might be sceptical of the claim that animals have moral rights, but maintain that, on account of their intrinsic value, an animal's interests (in, say, not being killed or tortured) must be taken into consideration. This latter thought can be given a strong or weak formulation. According to the strong formulation, (certain) animal interests count just as much as analogous human interests. For example, an animal's interest in not being tortured is regarded as being just as weighty as a human's interest in not being tortured. According to the weak formulation, animal interests count for something, and must be taken into account when we engage in practical reasoning, but they are less weighty than human interests. So, the intrinsic value of animals can be used to ground one of two strong views—(i) animals have rights,[3] or (ii) (certain) animal interests are as weighty as analogous human interests,[4]—or one weaker view—(iii) animals have interests that must be acknowledged, but animal interests count for less than human interests. For strategic reasons that I shall elaborate on below, the two stronger views are largely set aside for the remainder of the discussion.

So far we have noted that animal-protecting trade restrictions can have different aims and motivations. The harms that animal-protecting trade restrictions aim to prevent or reduce also vary in nature. A trade restriction might aim to protect an animal (or, more accurately, a species) from extinction, or it might aim to protect animals from harms that inflict suffering or death but that will not precipitate the extinction of their species. The harms that animal-protecting trade restrictions target may occur in the territory of the state implementing the restriction, in the territory of another state, or in an area beyond national jurisdiction. Given that international law grants states sovereignty over the biota found within their borders, restrictions that aim to protect animals outside the jurisdiction of the implementing state are more controversial than those that aim to protect animals within the jurisdiction of the implementing state.

---

[3] The classic defence of animal rights is Tom Regan, *The Case for Animal Rights* (Berkley and Los Angeles, CA: University of California Press, 1983). For a helpful overview of the literature, see Sue Donaldson and Will Kymlicka, *Zoopolis: A Political Theory of Animal Rights* (New York: Oxford University Press, 2011), Ch. 2.

[4] This view is associated with Peter Singer. See his *Animal Liberation: Second Edition* (London: Random House, 1990).

II

Objections

In what follows I consider, and rebut, a number of objections to the use of animal-protecting trade restrictions. Before I proceed, three clarificatory points should be made. First, my question concerns the permissibility of *unilateral* trade restrictions. I assume that states should pursue negotiated, multilateral, settlements before resorting to unilateralism, but I am interested in what states may do when such efforts fail. The second clarification concerns my treatment of ideas and arguments advanced by GATT dispute panels. Unlike the majority of commentators who have addressed the issues discussed here, I am not interested in the question of whether these panels accurately interpreted the GATT text upon which they relied when making their decisions. I am concerned with the *substance* of the panels' ideas and arguments, and not with whether those ideas and arguments can properly be said to have their source in the GATT text. This focus reflects the fact that this book is a work of normative political theory, not exegetical legal analysis.

Third, in the course of defending the use of trade restrictions to protect animals, I try not to appeal to the claim that animals have rights, or that animals have (certain) interests that are as weighty as analogous human interests. This is not because I think these claims are untenable. On the contrary, I find the case for animal rights compelling. I thus find the existence of many markets in animal-based products—and the practices of industrial killing and torture that those markets sustain—profoundly disturbing. In my view, justice and decency require the complete abolition of such markets.[5]

However, I cannot make the case for animal rights here, in a book about trade. Nor, given that I am in the minority on this issue, can I simply proceed on the assumption that animals have rights. I thus attempt to build my case for trade restrictions to protect animals on foundations that I hope will be more congenial to the majority of readers. I appeal to the instrumental[6] and inherent value of animals, and to the view that, on account of their intrinsic

---

[5] From an animal rights perspective, the adoption of trade restrictions for the purpose of, say, protecting dolphins looks morally arbitrary. Dolphins have a right not to be killed by virtue of certain characteristics that they share with countless other animals—cattle, sheep, pigs, chickens, etc.—that are killed and tortured in their millions in factory farms across the US and other industrialized countries. Our best reasons for protecting dolphins are also reasons for protecting these other animals. But the moral arbitrariness of trade restrictions such as those proposed by the MMPA is not, of course, a reason for animal rights activists to oppose those restrictions. That would be like opposing the abolition of slavery on the grounds that practices of racial segregation were not also being abolished.

[6] While I appeal to the instrumental value of animals, I do not invoke any instrumental uses that could be said to violate basic animal rights, if such rights exist. I refer to the role that animals can play in sustaining ecosystems, which is *useful* to us, but is not an example of *using* animals.

value, animal interests have some weight, and are relevant to our practical reasoning. This view, about the moral relevance of animal interests, undergirds the common conviction that animals should not be subjected to *excessive* or *unnecessary* suffering. In the US, this conviction receives some degree of legal expression in the Humane Methods of Slaughter Act (HMSA)—which requires that animals be 'rendered insensible to pain by a single blow or gunshot or an electrical, chemical or other means that is effective, before being shackled, hoisted, thrown, cast or cut'[7]—and in the Twenty-Eight Hour Law, according to which animals may not be confined 'in a vehicle or vessel for more than 28 consecutive hours without unloading'.[8] These laws are inadequate to achieve even the minimal aim of avoiding gratuitous suffering,[9] but their enactment is relevant as evidence of popular demand for basic animal protections. As the House Report of the HMSA observed: 'Witnesses have testified to having been sickened, physically as well as emotionally, upon learning of cruel abuses to livestock from which food they were eating or had eaten was derived.'[10]

Moreover, in recent years a small number of US states, responding to popular demand, have outlawed certain cruel factory farming practices that involve the use of sow gestation crates, veal crates, and battery cages.[11] Similarly, causing an animal to suffer unnecessarily is an offence under the UK's Animal Welfare Act, which determines whether suffering is unnecessary by considering, *inter alia*, 'whether the suffering could reasonably have been avoided.'[12] And New Zealand's Animal Welfare Act prohibits 'causing [an] animal to suffer . . . pain or distress that . . . is unreasonable or unnecessary.'[13] I offer this very brief and partial legislative survey in support of the claim that many people—and not just those of us who seek the abolition of animal exploitation—think that the interests of animals must be taken into account, and that the infliction of excessive or unnecessary suffering upon animals is unacceptable.[14]

---

[7] Quoted in Joan E. Shaffner, *An Introduction to Animals and the Law* (Basingstoke: Palgrave Macmillan, 2011), p. 107.

[8] Quoted in Shaffner, *Animals and the Law*, p. 107.

[9] 'In practice, these laws are ineffective. During the first 130 years of enforcement of the Twenty-Eight Hour law, no animals transported by truck, a primary means of transport in recent decades, were protected because the USDA [United States Department of Agriculture] did not interpret "vehicle" to include trucks! . . . Moreover, the law is rarely, if ever, enforced and the penalties are meaningless . . . Most importantly, however, 95 percent of all animals slaughtered for food are not protected under either law because fish, rabbits, and birds are not covered.' Shaffner, *Animals and the Law*, p. 108.

[10] Quoted in Shaffner, *Animals and the Law*, p. 106.

[11] Shaffner, *Animals and the Law*, p. 110.

[12] Quoted in Shaffner, *Animals and the Law*, p. 26.

[13] Quoted in Shaffner, *Animals and the Law*, p. 27.

[14] Of course, it makes no sense to ask whether a practice is necessary *in abstracto*. It makes sense only to ask whether a practice is necessary *to achieve a particular end*. If the end that a practice, P, is necessary to achieve is morally unacceptable, the fact that P is necessary to achieve that end does

With these points in mind, let us move on to consider objections to the use of animal-protecting trade restrictions. Four objections will be examined. These objections maintain that animal-protecting trade restrictions (i) sometimes discriminate, unjustifiably, among 'like products'; (ii) unjustifiably interfere with consumer freedom; (iii) unjustifiably interfere with the freedom of political communities to form their own policies and laws; and (iv) are often a disguised form of protectionism. My aim in addressing these objections is not purely negative; I hope that responding to these complaints will bring the value of the ends served by animal-protecting trade restrictions more sharply into focus.

Unjustifiable Discrimination among 'Like Products'

In the *Tuna–Dolphin* case, the GATT panel decided that by prohibiting the sale of tuna caught by Mexican fishing fleets while permitting the sale of tuna caught by US fleets, the MMPA unjustifiably discriminated between 'like products'. While Mexican tuna was harvested in a different manner to US tuna, that fact was deemed insufficient to justify discrimination. For discrimination between two products to be justified, the products themselves, and not just the associated process and production methods (PPMs), must be of a different character. The different harvesting methods used by Mexican and US fleets did not affect the character of the tuna itself, and therefore discrimination was unjustified.[15]

This argument prompts two questions. First, is it true that the different harvesting methods used by Mexican and US boats did not affect the character of the tuna caught?[16] And, second, can a moral basis be provided for the claim that discrimination is justified only when it tracks differences in the character of the products discriminated between, and not differences in the methods used to create those products? Consider the first question. It is true that the different fishing methods used by Mexican and US boats did not affect the *physical* properties of the tuna caught. However, it might be argued that even when the physical properties of products made with different production

---

not vindicate P. The law tends to assume that the slaughter of an animal for food is a morally acceptable end.

[15] *United States—Restrictions on Imports of Tuna: Report of the Panel (DS21/R—39S/155)*, 3rd September 1991, paras. 5.10–5.16 (available at: http://www.worldtradelaw.net/reports/gattpanels/tunadolphinI.pdf).

[16] This question is posed in Thomas J. Schoenbaum, 'Free International Trade and Protection of the Environment: Irreconcilable Conflict?', *The American Journal of International Law*, Vol. 86, 1992, pp. 700–27, at pp. 721–2. Schoenbaum asks: 'Is it possible to conclude that differences in the circumstances of production of items that may have the same characteristics at the point of importation justify their treatment as "unlike products"?' But Schoenbaum's question, unlike mine, is interpretive, rather than conceptual, in nature. He focuses on the meaning attributed to the term 'like product' by GATT jurisprudence. (His answer to the quoted question is negative.)

methods do not differ, those products may nevertheless have different natures by virtue of being produced in different ways. In other words, it might be argued that the process by which a product is made can endow that product with distinctive *non-physical* attributes that allow for it to be distinguished from other, physically identical, products.

This line of reasoning is leant intuitive support by the observation that we often do seem to think that the nature of a product is a function not just of its physical properties, but of facts about its genesis, and about its history more generally. For example, we think that the Mona Lisa and a copy of the Mona Lisa are different, and not merely distinct, even if they are physically identical, and we think that they are different by virtue of the fact that one was painted by Leonardo da Vinci, while the other was not. The genesis of the original confers upon the Mona Lisa a particular quality—a quality of authenticity—that the copy lacks.[17] Plenty of other examples come easily to mind. One's engagement ring is different to a physically identical ring available for purchase at the local jewellers. The former possesses sentimental value that is absent from the latter. And similar claims could be made about, say, a pendant one was given by one's late mother, or a charm worn by a soldier throughout a deadly conflict. Each of these items has significance, at least for the person to whom they belong, that other, physically identical, items lack, and they have that significance by virtue of facts about their history.

So the thought that Mexican tuna and US tuna might be unlike products, despite being physically identical, is at least intelligible. But what could distinguish Mexican and US tuna? By virtue of which attributes could the two products be regarded as unlike? One possible answer to this question is that the *ethical status* of the two products differs. It might be argued that tropical tuna caught with a purse seine is necessarily an unethical product, whereas tuna caught with a dolphin-safe net is not. But this reasoning looks sophistic. It seems more plausible to say that in the case of a product made with animal-harming methods it is not the product itself that is ethical or unethical, but rather the associated PPMs. The use of purse seine nets might be unethical, but that fact does not confer a distinctive character upon the fish caught. A product can be regarded as unethical when, say, it has an unethical function, or when its use has harmful side effects, but not simply by virtue of being produced in a certain way. (A child conceived as a result of rape is created in a deeply unethical way, but we do not infer from this that there is any sense in which the child herself is an unethical entity.)

---

[17] See the discussion in Robert E. Goodin, *Green Political Theory* (Cambridge: Polity Press, 1992), pp. 26–30.

Our first question—is it true that the different harvesting methods used by Mexican and US boats did not affect the character of the tuna caught?—can, I think, be answered affirmatively. Now let us consider our second question: can a moral basis be provided for the claim that discrimination is justified only when it tracks differences in the character of the products discriminated between, and not differences in the production methods used to create those products? It is here that the dispute panel's argument runs into trouble. We typically think that discrimination is unjustified when it fails to respect the maxim that like cases should be treated alike: if there are no relevant differences between two cases, there can be no acceptable grounds for treating those cases differently. By insisting that like products be treated alike, it may appear that the dispute panel is acting in accordance with this maxim. But when looking at two sets of *products* and attempting to determine whether we are dealing with like *cases*, all-things-considered, it is not sufficient to focus exclusively on the nature of the products themselves. Rather, we must also take into account the nature of the associated production methods. This is not because, if we do not, our description of the product itself will be inadequate, but because we will fail to undertake an adequately holistic examination of the cases we are considering, and may consequently overlook relevant differences between those cases.

To elaborate: in order to establish whether we are dealing with like cases, in any context, it is often not sufficient to compare only one aspect of the cases in question. A university hiring committee, for example, would not conclude that it were dealing with like cases simply on the grounds that each applicant had a comparable level of teaching experience; rather, the committee would seek to compare other relevant attributes, such as research aptitude. If the committee focused exclusively on teaching experience, its assessment would not be adequately holistic, and it would fail to establish whether there were relevant differences between the applicants. Similarly, in the context that we are interested in, if we focus exclusively on the nature of the products being offered for sale, we cannot conclude that there are no relevant differences between the cases under consideration, differences that could make differential treatment appropriate.

That asymmetric production methods can potentially constitute a relevant difference is brought sharply into focus by recognition of two points. First, different production methods are not ethically uniform. No one would deny that fact. Everyone would accept, for example, that production processes involving slave labour are necessarily unethical, whereas production methods using free labour are not necessarily unethical. Second, ethical asymmetries are typically regarded as the kind of thing that can justify different treatment of different cases. When I decide to stop inviting an old friend to social gatherings because I have discovered that he assaulted his wife, the grounds for my decision, which are ethical in character, are easily comprehended. These considerations enable us to formulate a reply to the dispute panel's argument. The reply maintains that asymmetrical PPMs can justify (or give us a *pro tanto* justification for) discriminating between two products even if the products themselves do not differ in character. The claim need not be that *any* asymmetry between PPMs can justify discrimination, but rather that discrimination can be justified by certain kinds of asymmetry, such as those that are ethical in nature. If one product is produced or processed in an ethical manner, while another, physically identical, product is produced or processed in an *un*ethical manner, that fact alone can justify (or provide a *pro tanto* justification for) differential treatment—e.g., permitting the sale of the former while prohibiting the sale of the latter.

These comments are sufficient to show that the panel's reasoning is deficient, but in order to defend animal-protecting trade restrictions we must do more than point out that PPMs can be unethical, and that asymmetries in the ethical status of PPMs can justify differential treatment: we must show that PPMs can be unethical when and because they harm animals. As I do not wish to appeal to the strong claims that animals have rights, or that (certain) animal interests are as weighty as analogous human interests, we will not be able to vindicate the claim that *all* PPMs that harm animals are *ipso facto* unethical. But the strong claims I am setting aside are not necessary to support the conclusion that *some* PPMs that harm animals are *ipso facto* unethical. As was noted earlier, the principle that humans should not inflict *excessive* or *unnecessary* suffering upon animals is widely accepted, and this principle can be used to show that some animal-harming PPMs are unethical by virtue of the kinds of harm they impose. Indeed, it does not seem hard to show that the principle is violated by the practice of setting nets on dolphins in order to catch the tuna with which they swim. It is not necessary to set nets on dolphins in order to catch tuna, and, by drowning dolphins, the practice inflicts particularly horrible deaths upon those dolphins that are caught.

In conclusion, the claim that discrimination can be justified only when it tracks differences in the character of the products discriminated between, and not differences in associated PPMs, looks unmotivated. The considerations adduced above support the view that governments can justify discriminating between a set of products made with animal-harming PPMs, on the one hand, and a set of identical products made with non-animal-harming PPMs, on the other, when and because the PPMs associated with the former violate the widely accepted principle that humans should not inflict excessive or unnecessary suffering upon animals.

In an interpretation of the GATT text offered in its *EC—Seals Products* report, the Appellate Body maintained that measures that apply equally to all countries can be de facto discriminatory if the adverse effects generated by those measures are not distributed equally among countries.[18] As one set of commentators has noted, this seems to have the extreme implication that 'every regulation that results in different market opportunities for products from different countries, regardless of the reason for the regulation and no matter how incidental that effect, is a *prima facie* violation of GATT...'[19] The upshot of the arguments I developed above is that, irrespective of their *legal* status, animal-protecting trade restrictions that have different consequences for different countries can be *morally* justifiable if the different consequences are attributable to differential treatment of animals. There is no *unjustifiable* discrimination if one set of countries bears a greater set of burdens by virtue of the fact that its laws permit the infliction of excessive or unnecessary suffering upon animals.

Unjustifiable Interference with Consumer Freedom

But now a second objection rears its head. According to this objection, governments should not interfere with consumer freedom by banning the importation of products made using methods that some of their citizens allegedly regard as unethical, but rather should allow those products to enter the marketplace and let citizens choose whether or not to buy them. Governments should not attribute ethical preferences to their citizens but rather enable citizens to express their preferences themselves.[20] They can do this by ensuring that products are appropriately labelled. Indeed, while the GATT dispute panel looked unfavourably on the US tuna embargo, it supported the US Dolphin Protection Consumer Information Act, which Mexico also challenged, and which allows firms to market tuna with a 'dolphin-safe' label

---

[18] Appellate Body Report, *European Communities—Measures Prohibiting the Importation and Marketing of Seal Products*, WT/DS400/AB/R and WT/DS401/AB/R (22 May 2014) (Henceforth, *EC—Seals Products*), paras. 5.94, 5.105, 5.110.

[19] Robert Howse et al., 'Sealing the Deal: The WTO's Appellate Body Report in EC—Seal Products', *American Society of International Law*, Vol. 18, No. 12, 2014 (original emphasis).

[20] In the past, GATT intolerance of animal- (and, more generally, environment-) protecting trade restrictions has often been criticized on the grounds that it is undemocratic. For example, William Snape and Naomi Lefkovitz write:

> At its core...the debate over PPMs and much of the trade/environment relationship is fundamentally about democracy. Who decides when and why trade restrictions based on PPMs are appropriate? Citizens of a country speaking through their legislature? Or an international trade organization, directly accountable only to member governments and career bureaucrats? (William J. Snape III and Naomi B. Lefkovitz, 'Searching for GATT's Environmental *Miranda*: Are "Process Standards" Getting "Due Process"?' *Cornell International Law Journal*, Vol. 27, 1994, pp. 777–815, at p. 781.)

The objection to animal-protecting trade restrictions currently under scrutiny in the text pushes back against this argument, suggesting that democratic values would be better served if citizens did not have to speak through their political representatives, but could instead speak for themselves in the marketplace.

provided they can demonstrate that it has not been caught in a manner that endangers dolphins.

I want to begin my analysis of this objection with a comment on labelling. The point I wish to make does not rescue animal-protecting trade restrictions from the objection we are considering, but it is important nonetheless. If labelling is to serve its purpose of ensuring that consumers are fully informed about the products available to them, and capable of making decisions that accurately reflect their preferences, it is not sufficient to label only those products that *have* been produced using methods that might be regarded as morally required; rather, it is also necessary to ensure that products that have *not* been produced using such methods are appropriately labelled. Marx famously contrasted the marketplace—a 'noisy sphere, where everything takes place on the surface and in view of all men'—with the 'hidden abode of production'.[21] In today's global economy, the production of animal products, in particular, remains a secretive affair, with considerable effort exerted in an attempt to conceal its brutal realities from consumers.[22] In the case of tuna harvesting, no such effort is required, for the obvious reason that the practice takes place at sea, far from prying eyes. Between the late 1950s and early 1990s, over seven *million* dolphins were killed with purse seine nets,[23] but this mass slaughter took place largely out of sight. Given the clandestine nature of production, it is unreasonable to expect consumers to deduce all potentially important facts about the methods used to produce the products available to them from the *absence* of an informational label. These considerations have been reflected in the labelling of eggs in the EU, where labels have been used to identify eggs laid by 'free range' chickens *and* eggs laid by chickens raised in cages. Through expensive advertising campaigns, companies relentlessly promote the idea that by purchasing their products consumers are promoting good outcomes. ('Buy this coffee or that smoothie and help save the planet.') Consumers are rarely confronted with the harms generated by their purchasing habits. Appropriate and explicit labelling can help redress this imbalance.

---

[21] Karl Marx, 'The Sale of Labour Power', in David McLellan (ed.), *Karl Marx: Selected Writings*, Revised Edition (New York: Oxford University Press, 2000), p. 492.

[22] Commenting on media coverage of abattoirs in the wake of the British horsemeat scandal in early 2013, the *Guardian* columnist John Harris observed: 'its visceral impact was not about whether the meat in question was from horses or cows, but the simple reality of the industrialised processes whereby sentient creatures are turned into what one former abattoir worker recently described in the Financial Times as "a block of frozen mush that's maybe 2ft by 2ft by 3ft". In an age when most people buy their meat from supermarkets and have rarely glimpsed a carcass, this points up one of 21st-century living's most messed-up aspects: the fact that most people eat meat, but recoil when they see what it entails.' John Harris, 'No more excuses. The only defensible option is to go vegetarian', *The Guardian*, 17 February 2013 (available at: http://www.theguardian.com/commentisfree/2013/feb/17/no-more-excuses-go-vegetarian/print).

[23] Snape and Lefkovitz, 'Searching for GATT's Environmental *Miranda*', p. 783.

Let us now consider an argument that responds more directly to the objection under scrutiny. According to this argument, for consumers to be able to express and satisfy their preference for goods produced in a non-animal-harming manner, such goods have to be available for purchase. If firms using animal-harming PPMs are more competitive than rival firms using non-animal-harming PPMs (perhaps because, by virtue of using animal-harming PPMs, they have lower production costs), the former might be able to drive the latter out of the market. If that happens, individuals with a preference for products made with non-animal-harming PPMs will lack opportunities to express or satisfy that preference. Trade embargos can ensure that consumers are not deprived of these opportunities.

It might be said that these consumers can express their preferences via the market simply by *refraining* from buying products made with animal-harming PPMs. But such omissions simply communicate the absence of a want; they do not communicate demand for an alternative. A more significant weakness of the argument sketched in the previous paragraph is that the market does not exhaust the avenues through which consumers can express their preferences. Consumers can also communicate their preferences through non-market channels (e.g., through petitions). This means that, contrary to what the argument purports to show, trade embargoes will not be necessary to ensure that consumers can express their preference for products made with non-animal-harming PPMs. It is true that an embargo might be needed to ensure that these consumers can *satisfy* (rather than merely *express*) their prefer-ences, but while an embargo could facilitate the satisfaction of preferences held by one set of consumers, the same embargo will impede the satisfaction of preferences held by another. Without a way of establishing whose prefer-ences should be accorded priority, the argument we have been considering is incomplete.

Some commentators note that what many consumers want is not simply the option of purchasing ethically produced goods, but the unavailability of unethically produced goods. Labelling enables such consumers to avoid unethically produced goods, but it does not prevent others from purchasing those products. Trade embargoes, by contrast, prevent the disfavoured prod-ucts from being sold in the domestic market, and therefore do a better job of ensuring that the preferences of certain consumers are satisfied.[24] But this line of reasoning shares one of the weaknesses of the previous argument we considered: it fails to establish why we should prioritize the interests of those consumers whose preferences are served by trade embargoes over the

---

[24] Robert Howse and Donald Regan, 'The Product/Process Distinction—An Illusory Basis for Disciplining "Unilateralism" in Trade Policy', *European Journal of International Law*, Vol. 11, No. 2, 2000, pp. 249–89, at pp. 273–4.

interests of those whose preferences are frustrated by trade embargoes. It is thus incomplete.

Let us consider another argument. This points out that the proposition that governments should leave ethical decisions to consumers, understood as a fully general claim, has implications that no one could reasonably accept. One such implication is that governments should permit trade in humans, and allow consumers to choose whether or not to engage in that trade. No one would accept that prohibiting trade in humans objectionably interferes with consumer freedom, for no one thinks it is morally permissible to contribute economically to practices such as slavery that egregiously violate human rights.[25] Thus, the claim under scrutiny would have to be made more specific. The claim would have to be that the particular kind of trade restrictions we are considering objectionably interfere with consumer freedom.

But *do* these restrictions interfere with consumer freedom in an objectionable way? Note that the restrictions proposed in the MMPA did not undermine the availability of any product that anyone might wish to purchase. As the GATT panel was eager to stress, the physical properties of tuna caught by US boats were no different to the physical properties of tuna caught by Mexican boats. What was made unavailable was not tuna, nor even a particular type of tuna, but rather tuna caught in a particular way. And while many consumers undoubtedly have a preference for tuna caught in a dolphin-safe manner, it seems highly unlikely that anyone has a preference for tuna caught in a manner that harms dolphins, other things being equal.

Many consumers do, of course, have a preference for *low-price* products, and products made or processed with animal-harming PPMs may often be cheaper than products made or processed with non-animal-harming PPMs. This forces us to consider whether a particular cost associated with animal-protecting trade restrictions (more expensive food) is proportionate to the benefit that those restrictions aim to bring about (less unethical treatment of animals). This question is made more difficult to answer by the fact that increases in food prices will be more of a burden for some individuals than for others. Even the richest societies have many members who struggle to afford nourishing food, and others for whom eating well has a sizeable opportunity cost. For example, many people have to choose between an acceptable diet, on the one hand, and heating their homes adequately during the winter, on the other. These observations flag-up a familiar problem: a measure taken to mitigate injustice in one sphere can often exacerbate injustice elsewhere if complementary measures are not introduced simultaneously. In this case, a

---

[25] Similarly, if animals have rights, it is not morally permissible to contribute to practices that subject them to torture or death. But, as mentioned in the text, I do not want to base my arguments on the claim that animals have rights.

measure designed to protect animals from unethical treatment risks aggravating the plight of the poor. This problem does not show that animal-protecting trade restrictions should be abjured. But it does show that if we introduce such restrictions without also making efforts to ameliorate the condition of society's worst-off members, the ethical gains that those restrictions can potentially realize will be offset, to some degree, by ethical losses elsewhere.

I have been considering the effects on consumer freedom of trade restrictions that prevent the importation of products made using certain kinds of animal-harming PPMs. I noted that restrictions such as those proposed by the MMPA do not undermine the availability of any products that consumers may wish to purchase. However, trade restrictions that prevent the importation of certain animal-based products per se, rather than products made using a particular method, *do*, of course, undermine the availability of certain products. How can such restrictions be defended against the claim that they constitute an objectionable form of interference with consumer freedom? When such restrictions target products derived from *endangered* species[26] they can be justified to those whose consumer freedom is reduced on the grounds that trade in endangered species imposes potentially huge costs (or 'externalities') upon third parties. Diminished biodiversity precipitated by species extinction poses a potential threat to all humanity. Complex and poorly understood interdependencies exist between species, and the extinction of one can have drastic, and often unanticipated, consequences for others. This is especially true of 'keystone species'—such as elephants and rhinoceroses (both of which are endangered and protected by trade prohibitions)—which dramatically influence the composition of the ecosystems in which they live.[27] One philosopher has compared the extinguishing of species to a game of Russian roulette: 'Each species lost without serious consequences has been a blank in the chamber. But how can we know before we pull the trigger?'[28] Those who wish to purchase products derived from endangered species clearly do not have the right to force the rest of us to participate in this game. And if they realized that the stakes were so high, it is unlikely that they would wish to participate themselves.

---

[26] See the *Convention on International Trade in Endangered Species of Wild Fauna and Flora* (CITES) (available at: http://www.cites.org/sites/default/files/eng/disc/E-Text.pdf).

[27] Edward O. Wilson, *The Diversity of Life* (London: Penguin Books, 1992), pp. 154–7.

[28] Bryan Norton, 'Commodity, Amenity, and Morality: The Limits of Quantification in Valuing Biodiversity', in Edward O. Wilson (ed.), *Biodiversity* (Washington, DC: National Academy Press, 1988), p. 205. Wilson asks: 'if enough species are extinguished, will the ecosystems collapse, and will the extinction of most other species follow soon afterward? The only answer anyone can give is: possibly. By the time we find out, however, it might be too late. One planet, one experiment.' *Diversity of Life*, p. 170. Even when the extinction of an animal species does not precipitate ecosystem collapse, it can harm humanity by, for example, triggering the demise of a species of flora with (known or unknown) medicinal properties.

Some trade restrictions target animal-based products that are not derived from endangered species. For example, the importation of seal products and cat and dog fur is outlawed throughout the EU. These restrictions can be justified on the grounds that the costs they impose on certain consumers are proportionate to the value of the ends they aim to achieve. The harms inflicted on cats, dogs, and seals in order to turn their bodies into consumer products are almost unspeakably heinous. Seals are clubbed to death in the first weeks of their lives, while cats and dogs are often skinned alive.[29] Even if we attribute less weight to animals' interests in avoiding suffering than to the analogous human interests, it seems clear that the costs imposed upon certain consumers by embargoes that prevent them from acquiring seal products and cat and dog fur are massively outweighed by the value of the protections such embargoes afford the animals from which those products are derived.

Unjustifiable Interference with Political Freedom

Let us move on to consider a third objection to animal-protecting trade restrictions. According to this objection, such restrictions disrespect the sovereign right of political communities to formulate their own policies and laws. In a second GATT dispute concerning the MMPA, the panel objected to the US tuna embargo on the grounds that, in the view of the panel, it was 'taken to force other countries to change their policies with respect to persons and things within their own jurisdiction'.[30] The panel claimed that this must have been the aim of the embargo, since it 'required such changes in order to have any effect on the conservation of dolphins.'[31]

The first thing to observe here is that even if it is true that the efficacy of the US embargo was contingent upon its ability to compel other countries to change their policies (I examine the truth of that proposition below), it is not true of all embargoes on products that are produced in a manner that harms animals. An embargo on an animal-harming product can promote the conservation—or, more generally, the protection—of vulnerable animals even if it does not induce other countries to alter their animal-harming policies. This is for the obvious reason that producers supply only enough of a product to satisfy market demand. Given that an embargo on an animal-harming product will reduce effective demand for that product, an embargo would result in decreased production of that product, and, *ceteris paribus*, fewer animals would be harmed.[32]

---

[29] PETA, 'The Chinese Fur Industry' (available at: http://www.peta.org/issues/animals-used-for-clothing/fur/chinese-fur-industry/).

[30] *United States—Restrictions on Imports of Tuna: Report of the Panel*, 16th June 1994, para. 5.24 (available at: http://www.worldtradelaw.net/reports/gattpanels/tunadolphinII.pdf).

[31] *United States—Restrictions on Imports of Tuna*.

[32] Howse and Regan, 'The Product/Process Distinction', p. 274.

The US tuna embargo was more complicated because it prohibited the importation of *all* tuna sold by countries that lacked adequate dolphin-protection standards, and not only tuna caught using dolphin-lethal methods. The GATT panel might be understood to have been claiming that *this aspect* of the embargo could promote the goal of dolphin conservation/protection only to the degree that it compelled foreign governments to change their policies. Unless an embargo on all tuna from a country lacking adequate dolphin-protection standards induced the government of that country to change its policies, an embargo targeting only tuna caught using dolphin-lethal methods, it might be argued, would be no less effective at promoting the conservation/protection of dolphins.

This argument fails. The US could reasonably maintain that an embargo targeting only tuna caught using dolphin-lethal methods would promote the conservation/protection of dolphins less effectively than the more comprehensive embargo it proposed, even if the latter did not compel the government to change its policies. The less comprehensive embargo would permit US citizens to buy products from companies that use dolphin-lethal methods, provided that the particular items they purchase were not secured using such methods, and would thus enable those companies to acquire from US citizens resources with which to fund the slaughter of dolphins. The less comprehensive embargo would conduce to the continued economic vitality of companies employing dolphin-lethal methods in a way that the comprehensive embargo would not.[33]

So far I have resisted the claim that the efficacy of an embargo on animal-harming products is dependent on its ability to compel foreign governments to change their policies. It does not follow, of course, that an embargo will not have the effect of compelling foreign governments to change their policies. In the event, Mexico did not yield to US pressure, and chose to endure the embargo rather than change its policies.[34] But things might have been different. Suppose the US market had been more important to Mexico, and the government had concluded that the option of not changing its policies were too costly to seriously consider. And suppose we accept that the US embargo had thereby *forced* the Mexican government to change its policies. Should we infer from that fact that the embargo was morally unacceptable? Would the US have acted wrongfully by forcing the Mexican authorities in this way? In order to answer this question, it is necessary to consider the nature of the costs that would have been imposed upon Mexico.

---

[33] Howse and Regan overlook this point when attempting to justify their refusal to defend 'country-based' measures. See Howse and Regan, 'The Product/Process Distinction', pp. 252, 269.

[34] The embargo was lifted in 2000 when Mexico, the US, and several other countries reached an agreement that, while not banning the use of purse seine nets, set limits on dolphin mortality rates.

It seems that the costs would have been exclusively economic in nature. It is not like Mexico has a cultural or moral commitment to the use of particular fishing methods. Certain technologies employed by Mexican fisheries in the Eastern Tropical Pacific would suddenly have been made redundant, and would have had to be replaced. Perhaps new fishing methods would have had to be learned. And perhaps income would have been foregone in the transitional phase between the use of old and new methods. Given that Mexico is a developing country, it is reasonable to think that the US would have had an obligation to minimize the transitional costs that its embargo would have imposed. It could have done this by, say, sharing information with Mexican fisheries, and by providing technical assistance. Indeed, when the US embargoed shrimp caught using technologies harmful to endangered sea turtles, it offered workshops and seminars explaining how alternative, turtle-safe technology works, and how it can be implemented at low cost.[35]

The cost associated with transitioning from the use of one set of technologies to another is not the only economic burden imposed upon poor countries by animal-protecting trade restrictions when such restrictions force them to change their policies. When poor countries are forced to conform to higher standards adhered to by richer countries, they lose the competitive edge that lower standards afford. Lower standards typically entail lower production costs, lower production costs entail lower prices, and lower prices entail greater success in the global marketplace. When an embargo forces poor countries to bring their standards into line with those of rich countries, the former forgo potential income gains, and thus might complain that the embargoing country has undermined their development prospects.

Moreover, rich countries can defend animal-protecting trade restrictions only by appealing to the very weak ethical principle that I have also been relying on, namely, that it is wrong to inflict excessive or unnecessary suffering upon animals. Rich countries cannot, in good faith, appeal to any stronger principles, because stronger principles are clearly violated by their own factory farming practices. But if permitting the use of PPMs such as those outlawed by the MMPA enables poor country firms to outcompete their international rivals, and thereby contributes to economic development, poor countries might argue that such PPMs do *not* impose excessive or unnecessary suffering upon animals; rather, the harms imposed are proportionate to the gains reaped.

This is a powerful argument, and one that must be taken seriously. If rich countries are to vindicate the use of animal-protecting trade restrictions against poor countries, they must ensure that such restrictions do not undermine those countries' development prospects. If a country lacks the capacity

---

[35] Robert Howse, 'The Turtles Panel: Another Environmental Disaster in Geneva', *Journal of World Trade*, Vol. 32, No. 5, 1998, pp. 73–100, at p. 97.

to develop—or to develop at an adequate pace—without violating minimal duties to non-human animals, then rich countries attempting to enforce compliance with those duties must be willing to bear the costs that compliance would otherwise impose on the poor.

Disguised Protectionism

Let us consider one final objection. According to this objection, trade restrictions ostensibly imposed to protect animals are often disguised forms of protectionism. Possible grounds for this objection are revealed by reflection upon the domestic farming practices of the US. Throughout this chapter I have used the US as an example of a state that has restricted trade in order to protect animals and enforce compliance with the principle that excessive or unnecessary suffering should not be inflicted. But the US itself massively violates this principle on a daily basis. The US has no federal laws to protect farm animals while on the farm,[36] and only a handful of states have introduced legislation to protect those animals.[37] Consequently, millions of farm animals across the US are subjected to horrendous and depraved acts of cruelty. For example, US farmers are legally permitted not only to castrate pigs, but to castrate them without first administering an anaesthetic.[38] (This practice is also common throughout Europe.[39]) Such practices flagrantly violate the principle that excessive or unnecessary suffering should not be inflicted upon animals. But this observation calls into question US motives for introducing trade restrictions such as those authorized by the MMPA. If US legislators are genuinely concerned about animal welfare, why do they not introduce federal laws to protect farm animals? Does the absence of such laws not reveal that the real aim of trade restrictions ostensibly imposed in order to reduce animal suffering is actually the protection of domestic industries from foreign competition?

Canada recently advanced an argument of this kind against the EC's ban on the importation of seal products. Describing Canada's argument, the Appellate Body wrote:

> Canada contends that a 'risk' to public morals in the European Union can be found to exist only if the evidence shows that 'the commercial seal hunts targeted by the ban exhibit a degree or incidence of animal suffering that falls below the standard or norm of right and wrong conduct in the context of animal welfare shown to prevail within the [European Union].' In this regard, Canada recalls that

---

[36] Shaffner, *Animals and the Law*, p. 104.   [37] Shaffner, *Animals and the Law*, pp. 110–11.
[38] Shaffner, *Animals and the Law*, p. 55.
[39] RSPCA, 'Pigs—Key Welfare Issues' (available at: https://www.rspca.org.uk/adviceandwelfare/farm/pigs/keyissues/-/articleName/FAD_AllAboutAnimalsPigsKeyIssues)

it presented evidence to show that 'EU policies and practices with respect to animal welfare included a tolerance for a certain degree of animal suffering, both for slaughterhouses and wildlife hunts.'[40]

The first thing to say here is that concerns of this kind cannot ground an objection to animal-protecting trade restrictions *tout court*, but only to the imposition of such restrictions by states that legally sanction practices that inflict upon animals excessive or unnecessary suffering. If a state can show that it does not sanction such practices, any animal-protecting trade restrictions it imposes are not vulnerable to the objection under scrutiny. The second thing to say is that the toleration of domestic practices that inflict excessive or unnecessary suffering upon animals does not necessarily impugn the imposition of trade restrictions ostensibly motivated by the conviction that the infliction of excessive or unnecessary suffering upon animals is unacceptable. The fact that legislators take action against one set of practices on the grounds that those practices violate a particular ethical principle but fail to take action against another set of practices that also violate that principle may simply reflect feasibility constraints. Tackling the former set might be feasible, while tackling the latter set might not. Indeed, a common explanation for the legal toleration of egregious factory farming practices in the US focuses on the considerable political power of the agricultural industry.[41]

If a state embargoes the importation of a set of products on the grounds that the production or processing of those products involves ethically unacceptable practices, while permitting the use of the same practices by domestic producers, the embargo will, admittedly, seem intuitively unfair, even if toleration of the disfavoured practices at the domestic level is explained by feasibility constraints. Such an embargo would place burdens upon foreign producers that are not borne by their domestic counterparts, despite the fact that the latter also engage in activities that are regarded as rendering the former liable to penalties. But consider the following scenario, to which the US tuna embargo conforms. Suppose that a state embargoes a set of products the production or processing of which involves an ethically unacceptable practice P (P-generated products), and also outlaws the domestic use of P, but fails to embargo a set of products the production or processing of which involves a practice Q (Q-generated products) that violates the same ethical principle as P, and also fails to outlaw the domestic use of Q. Suppose, further, that there is a plausible explanation for the asymmetrical treatment of P-generated products and Q-generated products, e.g., the latter are produced by a politically powerful industry, while the former are not. It seems to me that

---

[40] *EC—Seals Products*, para. 5.194 (footnotes omitted).
[41] Shaffner, *Animals and the Law*, p. 37.

the embargo on P-generated products is morally permissible. Importantly, the constraints imposed on foreign producers of P-generated products are also borne by domestic producers of P-generated products.

It is also worth noting in this context that while the US is morally permitted to embargo products made with animal-harming methods that are outlawed domestically, the US is itself an appropriate target for animal-protecting trade restrictions. Countries that have outlawed egregious animal-harming practices that are sanctioned by the US are morally entitled to impose restrictions on US imports in order to minimize the infliction upon animals of excessive and unnecessary suffering.

III

Conclusion

This brings my discussion of animal-protecting trade restrictions to a close. I do not claim to have replied to all of the objections that might be levelled against such restrictions, but I have replied to those objections most amenable to a philosophical response. In doing so, I hope to have also brought more sharply into focus the value of the ends that animal-protecting trade restrictions can serve.

4

The Harms of Trade III

Labour, Culture, and Development

In chapters 2 and 3, I considered a variety of ways in which serious physical harms are inflicted by trade, and defended the use of trade restrictions to prevent such harms. While such injuries are especially serious, they are not the only form of harm in which trade is implicated, nor are they the only ones that merit careful attention. Many of those who protest international trade deals are exercised by the threat those deals pose not to their physical safety, but to their socio-economic and cultural interests; they object to trade liberalization on the grounds that it destroys their jobs, shrinks their wages, and degrades their national culture, thereby undermining their standard of living. These harms are the subject of the present chapter.

The chapter unfolds as follows. Section I analyses the claim that trade restrictions should be used to nullify the threat that trade poses to jobs. Bracketing the special interests of developing countries, I argue that, while workers displaced by free trade can be compensated for their losses, trade restrictions can be justified if sufficient compensation is not forthcoming. Section II considers two alternative approaches to the problem of labour displacement—one advanced by Mathias Risse, the other by Aaron James—and identifies problems with each. Section III examines the claim that trade should be restricted in order to preserve cultural distinctiveness. Again bracketing the special interests of developing countries, I argue that a concern for cultural preservation can plausibly be thought to ground a case for restricting trade. However, in section IV, I add an important proviso: I argue that developed countries may restrict trade only on the condition that the restrictions they impose do not diminish the development prospects of poor countries. I suggest that, in practice, this condition seriously constrains the right of developed countries to protect their own workers by restricting trade. Section V notes that trade may impose socio-economic and cultural harms upon the developing world, and addresses developing country use of restrictive measures to prevent such harms.

I

Labour Displacement

I begin by considering whether restrictive measures can be justified on the grounds that free trade causes many workers in import-competing industries to lose their jobs. In section II, I will consider whether such measures can be justified on the grounds that they are necessary to preserve cultural distinct-iveness. The question posed in these sections is whether *developed* countries can justify the use of restrictive measures on the grounds I have mentioned, and for the time being I bracket the special claim that *developing* countries have to access developed country markets. Later in the chapter I will remove these brackets, and consider how the special claims of developing countries force us to revise our conclusions.

Advocates of free trade are far from oblivious to the concern that their preferred economic arrangements result in the destruction of jobs, and they have responded to the problem in a variety of different ways. One response is to point out that while free trade certainly imposes burdens on some groups, those burdens are outweighed by the benefits that accrue to others. A second response is to note that displaced workers can find new employment in expanding export industries. And a third response is to observe that those who lose from free trade can be compensated by the state. Let us consider each of these responses in turn.

Burdens Outweighed by Benefits

It is sometimes said that while some workers will certainly suffer as a result of free trade, these burdens are outweighed by the benefits that trade brings.[1] This response is undermined by the fact that it is insensitive to how the benefits and burdens of trade are distributed. This distribution-insensitivity obscures a number of important considerations. First, while the total gains from free trade may well outweigh the total costs, the gains are often highly diffuse, and the benefits received by any given individual are often small. By contrast, the burdens one bears as a result of losing one's job are, of course,

---

[1] See, for example, Douglas A. Irwin, *Against the Tide: An Intellectual History of Free Trade* (Princeton, NJ: Princeton University Press, 1996), p. 88.

sizeable.[2] One way of framing this point is to say that the defence of free trade under scrutiny rests upon an unacceptably reified conception of society. It identifies a social entity which enjoys large gains, when, in actuality, there is simply a multitude of individuals who either receive modest benefits or bear heavy burdens.

Second, in rich countries, the gains from trade will often accrue to those who are already relatively advantaged, while the costs will befall those who are relatively disadvantaged. The Stolper-Samuelson model of trade predicts that the gains will be captured by those who derive their income from abundant factors of production, while the costs will be incurred by owners of scarce factors.[3] This means that, in wealthy countries, the gains from trade liberaliza-tion go to (relatively advantaged) capital and skilled labour, while the costs are borne by (relatively disadvantaged) unskilled labour.[4] It is difficult to see how a society can justify an economic reconfiguration which harms the working poor only to enhance the prospects of those who are already better-off.[5]

In an article on the gap between economists and the US public over the issue of free trade, Cletus Coughlin observes that 'some oppose free trade because of their recognition that others will lose. This clash suggests that many in the general public differ from economists in how they weigh the costs and benefits of free trade policies.'[6] Elaborating, he notes that 'individuals are willing to support trade restrictions to improve the job and income prospects of low-income workers'[7] and that free trade's 'adverse effects for...low-income individual[s] might be viewed as outweighing the beneficial effect for...high-income individual[s].'[8] It is important to note that this is not an

---

[2] Cf. Aaron James, *Fairness in Practice: A Social Contract for a Global Economy* (New York: Oxford University Press, 2012), pp. 207–8.

[3] Wolfgang F. Stolper and Paul A. Samuelson, 'Protection and Real Wages', *Review of Economic Studies*, No. 9, 1941, pp. 58–73.

[4] Unskilled labourers will benefit from free trade qua consumers, but clearly the gains they enjoy in their capacity as consumers are outweighed by the costs they bear in their capacity as displaced workers.

[5] While unskilled labourers are disadvantaged relative to skilled labourers, they are not necessarily the least advantaged members of society. If it could be shown that free trade benefits the least advantaged, the case for job-preserving restrictive measures would be weakened. Fernando Tesón has argued that trade must be free precisely because it benefits the least advantaged members of the developed world (Fernando R. Tesón, 'Why Free Trade is Required by Justice', *Social Philosophy and Policy*, Vol. 29, No. 1, 2012, pp. 126–53, at pp. 137–8). Teson's argument rests on two empirical premises: (i) trade promotes growth, and (ii) growth is good for the poorest members of developed countries. Note that the second empirical premise is particularly controversial. The social scientists Richard Wilkinson and Kate Pickett have provided evidence that demonstrates that, while economic growth is crucial for poor countries, once a certain threshold of national affluence is crossed, continued economic growth ceases to contribute positively to human welfare (Richard Wilkinson and Kate Pickett, *The Spirit Level: Why More Equal Societies Almost Always Do Better* (London: Penguin Books, 2009), Ch. 1).

[6] Cletus C. Coughlin, 'The Controversy over Free Trade: The Gap Between Economists and the General Public', *The Federal Reserve Bank of St. Louis*, January/February, 2002, pp. 1–22, at p. 18.

[7] Coughlin, 'Controversy over Free Trade', p. 11.

[8] Coughlin, 'Controversy over Free Trade', p. 12.

empirical dispute, but rather a normative disagreement about how the benefits and burdens of trade should be weighted. On this point at least, the general public are not contesting the results of economic studies; rather, they are contesting the inferences economists have drawn from those results.

Expanding Export Industries

Let us now consider another response to the problem of labour displacement. It is often pointed out that while workers may lose their current jobs as a result of free trade, they will be able to find alternative employment in export-oriented industries expanding to meet global demand.[9] One notable weakness of this response is that it downplays the cost of losing one's job. While workers displaced by free trade may well be able to find new jobs, these are likely to pay lower wages. Citing figures from the US Trade Deficit Review Commission, Coughlin notes that

> [m]any displaced workers, especially those with much tenure, suffer not only during the period between jobs but also after they become reemployed. For example, the weekly earnings of all reemployed workers fell 5.7 percent on average during 1995–97. Those displaced from high-tenure jobs experienced a wage decline of over 20 percent.[10]

Moreover, the cost of transitioning from one job to another is not measured exclusively in terms of reduced earnings. Losing one's job can involve being ejected from a familiar environment which one may have grown to regard with affection; being separated from one's colleagues with whom one may have formed valuable relationships; being forced to adapt to a new, possibly more arduous, routine; and, more generally, being subjected to considerable anxiety. It should also be noted that workers' identities are sometimes bound up, to a greater or lesser degree, with their occupations. When they lose their jobs, their sense of identity can be undermined.

Compensation

These considerations motivate support for a third response to the claim that trade should be restricted in order to protect jobs. This response points out that the gains from trade can be redistributed in order to compensate those who are displaced. Moreover, compensation can go well beyond existing trade

---

[9] Irvin points out that this argument was first made, by a number of economists, at the turn of the eighteenth century. *Against the Tide*, pp. 54, 55, 58.

[10] Coughlin, 'Controversy Over Free Trade', p. 16. This point is also made in Dani Rodrik, *The Globalization Paradox: Why Global Markets, States, and Democracy Can't Coexist* (Oxford: Oxford University Press, 2011), pp. 56, 87.

adjustment assistance schemes (which often offer extended unemployment benefits, retraining, out-of-area job search allowances, and moving expenses). If displaced workers see their earnings decline, their income can be supplemented on an ongoing basis by the state, and non-pecuniary costs of the kind I described in the previous paragraph (which we might refer to as 'reductions in well-being') can also be offset by state payments.[11] Trade would then be Pareto efficient: some are made better-off while none are made worse-off.

Now, it might be argued that compensation is not necessary to justify the imposition of the various pecuniary and non-pecuniary costs I described above. The argument for compensation maintains that unskilled workers should be compensated for any reductions in income or well-being brought about by free trade. If a worker's wage or well-being under free trade is lower than it was prior to liberalization, she should receive state payments which ensure that her overall income/well-being level remains unchanged. But, it might be argued, this fetishizes the worker's initial wage/well-being level. Consider the claim that workers should be compensated for reduced earnings. Why, one might ask, should a worker's market-determined income level under autarky (or any regime falling short of completely free trade) be regarded as the income level which that worker must meet under free trade in order for justice to obtain? If the initial wage was regarded as just simply by virtue of the fact that it was the market wage, then, surely, the new wage should be regarded as just by virtue of the fact that, in an expanded, international, economy, *it* is now the market wage. Compensation is thus unnecessary in order to vindicate free trade. Alternatively, if the initial wage was regarded as just because, say, it was sufficient for the worker to enjoy an adequate standard of living, the new wage should be regarded as just provided that it is also sufficient for the worker to enjoy an adequate standard of living, and irrespective of whether it is as high as the initial wage. Again, compensation is unnecessary.

What should we make of this objection? If one endorses the libertarian view that justice entitles people to what they acquire through voluntary exchange, it is true that one is committed to the view that tax funded compensation is not only unnecessary, but also unjust. This should come as no surprise. But other, more plausible, conceptions of justice are more accommodating. Consider, first, the sufficientarian view, according to which justice requires ensuring that everyone can enjoy an adequate standard of living. If free trade reduces workers' living standards to below the specified adequacy threshold,

---

[11] In a footnote, Tesón voices support for '[d]omestic transfer policies' aimed at displaced labour ('Free Trade is Required by Justice', p. 138, n. 38). This support jars with his claim, made in the main text on the same page, that protectionist measures 'do not benefit persons or groups that, on any plausible theory of domestic or international justice, are entitled to a transfer of wealth in their favour'.

then, clearly, sufficientarians will maintain that justice requires either trade restrictions or compensatory transfer payments. If, by contrast, free trade lowers some workers' living standards, but not to a level below the sufficientarian threshold, compensation will not be *required* by justice, but neither will it be prohibited (unless, of course, the taxation required to fund compensation would inevitably put others below the threshold—but that seems unlikely). Other conceptions of justice provide resources with which to defend compensation as a requirement of justice. A Rawlsian view, for example, can maintain that, in the absence of compensatory transfer payments, free trade would create inequalities which are not necessary to benefit the least advantaged, and are thus in violation of the 'difference principle' (according to which inequalities are permissible only if they are maximally beneficial to the worst-off members of society). Compensatory transfers can also be endorsed from a 'luck egalitarian' perspective, which calls for the elimination of inequalities that cannot be attributed to choices made by the disadvantaged.

It is important to be clear about why luck egalitarians can endorse compensatory transfers. Luck egalitarians will recommend compensation not simply because trade liberalization itself is often beyond the control of those it disadvantages, a matter of chance rather than choice. After all, it is not difficult to identify a number of basic structural changes that are beyond the control of those they disadvantage but which do not offend against the luck egalitarian conception of justice. For example, the idle offspring of wealthy parents may be rendered worse-off than their industrious peers by a law (which, let us suppose, they resisted) introducing high levels of inheritance tax. But a luck egalitarian would not hold that such inequalities call for rectification. The reason that luck egalitarians can insist upon compensation in the trade case is that the disadvantages suffered by low-skilled workers in the kind of integrated market that liberalization creates will often be attributable to the natural and social lotteries whose influence luck egalitarians have always sought to extinguish. That is, those who fare poorly in a global market are often disadvantaged by the kinds of contingencies (social background, upbringing, genetic endowment, etc.) that luck egalitarian doctrine has, since the outset, regarded as paradigmatic sources of injustice. This contrasts with the inheritance tax case mentioned a moment ago in which a basic structural change beyond the control of those it disadvantages is intended to *mitigate* such contingencies. The problem that luck egalitarians will identify in the trade case is not that liberalization is itself often largely beyond the control of those it adversely affects, but rather that trade liberalization creates (or sustains in a modified form) an environment in which the worse-off are (further) disadvantaged by the kinds of bad brute luck that luck egalitarians have always recognized as generative of injustice. Those who lose out are disadvantaged because, unlike more fortunate individuals, they lack the skills needed to thrive in such an environment. The introduction of compensatory transfer payments in the wake of trade liberalization is simply a means of ensuring that society satisfies (or continues to satisfy) the demands of luck egalitarian justice in changed circumstances.[12]

One point which emerges from the foregoing discussion is that, when deciding whether or not compensation is morally required, we must defer to the correct conception of distributive justice.[13] If we believe that conception to be libertarian in character, compensation is not something that we will recommend. By contrast, if we hold a sufficientarian, Rawlsian, or luck egalitarian conception of distributive justice, we can (and, in some cases, should) endorse compensation. Let us assume that the correct conception of distributive justice is one that commits us to the view that free trade can be justified only if displaced workers are fully compensated for the losses they incur, and see where this takes us. We shall see that such an account can vindicate the conclusion that, under certain conditions, we should choose to restrict trade, rather than to liberalize trade and provide compensation.

Robert Goodin has distinguished between two types of compensation: *means-replacing compensation* and *ends-displacing compensation*.[14] Means-replacing compensation (Compensation 1) aims to 'provide people with equivalent means for pursuing the same ends (the same as before they suffered the loss, or as they would have pursued had they not suffered the disadvantage)'.[15] In other words, it replaces like with like.[16] Ends-displacing compensation (Compensation 2), by contrast, aims to 'provide [people] with equivalent satisfactions through different ends.'[17] In other words, it substitutes one sort of pleasure for another,[18] or 'compensat[es] people in one realm for losses suffered in another realm entirely.'[19] Both types of compensation leave people as well-off as they would have been in the absence of the loss for which they are compensated, but whereas Compensation 1 leaves people 'identically situated with respect to exactly the

---

[12] Note that compensating individuals who lack the skills needed to thrive in an integrated market is a reactive measure. It may seem that a preferable approach would be the *proactive* one of ensuring that the individuals in question possess the relevant skills. This approach can address skill-deficits attributable to social factors (such as inadequate education), but to the extent that natural factors (genetic endowment) remain a source of the problem, compensation will still be required.

[13] Cf. Mathias Risse and Gabriel Wollner, 'Critical notice of Aaron James, Fairness in Practice: A Social Contract for a Global Economy', *Canadian Journal of Philosophy*, Vol. 43, No. 3, 2013, pp. 382–401, at pp. 391–2, 397–8.

[14] Robert E. Goodin, 'Theories of Compensation', *Oxford Journal of Legal Studies*, Vol. 9, No. 1, 1989, pp. 56–75, at p. 60.

[15] Goodin, 'Theories of Compensation', p. 60.

[16] Goodin, 'Theories of Compensation', p. 61.

[17] Goodin, 'Theories of Compensation', p. 60.

[18] Goodin, 'Theories of Compensation', p. 61.

[19] Goodin, 'Theories of Compensation', p. 63.

same set of ends', Compensation 2 leaves people 'differently off than they would have been.'[20]

Goodin is critical of policies that generate costs that can be offset only by ends-displacing compensation. Such policies, Goodin writes, amount to 'forcibly shifting [people] from one set of plans and projects to another', and thus compromise individual autonomy, which is a 'central tenet of the liberal ethos.'[21] Labour-displacing trade liberalization is clearly a policy of this sort. When workers are displaced from one job, and reemployed elsewhere, they are 'forcibly shift[ed] . . . from one set of plans and projects to another.' When they receive pecuniary compensation for this loss (which is the only kind of compensation available), they are compensated 'in one realm for losses suffered in another realm entirely.' One might argue that certain jobs are mere means (i.e., for obtaining income) and not 'projects'. But given that displacement entails the kinds of well-being-reducing costs I identified earlier (ejection from a familiar environment, separation from one's colleagues, etc.), it remains true that pecuniary compensation (which, again, is the only kind of compensation available) is an instance of Compensation 2. Does it follow from Goodin's critique of Compensation 2 that free trade should be eschewed?

Not necessarily. In the final paragraph of his paper Goodin acknowledges that there can be 'all sorts of reasons' for or against pursuing a particular policy, and the fact that it is not possible to grant means-replacing compensation to those who will lose out is 'just one among many'.[22] He concludes that 'on balance we may well decide that it is best to go ahead with the policy', even though, because Compensation 2 is the only form of compensation available, it is not true that those who suffer a loss 'have no grounds for complaint.'[23] This conclusion strikes me as correct. Elaborating, we can say this: provided that ends-displacing pecuniary compensation is sufficiently generous, some policies which comprise autonomy to some degree can be tolerated.

In this connection, it is important to inquire about the size of the gains that labour-displacing trade liberalization can be expected to generate. If the expected gains are small, they might be inadequate to fund sufficiently generous compensation (and thus insufficient to ensure that trade is Pareto efficient). The size of the gains from trade-liberalizing policies depends on, *inter alia*, how liberal trade was to begin with. *Ceteris paribus*, a highly protectionist country stands to gain much more from freeing trade than a relatively liberal country stands to gain from pursuing further liberalization. Given that trade barriers among today's developed countries are generally very low, it is

---

[20] Goodin, 'Theories of Compensation', p. 60.
[21] Goodin, 'Theories of Compensation', pp. 68–9.
[22] Goodin, 'Theories of Compensation', p. 75.
[23] Goodin, 'Theories of Compensation', p. 75.

possible that the gains these countries can expect from further liberalization would be inadequate to fund sufficient compensation for displaced workers.[24]

Whether the gains from trade will be sufficient in this way depends on just how generous pecuniary compensation has to be in order to be adequate, and specifying that level will not be easy. But what we can say is this: when the gains from trade are inadequate to fund sufficient compensation for displaced workers, trade should be restricted (provided, of course, that the correct conception of justice commits us to the view that compensation is necessary to vindicate free trade). Trade should also be restricted if sufficient compensation is not forthcoming for some other reason (e.g., if the provision of compensation is politically infeasible, because citizens are not willing to support it).

II

Two Alternative Approaches

In section I, I argued that our response to the problem of labour displacement should be informed by our conception of distributive justice. If the correct conception of distributive justice is sufficientarian, Rawlsian, or luck egalitarian in nature, we can (and, in some cases, should) recommend the introduction of compensatory transfer payments. If the gains from trade are inadequate to fund sufficient compensation (or if sufficient compensation is unavailable because, say, its provision is politically infeasible), trade should be restricted. In this section, I consider two alternative approaches to the problem of labour displacement. The first of these is taken by Mathias Risse, while the second is taken by Aaron James. I will argue that both approaches have shortcomings, but that Risse's contains an important insight that I shall later integrate into my own account.

Risse's Approach to the Problem of Labour Displacement

Risse asks whether domestic workers 'have a claim for compensation from their government' if they are harmed by the maintenance of oppressive or lower labour standards abroad.[25] He claims that an affirmative answer can be given to this question if domestic labour standards are adopted for moral reasons; that is, if they are motivated by 'a certain view of the person, and

---

[24] James, *Fairness in Practice*, p. 214.
[25] Mathias Risse, 'Fairness in trade I: obligations from trading and the pauper-labor argument', *Politics, Philosophy & Economics*, Vol. 6, No. 3, 2007, pp. 355–77, at p. 366.

the kind of protection to be granted to persons.'[26] More specifically, he argues that domestic workers have a claim to redress if domestic labour standards are grounded in the view that in order to 'avoid setting incentives to treat people badly and out of respect for those who have been treated badly, nobody should benefit from poor treatment of others in any way.'[27] If domestic standards are undergirded by this view, then consistency-based considerations serve as reasons for governments to formulate trade policy in a way that does not provide foreign competitors with incentives to treat their workers poorly, or enable them to benefit from doing so. We must be sensitive to the fact that by importing goods produced in countries with low or oppressive labour standards, and thus creating demand for those goods, we are creating such incentives, and thereby acting contrary to our own moral reasons. Risse concludes that domestic parties who are economically vulnerable as a result of low or oppressive standards abroad 'deserve' some form of redress.[28]

Four points should be made here. First, Risse equivocates between suggesting that (i) *workers* should be *compensated*, and (ii) *industries* should be *protected*.[29] Only the latter view is supported by Risse's proposition that government intervention is called for in order 'to avoid setting incentives to treat people badly and to keep others (for example, foreign competitors) from benefiting from such situations.'[30] Protecting domestic industries (with tariffs, subsidies, etc.) will prevent foreign competitors from benefitting from treating their workers poorly (by offsetting the competitive advantage that such treatment affords), but simply offering domestic workers *ex post* compensation for harms already inflicted by successful foreign competitors will not.

Second, foreign competitors are not the only ones who benefit from the importation of goods produced under low or oppressive conditions. Consumers in the importing country also benefit (i.e., from lower prices). This benefit—like the benefit to foreign competitors—will not be eliminated by compensating workers (though it may be offset by taxes introduced to fund compensation). If we think that we have reasons to prevent one set of individuals benefitting from the maltreatment of others, then this fact constitutes another ground for restricting imports from countries with low or oppressive standards, rather than for permitting imports and compensating workers.

Third, if government protection of domestic industries is required on the grounds that it is necessary 'to avoid setting incentives to treat people badly and to keep others . . . from benefiting from such situations', then while duties of protection are duties *regarding* domestic workers, they are not duties *owed to*

---

[26] Risse, 'Fairness in trade I', p. 367.   [27] Risse, 'Fairness in trade I', p. 367.
[28] Risse, 'Fairness in trade I', p. 367.
[29] Risse speaks of compensation for workers at p. 366 and 367, of compensation and 'aid' for industries at p. 367, and of 'protection' for industries at p. 368.
[30] Risse, 'Fairness in trade I', p. 367.

domestic workers. Rather, the duties are owed to foreign workers whose poor treatment we believe no one should benefit from or incentivize. Thus, to the extent that domestic workers 'deserve' redress, they do so only in a very loose sense of that term. What Risse's argument suggests is that trade restrictions should be put in place because they stop people incentivizing and benefitting from the maltreatment of workers in other countries, not because domestic workers have any kind of independent claim to them. The case for restrictions is grounded in the claims of foreign workers, not our own.

Fourth, Risse concludes his discussion by suggesting that the optimal solution may be to permit trade and redistribute the surplus it yields so that domestic workers do not lose out,[31] but the foregoing observations impugn this suggestion. Such redistribution does not prevent trade incentivizing, or enabling people to benefit from, the poor treatment of foreign workers. It promotes the interests of domestic workers, whom our duties regard, but not those of the developing country workers to whom our duties are owed. The problem here is that Risse's discussion elides two distinct concerns—one about domestic workers, the other about foreign workers—and his policy proposal (permit trade and redistribute the gains among the domestic population) addresses the former only by neglecting the latter.

As I mentioned above, I am bracketing the interests of the developing world until section IV. I will briefly return to Risse's observations about incentivizing maltreatment of foreign workers in that section. (The claim that domestic workers have a distinctive complaint when they are adversely affected by low labour standards abroad is explored further, from a different angle, in chapter 5.)

James's Approach to the Problem of Labour Displacement

Aaron James's approach to labour displacement is provided by his principle of Collective Due Care. According to this principle:

> trading nations are to protect people against the harms of trade (either by temporary trade barriers or 'safeguards,' etc., or, under free trade, by direct compensation or social insurance schemes). Specifically, no person's life prospects are to be worse than they would have been had his or her society been a closed society.[32]

Elaborating on how this principle should be applied, James writes: 'given a manifest specific injury, in some particular context, we compare the person's condition with how well his or her life would have gone had his or her society (perhaps gradually) chosen autarky roughly around his or her birthday.'[33]

---

[31] Risse, 'Fairness in trade I', p. 368.   [32] James, *Fairness in Practice*, p. 203.
[33] James, *Fairness in Practice*, p. 211.

James's principle expresses his view that we should attach greater significance to burdens imposed by trade liberalization than to burdens imposed by autarky (or some regime that falls short of fully free trade). James attempts to motivate support for this view by appealing to the intuition that rendering someone worse-off is more objectionable than denying someone a benefit, at least when the individual whose condition is worsened is not more advantaged than the individual who is denied a benefit. He writes: 'Other things being equal, the objection "I am made worse off" is more powerful than "I could have been better off," in which case either market protection or compensation of the loser carries the day.'[34] Elaborating, James suggests that

> special presumptive weight is to be accorded to ways someone's condition is worsened, relative to what it was at some previous time (i.e., by a historical baseline of comparison), or what it would have been had the policy change in question not occurred (by a subjunctive-historical baseline). At least when other things are equal, worsenings are not on the same footing as mere opportunity costs, or ways one could have done better although one's condition is not worsened in either of the above ways.[35]

Let us begin our assessment of James's argument by considering his claim that special presumptive weight should be ascribed to ways in which someone's condition is worsened in subjunctive-historical terms. In order to evaluate this claim, let us spell out its implications in greater detail. Suppose that, at time T, which is a condition of autarky, X and Y both have a 'well-being' level of 15. Suppose, further, that if autarky is retained, then, at time T + 1, X's well-being level will increase to 17, while Y's well-being level will increase to 16. By contrast, if trade is liberalized, then, at time T + 1, X's well-being level will increase to 16 (meaning that X would be made worse-off according to a subjunctive-historical baseline), while Y's welfare level will increase to 17. James's view tells us that in this situation we are to ascribe special presumptive weight to the way in which X's position would be worsened (in subjunctive-historical terms) by a shift to free trade. Avoiding this worsening, perhaps by refusing to liberalize trade, should take priority over avoiding the opportunity cost that Y will suffer if we maintain the status quo. This is despite the fact that X and Y are identically situated, and despite the fact that the benefits each stands to reap, and the costs each stands to incur, are identical in size.

How could we account for this judgement? Keep in mind that we are not considering a case in which trade liberalization would make X worse-off than he had been at an earlier stage of his life. Rather, we are considering a case in which X is deprived of *future* benefits that he *would* have enjoyed had trade not been liberalized. Why should we regard that deprivation as any more

[34] James, *Fairness in Practice*, p. 207.   [35] James, *Fairness in Practice*, p. 207.

significant than the one suffered by Y when autarky is maintained? James does not provide an answer to this question, so we are left to speculate. We could justify ascribing presumptive weight to X's 'loss' if we thought that special significance should be attributed to the fact that X's loss under free trade is traceable to a policy change (occurring within his lifetime)—namely, trade liberalization—whereas Y's loss under autarky is not traceable to a policy change (occurring within her lifetime). But why attribute special significance to that fact? Perhaps an unarticulated concern about 'rug-pulling' is doing some of the work in James's account. Maybe the thought is that we should take into consideration the fact that X may have formulated plans based on his expected future earnings under autarky, and that to free trade now would be to undermine his 'legitimate expectations'. But, as we have seen, James's view tells us that we should attribute special significance to burdens imposed upon X by trade liberalization if his future prospects are worse than they would have been had a decision to favour autarky over trade been made *around the time of his birthday*. If the contrary decision had been made around this time, X would not, as a sane adult, have formulated any plans based on future earnings that could be expected only if that decision had *not* been made. Thus, a concern about rug-pulling does not arise. It is difficult to know, then, what motivates James's claim.

Puzzlingly, at one point James suggests that we should attach greater significance to the burdens imposed on X even if Y's loss *is* traceable to a policy change. He writes: 'even if the harm [to X] is simply prevented, by retaining *or imposing* a trade barrier, [Y] may be no worse off than before; [she] simply [is] not afforded a benefit.'[36] But if Y is worse-off relative to how she would have fared had a trade barrier not been imposed, then she is worse-off relative to a subjunctive-historical baseline, and James's own account tells us that we should attach special presumptive weight to the burdens she incurs.

Suppose we were to retain James's account, but excise the clause about subjunctive-historical harms. That is, suppose we held that special presumptive weight should be accorded only to ways in which someone's condition is worsened relative to what it was at some earlier time of their life. Would this revision be sufficient to salvage James's account? It seems plausible to hold that making one individual worse-off than she was at an earlier stage of her life simply in order to grant a comparable benefit to a similarly situated individual is worse than denying the benefit and refraining from worsening either person's condition. But notice that, if we are assuming—as James does at this stage of his argument—that trade and autarky generate comparably sized benefits and burdens for similarly situated individuals, then, while this

---

[36] James, *Fairness in Practice*, p. 207 (emphasis added).

judgement lends support to the claim that autarkic societies should eschew trade liberalization (when compensation is unavailable), it can also lend support to the claim that liberalized societies should eschew the introduction of restrictive measures, at least when such measures would render some individuals worse-off than they were at an earlier stage of life simply in order to confer benefits on others. The judgement in question does not identify anything special about harms imposed by liberalization relative to harms imposed by the introduction of protective measures.

Throughout this subsection I have worked with James's 'all else equal' clause. That is, I have assumed that those who benefit from free trade and those who lose from free trade are similarly situated, and I have assumed that the benefits and burdens in question are of a comparable magnitude. Now, as we saw earlier in the chapter, and as James recognizes, in the real world the 'all else equal' clause is not actually satisfied. Those who lose from free trade are typically unskilled workers who are economically worse-off than the owners of capital who benefit from free trade, and the losses suffered (labour displacement and wage suppression) are typically greater than the benefits enjoyed by any particular individual. One can appeal to this fact in order to justify ascribing special significance to the burdens that free trade creates, and to justify restricting trade when compensation is unavailable. But then one is not justifying one's position in the way that James recommends. Rather, James's argument is set aside. My aim here has not been to question James's conclusion—which, as demonstrated earlier in the chapter, can be defended on independent grounds—but rather to challenge his argument.

III

Cultural Degradation

We shall return to the issue of labour displacement in section IV, but for now let us move on to consider another perceived harm associated with trade liberalization. Free trade is sometimes resisted on the grounds that it undermines cultural distinctiveness. Many fear that global free markets have a homogenizing effect on world culture, and believe globalization to be a synonym for American cultural imperialism. Public opinion in France is particularly hostile to globalization, and much of this hostility has its source in concerns about free trade undermining France's unique cultural identity. French politicians have argued vociferously for a principle of 'cultural exception', according to which trade in cultural goods is to be exempt from GATT/ WTO rules, and they have pursued a variety of policies that aim to protect France's cultural heritage from market forces. These policies include quotas requiring that 60 per cent of audiovisual broadcasts be of European origin, subsidies for French film studios (funded by taxation on cinema tickets for domestic and foreign films), and schemes that educate schoolchildren about French cuisine.[37]

A concern for cultural preservation has been used not only to justify restrictions on the free movement of goods across state borders, but also to justify restrictions on the free movement of people. Michael Walzer, for example, has argued as follows:

> The distinctiveness of cultures and groups depends upon closure and, without it, cannot be conceived as a stable feature of human life. If this distinctiveness is a value, as most people...seem to believe, then closure must be permitted somewhere. At some level of political organization, something like the sovereign state must take shape and claim the authority to make its own admissions policy, to control and sometimes restrain the flow of immigrants.[38]

There is, however, an obvious, and perhaps important, asymmetry between the way in which immigration may undermine cultural distinctiveness, and the way in which free trade may undermine cultural distinctiveness. In the former case, it is obvious enough that the decision to immigrate is made not by those whose culture is threatened by immigration, but rather by the foreigners who constitute that threat. However, in the case of trade, the decision to move culture-threatening goods into a culturally vulnerable society is made not just by the outsiders whose goods pose the threat, but also by the members of the society whose culture is threatened. Sellers offer their goods to individuals in foreign markets, and it is up to those individuals to accept or decline the offer.

This fact may be used to ground the following argument against culturally motivated government restrictions on free trade. If people wish to preserve their culture, and believe that the proliferation of certain goods is inimical to cultural preservation, they can simply refrain from purchasing the goods in question. If they buy culture-threatening goods, they consent to any cultural degradation which ensues. International markets, the argument goes, present

---

[37] On the French cultural exception, see, for example, Thomas Bishop, 'France and the Need For Cultural Exception', *New York University Journal of International Law and Politics*, Vol. 29, 1996–7, pp. 187–92; Judith Beth Prowda, 'U.S. Dominance in the "Marketplace of Culture" and the French "Cultural Exception"', *New York University Journal of International Law and Politics*, Vol. 29, 1996–7, pp. 193–210; Sophie Meunier, 'The French Exception', *Foreign Affairs*, July/August, 2000, pp. 104–16; Philip H. Gordon and Sophie Meunier, 'Globalization and French Cultural Identity', *French Politics, Culture & Society*, Vol. 19, No. 1, 2001, pp. 22–41. Related concerns are noted in Kok-Chor Tan, *Justice without Borders: Cosmopolitanism, Nationalism, and Patriotism* (Cambridge: Cambridge University Press, 2004), p. 120, and in Malgorzata Kurjanska and Matthias Risse, 'Fairness in Trade II: Export Subsidies and the Fair Trade Movement', *Politics, Philosophy & Economics*, Vol. 7, No. 1, 2008, pp. 29–56, at pp. 38–9.

[38] Michael Walzer, *Spheres of Justice* (New York: Basic Books, 1983), p. 39.

consumers with a set of choices, and the choices consumers make reflect their preferences. If citizens value cultural preservation, they will express that preference in the marketplace by not buying culture-threatening goods. If, on the other hand, they choose to purchase culture-threatening goods, they clearly do not have the preferences that their government attributes to them. It is therefore both unnecessary and illegitimate for governments to step in and prevent (or limit, or interfere with in whatever way) the sale of certain goods on grounds of cultural preservation. Governments should stop speaking on their citizens' behalf, and allow them to speak for themselves. Objecting to, for example, the Americanization of French culture is unreasonable because it has been *consented* to by the French people.

Let us consider three arguments which might be employed in an attempt to defuse this objection to culturally motivated trade restrictions. Ronald Dworkin has argued that it is incoherent to claim that the market gives people the culture they want. This is because what people want—the cultural products they choose to consume—is conditioned, to a considerable extent, by the cultural environment in which they reside.[39] Culture provides not only valuable experiences but also the apparatus we use to value them.[40] In Dworkin's words, our cultural 'environment provides the spectacles through which we identify experiences as valuable'.[41] Dworkin suggests that arguments for the view that the market satisfies people's cultural preferences are undermined by the fact that such 'argument[s] cannot work without some way to identify…what people—in the present or future—want by way of culture; and culture is too fundamental, too basic to our schemes of value, to make questions of that kind intelligible.'[42]

This bold claim relies on a conflation of two distinct aspects of culture, which, later in his essay, Dworkin is careful to distinguish. On the one hand, there are specific cultural experiences (reading a novel, watching a film, etc.), and, on the other, the 'structural frame' which enables us to value those experiences.[43] This structural frame, Dworkin explains, is a kind of language, or 'a special part of the language we now share.'[44] So, put more moderately, Dworkin's thesis is that while we can identify the specific cultural experiences people want, they want those experiences only because they have inherited a particular structural frame.

---

[39] Ronald Dworkin, *A Matter of Principle* (Oxford: Oxford University Press, 1985). Dworkin initially deploys this argument against the claim that public subsidies ensure that people get the culture they want, but he goes on to point out that the argument also undermines the claim that the market gives people the culture they want.

[40] Dworkin, *A Matter of Principle*, p. 228.   [41] Dworkin, *A Matter of Principle*, p. 228.

[42] Dworkin, *A Matter of Principle*, p. 228.   [43] Dworkin, *A Matter of Principle*, p. 229.

[44] Dworkin, *A Matter of Principle*, p. 231.

Rather than defusing the objection with which we began, the foregoing observations actually strengthen the case of those who oppose culturally motivated trade restrictions on the grounds that such restrictions override people's preferences. Drawing on Dworkin's insights, those opponents can point out, for example, that despite inheriting a structural frame that makes them especially amenable to appreciating distinctively French cultural phenomena, many French people have chosen to embrace the cultural products of the USA. The fact that these preferences were shaped in an environment hostile to their formation lends them a certain authenticity. They seem authentic in the same way that the Christian views of an individual raised in a staunchly atheist family seem authentic. Consequently, government attempts to override such preferences seem more, rather than less, objectionable.

A second response to the argument against culturally motivated trade restrictions that we have been considering challenges the idea that anyone actually consents to cultural homogenization simply by making certain decisions in the market. According to this response, it is a mistake to think that individuals will not only the outcomes of their own decisions, but also the outcomes generated when numerous other individuals make similar decisions. It is true that we sometimes want to criticize individuals for making decisions that, when combined with similar decisions made by others, foreseeably bring about regrettable states of affairs. But that is very different to saying that those individuals consent to those states of affairs.

When an individual purchases an item in a market, all she consents to is that particular transaction, not to the cumulative effects of all similar transactions. When a French citizen purchases American fast food, or a ticket to see an American film, all she consents to is those purchases, not the disappearance of French cuisine or French cinema, which might result if many other French citizens make similar purchases. It is therefore false to suggest that a government necessarily overrides the preferences of its citizens when it acts to alter a state of affairs that has been brought about by the set of individual choices they have made in the marketplace.

Now, it might be said that restrictions that aim to prevent cultural change are objectionable not because the affected parties have consented to such change, but simply because cultural change has been brought about by the voluntary actions of affected parties. I would suggest that a large part of the appeal of this claim is attributable to the ease with which it is confused with the similar but distinct claim that restrictions are objectionable because cultural change is brought about *voluntarily* by the affected parties, which is just an alternative formulation of the consent-based argument we have been considering.

Voluntarily performing an action, or set of actions, that brings about a particular state of affairs is not the same as voluntarily bringing about that state of affairs. When we say that a state of affairs, X, was brought about voluntarily by P, we typically mean something like this: '(i) from a variety of reasonable options available to her, P (ii) chose to perform (was not coerced into performing) an action, or set of actions, A, (iii) in the knowledge that the performance of A would bring about X.' Satisfaction of conditions (i) and (ii) ensures that P's performance of A is voluntary, while the satisfaction of all three conditions is needed to ensure that P's bringing about X is voluntary. If condition (iii) is not satisfied—if P performed A without understanding that the performance of A would bring about X—we can still say that P performed A voluntarily (if conditions (i) and (ii) are satisfied), but it does not seem accurate to say that P voluntarily brought about X.

At the heart of the claim that cultural change is brought about voluntarily by the affected parties (which, as I said, is just another way of formulating the consent-based argument that we have already discussed) is the thought that cultural change reflects the preferences of those who are affected. The new argument we are now considering makes no reference to the preferences of affected parties: it does not follow from the fact that P voluntarily performs an action, or set of actions, A, that, perhaps in conjunction with actions performed by others, causes a particular state of affairs, X, to obtain, that X reflects P's preferences. For P may not have realized that her performance of A would contribute to causing X. Indeed, it is unlikely that the average consumer appreciates how her individual purchases might affect her national culture. Consumers consider their purchases is isolation, not in conjunction with the purchases that others might make, and which, taken cumulatively, might precipitate cultural change.

But the mere fact that cultural change is precipitated by the voluntary actions of (some subset of) the affected parties, considered in isolation from the question of whether or not the affected parties voluntarily brought about cultural change, does not seem to carry enough weight to ground a strong argument against culturally motivated trade restrictions. To be sure, such restrictions interfere with transactions that would otherwise be entered into voluntarily, but the argument we are considering gives us no reason to think that the *outcome* of those transactions would have been voluntarily brought about, and that seems to be a crucial consideration.

I said that the average consumer does not consider her purchases in conjunction with the purchases of others. But it might be objected than in a scenario where the government is actively warning its citizens about the threat of cultural degradation, consumers *will* think of their purchases in this way. And if they choose to go ahead and make certain purchases, despite being informed of the ways in which those purchases may erode the national culture, then, it could be argued, this serves as evidence that they do not share the cultural preferences of their political representatives. The obvious response to this objection is that consumers face a collective action problem. They know that if many of their fellow citizens are refraining from making culture-threatening purchases, their own purchases will not be sufficient to offset their efforts. Conversely, they know that if their fellow citizens are *not* refraining from making culture-threatening purchases, abstinence on their part will be futile. Thus, even in a scenario where the government is promulgating information about cultural degradation, a consumer's choice to continue purchasing culture-threatening goods need not imply that she does not value her national culture.

A third response to the claim that cultural homogenization, when it occurs, is consented to, concedes that *some* individuals may consent, but argues that others do not, and maintains that if the market is given free reign, the preferences of some will be disregarded. This response might be countered in the following way: while certain individuals do not consent to cultural homogenization, those individuals constitute a minority that has been 'outvoted' in the marketplace, and, if we respect democratic values, there is no reason to think that such a minority has a legitimate claim to redress.

This argument is not decisive. To begin with, note that trade-restricting measures aimed at preserving cultural distinctiveness do not necessarily deprive the majority of what they want. Subsidies for French film studios, for example, do not prevent the majority from enjoying American blockbusters (if that is what the majority enjoys); rather, they simply ensure that American competition does not undermine the ability of French studios to cater to different tastes.

Still, the majority are being asked to contribute to the production of goods that they do not themselves consume, and perhaps this is objectionable. But note that demanding that the majority subsidize minority tastes is not necessarily undemocratic in the way that the above objection suggests. The preferences consumers express in the market do not provide us with a reliable indication of which policies citizens would support in a democratic forum. It is entirely possible that people would vote in favour of measures aimed at supporting the production of certain cultural goods, even if they do not consume those goods themselves. People who choose to vote in such a way might be motivated by the thought that it is unfair for one group to enjoy less welfare than another simply by virtue of the fact that the former has been burdened with preferences that, unlike the preferences of the latter, are not adequately catered to by the market.[45] (And if we endorse the principle underlying this thought, whether or not voters *are actually* motivated by it is, in one sense, beside the point. We can say that they *should* be motivated by

---

[45] This suggestion is inspired by G. A. Cohen's discussion of 'expensive tastes' in 'On the Currency of Egalitarian Justice', *Ethics*, Vol. 99, No. 4, 1989, pp. 906–44.

it if they are to treat their fellow citizens with the equal respect to which they are entitled.)

Dworkin is well known for challenging state intervention on behalf of those whose tastes are relatively poorly served by the market. Such intervention, he argues, will often fail to pass what he calls the 'envy test'. According to the envy test, redistribution from one set of individuals to another constitutes a demand of distributive justice only if the latter can be said to envy the position of the former. But, Dworkin argues, those whose tastes are ill-served by the market often will not envy those whose tastes are more easily satisfied. One way in which this can be revealed is by the fact that the former would often not be willing to substitute (if they could) the latter's preferences for their own. If those whose preferences are for films such as *Blue is the Warmest Colour* could take a pill that would enable them to derive comparable aesthetic pleasure from *Captain America*, it is reasonable to conjecture that they would decline to do so; for, film connoisseurs *identify* with their preferences, and regard them as superior to those of individuals who can be satisfied by mindless popcorn fodder.[46] Dworkin's argument challenges the defence of culturally motivated trade restrictions offered in the previous paragraph, and grounds a distinct objection to such restrictions. In a global market, some individuals will find their preferences more difficult or costly to satisfy than those of others, but provided that these individuals do not envy those whose preferences are more easily satisfied, policies that redistribute from the latter to the former are inappropriate.

Dworkin's argument is intended to demonstrate that the mere fact of inequality of welfare attributable to differentially satiable preferences cannot support regarding redistributive measures as a demand of distributive justice. It does not follow from the mere fact that global markets make one individual's tastes more difficult or costly to satisfy than another's that state intervention is required or permissible. But Dworkin's argument does not establish that culturally motivated redistributive trade restrictions will never be a requirement of distributive justice. For, beyond a certain degree of cultural degradation, those whose cultural preferences are neglected presumably *would* begin to envy those with different preferences, and would consequently be willing to trade places. One may not be willing to surrender their tastes in a world in which their satisfaction is difficult or costly in a mere relative sense, but in a world in which their satisfaction is difficult or costly in *absolute* terms, with the consequence that one's preferences are rarely, if ever, satisfied, the

---

[46] Ronald Dworkin, *Sovereign Virtue: The Theory and Practice of Equality* (Cambridge, Mass: Harvard University Press, 2000), p. 291. For an extended treatment of these ideas, to which I am indebted, see Tom Parr, 'How to Identify Disadvantage: Taking the Envy Test Seriously' (Political Studies).

renunciation of those preferences is likely to become something that one is willing to countenance. In a scenario of this kind, the upshot of Dworkin's argument is that justice would sanction the introduction of redistributive trade restrictions.[47]

So, a case can be made for the claim that trade should be restricted in order to mitigate the harm of cultural degradation, and that case is not defeated by any of the objections considered above. But the case for culture-protecting trade restrictions—like the case for worker-protecting trade restrictions—is incomplete, as I have so far bracketed the interests of the developing world. It is now time to lift those brackets, and to ask whether recognition of the interests of poor countries forces us to revise the provisional conclusions reached here and in section I.

IV

The Special Interests of the Developing World

It is widely held that participation in world trade can facilitate development, and enable poor countries to mitigate the extreme poverty that afflicts so many of their people. One type of participation in world trade is the export-ation of domestically produced goods and services, and, obviously, a country can engage in this form of participation only if the markets of other countries are open. If rich countries close their markets to developing-world exports, they deny poor countries a crucial opportunity to develop.

How, if at all, do these observations affect the arguments developed above? To begin with, how do they affect the claim that rich countries may restrict trade in order to protect their cultural heritage? The special interests of devel-oping countries prompt the following qualification: it is permissible for rich countries to protect their cultural heritage by restricting trade *provided that such restrictions do not diminish the development prospects of poor countries*. This qualification is necessitated by the fact that the development interests of poor countries outweigh the cultural interests of developed country citizens.

Given that threats to cultural distinctiveness typically come from other rich countries, I doubt that this qualification has much practical significance. Still, if cultural threats were to emanate from the developing world, rich countries would not be morally permitted to shelter themselves from such threats by restricting trade. Moreover, if economists could demonstrate that

[47] Given Dworkin's claim that the level of redistribution required is determined by a hypothetical insurance market, the degree of redistribution that his argument would sanction is likely to be smaller than that sanctioned by the Cohen-inspired argument considered earlier.

culture-protecting measures among developed countries indirectly under-mine development efforts in poor countries, such measures would again be impermissible.

In the first section of this chapter I argued for the following conclusion: if the correct conception of justice commits us to the view that compensation (of a certain level) is required to vindicate free trade, we are also committed to the view that trade should be restricted if sufficiently generous compensation is not forthcoming. The special interests of poor countries prompt a revision to this conclusion that is analogous to the revision made above to the claim about the permissibility of culture-preserving restrictions: if sufficiently gen-erous compensation is not forthcoming, rich countries should restrict trade in order to protect their workers *provided that such restrictions do not diminish the development prospects of poor countries.*

This revision is likely to have greater practical significance than the previous one. This is because the threat to workers in rich countries often comes from the developing world; labour displacement is often precipitated by cheap imports produced by low wage labour in poor countries. When trade promotes development but also displaces domestic workers, free trade should be pro-moted even if it will not produce gains large enough to fund compensatory transfer payments. In such cases, compensation can still be provided if the state draws on revenues raised through general taxation. If compensation is not forthcoming because its provision is politically infeasible (i.e., if citizens are unwilling to support it), free trade must still be favoured, despite the fact that it will inflict uncompensated harms on the working class. In such a scenario, the case for free trade is grounded in the fact that the interests it serves are more fundamental than those it frustrates. A peasant farmer's interest in subsistence is more important than the interest of an unskilled domestic worker in maintaining her current job. To be sure, if domestic workers are not compensated for their losses, injustice obtains, but this injust-ice must be regarded as the lesser of two evils.[48]

Consider an analogy. Anne, who is desperately poor, has made a deal with Ben, who has agreed to airdrop food parcels into the area where Anne lives. Christine can coordinate with Ben, at negligible cost to herself, and thereby ensure that the parcels are delivered safely. But Christine, who is unwilling to make small sacrifices for the sake of strangers, refuses to do so. If Ben goes ahead and makes the delivery without Christine's assistance, David—who is much better-off than Anne, and who does not need the food parcels in order to satisfy his basic needs—will inevitably be injured. He will be struck by

---

[48] The overriding importance of the interests of developing countries is noted in Kurjanska and Risse, 'Fairness in Trade II', p. 39.

falling parcels and suffer a broken arm. I have the capacity to remotely disable the release-mechanism on Ben's plane. If I do this, Ben will be unable to make the delivery, David will escape harm, and Anne will starve to death.

It seems clear that I should not disable the release-mechanism. Anne's interest in not starving is more fundamental than David's interest in avoiding a broken arm. Similarly, we should not block international exchanges that could enable the world's poor to claw their way out of severe poverty, simply in order to protect relatively affluent workers in wealthy countries from harms that their fellow citizens could—but do not—mitigate by providing compensation. To be sure, if Ben makes the delivery without Christine's assistance, David will sustain an injury that he would not have suffered had Christine only done her bit. And that is unjust. Analogously, if free trade is not supplemented with compensatory transfer payments, the domestic working class will incur socio-economic costs larger than those they would have borne had their fellow citizens done their bit. And that is also unjust. But these outcomes are *less* unjust than ones where Anne and the world's poor are forced to starve.

Some will maintain that the interests of domestic workers should be given extra weight on account of the fact that they are the interests of our fellow nationals or fellow citizens. But even if we grant this, the extra weight that could plausibly be accorded will not be sufficient to justify prioritizing the satisfaction of these interests over the satisfaction of the more basic interests of the global poor. Moreover, it should be stressed that the dilemma we are considering arises only when political communities refuse to take available measures that could ensure that justice prevails both within and beyond their borders (i.e., by supplementing free trade with compensatory transfer payments). In the case we are examining, there is no fundamental, intractable conflict between the interests of a political community's members, on the one hand, and the interests of outsiders, on the other.

I have said that it is impermissible to restrict trade that is beneficial to the world's poor, even when doing so is necessary to protect domestic workers. In response, it might be said that a state can permissibly impose restrictions if it takes steps to offset the harms that those restrictions inflict; that is, if it ensures that the benefits that trade could bring to the world's poor are provided in some other way. The world's poor are entitled to a route out of poverty, but, it might be said, they are not entitled to *any particular* route. If two modes of equally effective poverty alleviation are available, it is permissible to substitute one for the other, and we may have good reason to do this if one mode has harmful side effects, while the other does not.

This is correct, and, in fact, I have already acknowledged that states ought to favour one mode of poverty alleviation (free trade plus compensation) over another (free trade without compensation) on the grounds that the former lacks the harmful side effects associated with the latter. But it might be said that there are *other*, non-trade-related, modes of poverty alleviation (foreign aid, for example) that a state can permissibly substitute for trade liberalization. Two considerations reduce the significance of this point. First, we have been considering a case in which a community refuses to employ redistributive measures in order to compensate its workers for harms inflicted by trade. If a community is unwilling to redistribute wealth in order to benefit its own citizens, it is hard to see why it would be willing to redistribute wealth for the sake of foreigners. Second, world poverty is an extremely difficult issue, and there is much disagreement over the relative efficacy of different ways of addressing it. But it is widely believed that poor countries benefit greatly when they have access to markets in the rich world. Thus, by restricting trade, rich countries will often be closing off one of the most promising avenues available to the poor. They may not permissibly do this unless they can demonstrate convincingly that they are providing an alternative that is at least equally effective, and that will be very difficult.

Nothing I have said here should be taken to imply that developed countries should *never* restrict trade with developing countries. I said that participation in world trade can help alleviate poverty in the developing world, but not all trade will be beneficial in this way. For example, rich countries do not benefit the global poor by purchasing resources from despotic regimes that use the funds generated by such sales to augment their power.[49] Moreover, as Risse observes, and as was recorded earlier, importing goods from countries with low labour standards may incentivize the maintenance of those standards, and thus the maltreatment of the world's working poor. When this is the case, we have a *pro tanto* reason to suspend trade, a reason that can be overturned only when it is clear that suspension will make matters worse, all-things-considered. I return to the issue of trading with countries that maintain low labour standards in chapter 5.

My claim has been that developed countries cannot justifiably restrict trade with those in the developing world, when doing so will impede the latter's development prospects, on the grounds that doing so is necessary to protect domestic workers or preserve cultural distinctiveness. However, as I have just noted, there are undeniably other grounds on which developed countries can justifiably restrict trade with developing countries: they can do so when such restrictions are in the interests of the global poor.

---

[49] Leif Wenar, 'Property Rights and the Resource Curse', *Philosophy & Public Affairs*, Vo. 36, No. 1, 2008, pp. 2–32.

V

Restrictions in Developing Countries

I have considered whether, in order to avoid the harms of labour displacement and cultural degradation, developed countries may permissibly restrict trade with other developed countries, and whether developed countries may permissibly restrict trade with developing countries. I have not yet considered whether trade imposes harms on the developing world that its members can, and may permissibly, prevent by restricting trade with developed countries. It is to that question that we should now turn.

If trade produced harms that developing countries could guard against by restricting trade with developed countries, I doubt that any sensible person would deny their right to do so. Developing countries cannot be expected to exacerbate their own plight simply in order to benefit already advantaged members of the rich world. But the question of whether trade imposes harms that developing countries can deflect with protective measures is fiercely contested.

Some economists think that by restricting trade, poor countries shoot themselves in the foot; others maintain that restrictive measures can enable poor countries to evade significant harms.[50] The most well known, and robust, argument in favour of restrictions is the 'infant industry argument'. Famously defended by John Stuart Mill, the infant industry argument maintains that if liberalization takes place prematurely, trade can stunt the development of new firms that are not ready to compete in the global market. Unless these firms are sheltered in the early years of their existence, and given the opportunity to grow, they will never be able to get off the ground. If trade is to facilitate, and not stifle, development, it must be preceded, or accompanied, by (selective) restrictions that ensure that a country's engines of growth are not washed away by the tides of the global economy.[51]

A number of eminent economists have argued that the infant industry argument has been vindicated by recent economic history. For example, Andrew Charlton and the Nobel Prize winner Joseph Stiglitz observe that, in the latter half of the twentieth century, East Asian economies achieved miraculous levels of growth while pursuing two-track trade policies whereby

---

[50] Tesón's claim that the debate over developing-country protectionism 'suffers from a fatal rhetorical glitch caused by the public's failure to understand the economics of trade' ('Free Trade is Required by Justice', p. 138) is thus misleading.

[51] For discussion, see Irvin, *Against the Tide*, Ch. 8. The importance of infant industry protection in developing countries was recognized in a revised preamble to the GATT, according to which developing countries 'should enjoy additional facilities to enable them ... to maintain sufficient flexibility in their tariff structure to be able to grant the tariff protection required for the establishment of a particular industry.' *The General Agreement on Tariffs and Trade*, Article XVIII, p. 29 (available at: http://www.wto.org/english/docs_e/legal_e/gatt47_e.pdf)

industries deemed not ready to compete globally were protected from foreign competition, while export-ready industries were promoted.[52] They also point out that, during the same period, a number of Latin American countries achieved rapid growth by adopting a strategy of import-substituting industrialization whereby consumer goods, rather than being imported from abroad (as had been done in the past), were produced by domestic firms, while the importation of foreign goods was restricted.[53] Moreover, other notable economists, such as Cambridge University's Ha-Joon Chang, have shown that, in restricting imports and promoting domestic industries, governments in East Asia and Latin America were simply following the example set by the governments of developed countries in North America and Western Europe.[54]

Stiglitz and Charlton are keen to stress that the debate about trade and development is characterized by a considerable degree of uncertainty. 'Economists', they observe, 'have learned much about the process of economic development, but there is still a lot that [they] do not know'.[55] They infer from this uncertainty that it is wrong to pressure developing countries into liberalizing their markets, as the major international economic institutions have often done in the past. '[D]eveloping countries', they write, 'should be given the freedom to develop their own policy strategies tailored to their own idiosyncratic circumstances.'[56] To my mind, this seems like a sensible conclusion. Whether poor countries benefit from opening their markets is a question that can be answered only by economists, and not by political philosophers. But until it is answered, we have no reason to criticize developing-country governments that maintain restrictive measures in an attempt to nurture infant industries. By doing so, they are not wronging their own citizens, and they are certainly not wronging citizens of the developed world.

Before concluding this chapter, we should note that economic grounds are not the only ones on which poor countries can build a case for restricting trade. The concern about cultural degradation discussed above also arises in relation to the developing world. All of the arguments given in defence of culturally motivated trade restrictions earlier in the chapter also apply in this context. Moreover, there may be reasons to think that poorer countries are especially vulnerable to cultural domination. This worry is expressed by Kok-Chor Tan, who argues that global inequality leaves developing countries exposed to cultural-imperialist practices. He writes:

---

[52] Joseph E. Stiglitz and Andrew Charlton, *Fair Trade for All: How Trade can Promote Development* (Oxford: Oxford University Press, 2005), p. 16.
[53] Stiglitz and Charlton, *Fair Trade for All*, p. 19.
[54] Ha-Joon Chang, *Bad Samaritans: The Myth of Free Trade and the Secret History of Capitalism* (New York: Bloomsbury Press, 2008), Ch. 2.
[55] Stiglitz and Charlton, *Fair Trade for All*, p. 17.
[56] Stiglitz and Charlton, *Fair Trade for All*, p. 17.

economic inequality can...directly threaten the cultural life of a community by creating a pipeline in which cultural goods and influences flow only one way, from the rich to the poor. Rich countries are better able to produce, globally market and promote mass cultural products than poor countries. Simply put, global economic inequality makes for a highly unequal global cultural marketplace, making it difficult for some countries to protect their local cultural practices, thereby challenging their right to cultural self-determination.[57]

Poor countries might sometimes be justified, then, in restricting trade not only in order to shelter nascent industries, but also in order to preserve their cultural distinctiveness.

However, we must be alert to the fact that rhetoric about culture is often invoked in an attempt to shield from scrutiny repressive social practices. As Simon Caney notes: 'Terms like "culture" and "cultural identity"...sound attractive and benign but...cultures can be cruel, oppressive, exclusionary, and violent.'[58] Thus, when trade and culture collide, it is not always the former that should yield. Reflecting on the globalization 'of cheap, cultural-consumption goods—fashion, drinks, fast food, popular music, TV and movies', Michael Mann notes that this process is 'subverting many local norms and rituals that govern such important social spheres as marriage practices, parent-child relations and the submission of women.'[59] There is clearly no reason to assume that these subversions will invariably be for the worse. Even Marx recognized the progressive role that the capitalist revolution played in displacing feudalism,[60] and if contemporary global markets play a similar role in releasing the stranglehold of oppressive and patriarchal social norms in parts of the developing world, then that should be welcomed, not regretted. When any government appeals to the value of culture in an attempt to justify trade restrictions, we must ensure that the language of culture is not being abused to serve unjust ends.

VI

Conclusion

A word of caution is in order. A number of the arguments advanced in this chapter depend on contestable positive theses. If alternative theses are

---

[57] Tan, *Justice Without Borders*, p. 120.

[58] Simon Caney, *Justice Beyond Borders: A Global Political Theory* (Oxford: Oxford University Press, 2005), p. 89.

[59] Michael Mann, 'Globalization and September 11', *New Left Review* 12, November–December 2001, pp. 51–72, at p. 64.

[60] See, for example, Karl Marx and Friedrich Engels, *The Communist Manifesto*, in David McLellan (ed.), *Karl Marx: Selected Writings*, Revised Edition (New York: Oxford University Press, 2000).

vindicated, our normative outlook may change. A philosophical perspective, then, cannot substitute for an economic one. But the converse is also true, and I hope that this chapter has helped to illuminate that fact. Just as philosophers must turn to economics in order to understand the effects that trade and protectionism will have, so economists must turn to philosophy in order to know what to infer from the economic conclusions they reach.

We should therefore be glad that political philosophers have finally begun to address debates over labour displacement, cultural degradation, and development. Still, with developed-world trade barriers at an all-time low, we might wonder whether the owl of Minerva is spreading its wings only after dusk has fallen. There are at least three reasons why this is not the case. Firstly, rich countries continue to protect markets of vital importance to the developing world. For example, the EU and US continue to pay large domestic subsidies to their farmers, thereby undermining the capacity of farmers in the Global South to earn a living. Secondly, just because trade barriers are low today, there is no guarantee that they will remain low. National borders were open at the end of the nineteenth century, but were slammed shut again at the beginning of the twentieth. Thirdly, and perhaps most interestingly, we can imagine a possible future in which today's poor countries have achieved development without entirely liberalizing their markets. In such a future it will inevitably be asked whether these countries may permissibly retain trade barriers in order to protect jobs and preserve cultural distinctiveness. Thus, theorizing about trade can hopefully yield answers to important questions that, in addition to exercising present generations, may also confront our descendants.

5

The Opportunities of Trade

In chapters 2–4 I considered various harms associated with trade, and with participation in the trade regime. I argued that there are harms that cannot be inflicted permissibly, at least without compensation, and that trade must sometimes, therefore, be restricted in order to prevent their infliction. Having examined the burdens of trade, we should turn now to look at its benefits, and at how those benefits should be distributed. Trade enables each country to augment its income, and, in chapter 6, I will consider the claim that justice imposes constraints on how these income gains are shared. In this chapter, I consider a more common, and less demanding, view, according to which justice requires not a particular outcome, but rather a specific distribution of opportunities. The trade regime provides its members with opportunities to access the markets of others, and, according to the procedural approach explored in this chapter, these opportunities must be allocated in a particular way. More specifically, the distribution of these opportunities must conform to an ideal of 'formal equality'.

The notion of formal equality is at the heart of the WTO's approach to market access. According to this ideal, all member states are to receive and offer equal, or uniform, treatment. This commitment to formal equality is expressed in various ways. It is expressed, for example, in the principle of non-discrimination (embodied in the Most Favoured Nation and National Treatment rules) and the principle of reciprocity. The Most Favoured Nation rule (MFN) requires WTO member states to refrain from treating any members less favourably than they treat others. If a state offers a privilege (e.g., a tariff concession) to another state, it must extend that privilege to all WTO members. The National Treatment rule (NT) requires states to refrain from treating imports less favourably than they treat domestically produced goods; once foreign goods have passed customs and entered the domestic market, the taxes and regulations that apply to them must not differ from those applied to domestic products. And the principle of reciprocity requires states to match the liberalization efforts of others; if, during a round of negotiations, one state promises to cut tariffs by x per cent, other states are also expected to cut tariffs by x per cent.

Formal equality has been championed by developed countries, but it has been challenged by poorer members of the trade regime. Throughout the trade regime's history, developing countries have sought various forms of preferential treatment—often referred to as 'special and differential treatment' (SDT)[1]—and their requests have sometimes been granted.[2] For example, Part IV of the GATT, which was added in 1965, restricts the application of the reciprocity principle to developed countries, and the Generalized System of Preferences (GSP), initiated in 1968, permits developed countries to deviate from MFN by imposing lower tariffs on imports from developing countries. Also, developing countries have sometimes enjoyed the freedom to refrain from signing agreements that they felt were not in their interest. During the Tokyo Round of negotiations, for example, many developing countries were able to refrain from signing a number of agreements on reducing the incidence of non-tariff barriers. In recent years, new forms of SDT have been mooted—including technology transfers from developed to developing countries, and payments to help the latter implement obligations and to build their negotiating capacity—but opponents of SDT have not gone away.

This chapter considers whether we have moral reasons to endorse formal equality within the trade regime. The general thrust of my argument is that formal equality, as that idea has been interpreted and applied in the context of trade, is not an ideal to which we should aspire. But, as will become clear, the issue cannot be fully resolved through philosophical analysis alone. The chapter is structured as follows. The first section elaborates upon the idea of formal equality and its rationales, identifies several positive arguments for departing from formal equality, and responds to a number of objections to SDT. Next, in section II, I consider in more detail one specific element of formal equality in the trade regime, namely, the principle of reciprocity. Three distinct reciprocity principles are identified, none of which, it is argued, should be regarded as a requirement of fairness. Section III considers a more recent interpretation of formal equality that requires trading countries to 'harmonize' domestic laws and policies. I argue that harmonization is not required by fairness.

---

[1] On SDT see, for example, Christopher Stevens, 'Special and Differential Treatment', in Ivan Mbirimi et al. (eds.), *From Doha to Cancun: Delivering a Development Round* (London: Commonwealth Secretariat, 2003); Alexander Keck and Patrick Low, 'Special and Differential Treatment in the WTO: Why, When, and How?', in Simon Evenett and Bernard M. Hoekman (eds.), *Economic Development and Multilateral Trade Cooperation* (New York: Palgrave Macmillan, 2006); Michael J. Trebilcock and Robert Howse, *The Regulation of International Trade 3rd Edition* (New York: Routledge, 2005), Ch. 15.

[2] See Chin Leng Lim, 'The Conventional Morality of Trade', in Chios Carmody et al. (eds.), *Global Justice and International Economic Law: Opportunities and Prospects* (New York: Cambridge University Press, 2012).

I

Formal Equality and Preferential Treatment

Is formal equality within the trade regime desirable? Should we heed calls to abolish SDT, or seek to maintain and extend it? We can start to answer these questions by examining in more detail the idea of formal equality and the considerations that support it. Note that formal equality is an ambiguous concept. It is used to refer both to the claim that (i) all individuals (or all members of a particular practice) must receive equal (uniform, identical) treatment,[3] and to the claim that (ii) all individuals (or all members of a particular practice) *who are comparable in relevant respects* must receive equal (uniform, identical) treatment—that is, to the principle that like cases should be treated alike.[4] Given that any statement of (ii) presupposes an account of which respects are relevant, (ii) can easily collapse into (i). Suppose a university claims to adhere to the principle that like cases should be treated alike. And suppose that individuals are deemed to be alike provided that they are members of the university. It follows that the university's policy of treating like cases alike is indistinguishable from a policy of treating all members identically.

One might say that when developed members of the trade regime champion the idea of formal equality, they are championing the idea that like cases should be treated alike. But, to the degree that this is true, the developed-country advocates of formal equality have worked with an implicit account of relevant respects according to which member states and their citizens are not deemed to be unalike by virtue of differential levels of economic development. The developing countries and their citizens may be poorer than the developed countries and developed-country citizens, but both sets of countries, and both sets of citizens, are deemed to be alike in all respects that are relevant, and it is said that they should therefore receive, and be expected to offer, uniform treatment.

Formal equality within the trade regime might be endorsed for a variety of pragmatic reasons: when expectations are uniform it may be easier for states to identify what is required of them; uniform rules are easier to administer and enforce; and uniform rules might facilitate the process of trade liberalization. Formal equality might also be defended for reasons of equity. Departures from formal equality often confer advantages upon one set of individuals, and if all

---

[3] See, for example, Patricia Hughes 'Recognizing Substantive Equality as a Foundational Constitutional Principle', *Dalhousie Law Journal*, Vol. 22, No. 5, 1999, pp. 1–29, at p. 27; Lim, 'Conventional Morality of Trade'.

[4] See, for example, John Rawls, *The Law of Peoples* (Cambridge, MA: Harvard University Press, 1999), p. 65; Catherine Barnard and Bob Hepple, 'Substantive Equality', *Cambridge Law Journal*, Vol. 59, No. 3, 2000, pp. 562–85, at pp. 562–4.

individuals are deemed to be alike in relevant respects the conferral of such advantages can be seen as unfair. If there are no relevant differences among individuals, there can be no grounds for treating one set differently and more favourably than others. The problem with this argument when applied in the context of trade is that it is very difficult to defend the claim that all members of the trade regime are alike in relevant respects. More specifically, the claim that differential levels of economic development do not constitute a relevant difference is highly suspect. Indeed, the fact that some members of the trade regime are very poor gives us a strong *pro tanto* reason to depart from formal equality, and to advocate preferential treatment for poorer states.

The case for departing from formal equality and offering special and differential treatment to poor countries can be given several more specific rationales. First, one might advocate SDT on the grounds that it enables wealthy states to discharge positive duties to alleviate severe global poverty. Many philosophers have defended the claim that citizens of affluent countries have positive duties to assist the world's poor, at least when they can do so at little cost to themselves, and one might argue that SDT provides an opportunity to discharge such duties. Alternatively, one might advocate SDT on the grounds that it enables wealthy states to discharge rectificatory duties—that is, duties to compensate for the infliction of harm. According to some critics, rich countries are guilty not (or not merely) of failing to discharge positive duties to help the poor, but of violating negative duties to refrain from harming them. Scholars and activists who take this view hold that rich countries are implicated in the poor's plight. Colonial practices have inflicted long-lasting damage on poor countries, and the contemporary global order is structured in a way that continues to undermine their development prospects.[5] If rich countries are guilty as charged, their primary duty must be to stop inflicting harm. But they will also have duties to compensate for harms they have already caused. SDT might, then, be justified as a way of discharging those rectificatory duties: giving poor countries extra now might be seen as a way of making up for what the rich have taken in the past. In order for these two arguments to go through, one would have to show not only that SDT is, in fact, an effective tool for discharging positive and rectificatory duties, but also that there are not acceptable alternatives that do not involve deviations from formal equality.

SDT might also be defended on the grounds that it is necessary to ensure that participation in the trade regime is not disproportionally onerous for

---

[5] Thomas Pogge's oeuvre offers the most sophisticated statement of this view. See, for example, Thomas Pogge, *World Poverty and Human Rights: Second Edition* (Cambridge: Polity Press, 2008). For a helpful overview of the literature on the effects of colonial practices on economic development, see Nathan Nunn, 'The Importance of History for Economic Development', *Annual Review of Economics*, Vol. 1, 2009, pp. 65–92.

poor countries. Given the huge differences between the abilities and needs of developed and developing countries, a set of rules with which the former can easily comply might be excessively demanding for the latter. Complying with WTO rules is often more demanding for poor countries, for a variety of reasons: poor countries have weaker safety nets, and are thus less able to assist workers displaced by trade liberalization; their administrative systems typically require greater reform; and implementing trade agreements requires expenditure of resources that could otherwise be spent on development programmes.[6] It can therefore be argued that differential treatment is appropriate, as it can ensure that poor countries are not unduly burdened, and that the opportunities of trade are not offered at too high a price.[7]

Each of the arguments briefly sketched above provides resources with which to justify departures from formal equality, and vindicate preferential treatment for poor countries. But these arguments might be countered with a variety of objections, to which we should now turn our attention.

Objections

It might be argued that SDT (i) undermines the bargaining power of poor countries; (ii) is unfair; or (iii) directly harms the economies of poor countries. Let us consider these three objections in turn.

Diminished Bargaining Power

It is sometimes argued that SDT is counterproductive because it undermines the bargaining power of the poor. According to this argument, poor countries will be granted access to important markets in the developed world only if they offer rich countries something in return. But SDT permits and encourages poor

---

[6] Joseph E. Stiglitz and Andrew Charlton, *Fair Trade for All: How Trade can Promote Development* (Oxford: Oxford University Press, 2005), Ch. 13.

[7] In addition to finding some rules especially burdensome, poor countries may be unable to take advantage of certain options that WTO rules ostensibly make available to all. Consider the WTO's Dispute Settlement Understanding. When a member state is found to have violated a trade agreement, injured parties are permitted to take retaliatory action. But this permission is often of little use to poor countries. While rich countries can effectively force others to comply with trade agreements by threatening to withhold market access from those who do not, analogous threats made by poor countries lack force: the harms they can inflict by impeding access to their markets are not large enough to compel wealthy countries to alter their behaviour. Given their inability to take advantage of existing arrangements, developing countries have argued that, when rich countries harm poor countries by violating trade agreements, the latter should be permitted to engage in *collective* retaliation. The thought is that while retaliatory action taken by a single developing country will have little impact, retaliatory action taken by *multiple* developing countries acting in concert will be considerably more effective. See Robert E. Hudec, 'Broadening the Scope of Remedies in WTO Dispute Settlement', in Friedl Weiss and Jochem Wiers (eds.), *Improving WTO Dispute Settlement Procedures* (Folkestone: Cameron May Publishers, 2000).

countries to offer few concessions, and, consequently, they receive little from the rich. The objection is well articulated by Peter Lichtenbaum, who writes:

> Developing countries have been unable to obtain significant concessions on products of interest to them from developed economies by failing to participate in the exchange of reciprocal reductions in trade barriers. For example, industrialized countries singled out textiles and agriculture, which are important products for developing countries, and subjected these industries to extremely high import restrictions... [T]he long-term interests of developing countries may be better served if they were able to improve their negotiating position by offering to liberalize their economies and open their markets to import competition. In this way, developing countries could bargain more effectively to obtain market access on products of interest to their economies.[8]

It is important to be clear about what it being said here. The claim is not that SDT *directly* or *necessarily* hurts the interests of poor countries. Rather, the claim is that when poor countries avail themselves of the opportunities made available by SDT, rich countries react in a particular way—namely, they single out products of special importance to poor countries and impose upon those products inordinately high tariffs. Rich countries give with one hand—by acceding to demands for SDT—but take away with the other. Now, it should be obvious that the argument currently under scrutiny—SDT should be abandoned because it hurts the interests of the poor—cannot be made in good faith by rich members of the WTO. The rich cannot object to SDT on the grounds that it is bad for the poor if it is their own voluntary actions that *make* it bad for the poor. As G. A. Cohen famously pointed out:

> an argument changes its aspect when its presenter is the person, or one of the people, whose choice, or choices, make one or more of the argument's premises true. By contrast with other presenters of the same argument, a person who makes, or helps to make, one of its premises true can be asked to justify the fact that it is true.[9]

Poor countries might decide that, given how the rich have acted in the past, and can be expected to act in the future, they have prudential reasons for eschewing SDT. But things are very different for rich countries. We can ask rich countries to justify their decision to act in the way they do when poor countries make use of the options given to them by SDT, and an acceptable justification is unlikely to be forthcoming.

---

[8] Peter Lichtenbaum, '"Special Treatment" vs. "Equal Participation:" Striking a Balance in the Doha Negotiations', *The American University International Law Review*, Vol. 17, No. 5, 2002, pp. 1003–43, at 1017–18 (footnote omitted). Cf. Constantine Michalopoulos, 'Developing Country Strategies for the Millennium Round', *Journal of World Trade*, Vol. 33, No. 5, 1999, pp. 1–30, at p. 25; and Ethan Kapstein, *Economic Justice in an Unfair World: Toward a Level Playing Field* (Princeton, NJ: Princeton University Press, 2006), pp. 70–1.

[9] G. A. Cohen, *Rescuing Justice & Equality* (Cambridge, Mass: Harvard University Press, 2008), pp. 38–9 (footnote omitted).

Unfairness

Special and differential treatment is sometimes compared to domestic affirmative action policies that require firms and universities to give preferential treatment to applicants from disadvantaged groups.[10] If affirmative action and SDT are comparable, the latter may be vulnerable to some of the objections commonly levelled at the former. Let us consider this possibility. Perhaps the strongest objection to affirmative action is that it unfairly deprives talented individuals of jobs and university places that they would have secured in the absence of affirmative action. Those who make this objection sometimes acknowledge that we are not dealing with like cases, but maintain that differential treatment is nevertheless unfair.

The most obvious analogue to this objection focuses on the effects of SDT on rich-world firms. These firms may be denied access to certain markets, their developing-world competitors will be strengthened, and their economic vitality may well be undermined. We can begin to formulate a response to this objection by considering how one should reply to the complaint that affirmative action denies talented individuals access to positions that would otherwise have been available to them. Notice that this complaint invokes an inappropriate counterfactual. The relevant counterfactual consideration is not who would have secured which position in a scenario identical to the status quo except for the absence of affirmative action policies, but rather who would have secured which position in a scenario in which (i) affirmative action policies were never introduced *and* (ii) where the injustices that motivated those policies never occurred. While it is surely true that in a society disfigured by racial injustice certain white applicants would be offered jobs and university places that they would not have been offered had affirmative action programmes been in operation, it is much less likely that those same applicants would have been offered those positions had segregation and other forms of racial injustice not incapacitated potential black competitors.

Similarly, one might argue that rich-world firms are invoking an inappropriate counterfactual when they complain that they are denied opportunities that they would have enjoyed if SDT had never been introduced and all other variables had remained the same. The relevant counterfactual, it can be argued, is how those firms would have fared if (i) SDT had never been introduced *and* (ii) many of their foreign rivals were not operating in countries crippled by colonial plunder and the extant machinery of global injustice. If we endorse the second of the three positive arguments for SDT adumbrated in the previous subsection—according to which rich countries are complicit in

---

[10] Gillian Moon, 'Trade and Equality: A Relationship to Discover', *Journal of International Economic Law*, Vol. 12, No. 3, 2009, pp. 617–42, at pp. 622–3; Kapstein, *Economic Justice*, p. 70.

the creation and maintenance of world poverty—this response is readily available to us.

Equally pertinent is the fact that even in a free global market without SDT, the most efficient rich-world firms would not prosper simply by virtue of being the most efficient. To the degree that rich-world firms object to SDT on the grounds that it enables less efficient companies based in developing countries to outcompete them in the global market, they are betraying their economic ignorance; they may be outdone by their less efficient foreign rivals even in the absence of SDT. Domestic firms in Industry A may be more efficient than their foreign counterparts, but the theory of comparative advantage tells us that if firms in Industry B are even more efficient vis-à-vis *their* foreign counterparts, the firms in Industry A will lose out from free trade.[11]

In the US, practices such as affirmative action that sanction granting preferential treatment to certain groups of citizens are sometimes accused of violating the Fourteenth Amendment of the Constitution, which guarantees 'equal protection of the laws'. SDT practices which grant preferential treatment to certain countries, and deviate from MFN, NT, and the reciprocity principle, may be conceived as analogous transgressions. It is thus instructive to consider how the US courts have responded to these accusations.[12]

In order to assess claims that a piece of legislation violates the equal protection clause of the Constitution, the American courts follow a two stage procedure. The goal of the first stage is to establish whether the law in question seriously disadvantages what the Supreme Court has referred to as a 'suspect class', namely, a group 'saddled with such disabilities, or subject to such a history of purposeful unequal treatment, or relegated to such a position of political powerlessness as to command extraordinary protection from the majoritarian political process.'[13] If the law seriously disadvantages a suspect class then the purpose of the second stage is to subject the law to 'strict scrutiny'. If, on the other hand, those disadvantaged by the law do not belong to a suspect class, the law is subjected to 'relaxed scrutiny'. A law subject to strict scrutiny will be regarded as unconstitutional unless the disadvantage it generates can be shown to be necessary for the protection of a 'compelling' governmental interest. By contrast, a law subject to relaxed scrutiny will be regarded as constitutional unless it can be shown to serve no purpose whatsoever.

Suppose we were to assess SDT using a similar procedure. It seems that SDT should be subject only to relaxed scrutiny, for the rich-world firms it

---

[11] On this point, see Douglas A. Irwin, *Free Trade Under Fire*, 3rd ed. (Princeton: Princeton University Press, 2009), pp. 33–4.

[12] The following paragraph draws on Ronald Dworkin, *Sovereign Virtue: The Theory and Practice of Equality* (Cambridge, Mass: Harvard University Press, 2000), pp. 412–13.

[13] Justice Powell, quoted in Dworkin, *Sovereign Virtue*, p. 412.

disadvantages clearly do not belong to a suspect class. Thus, SDT would be vindicated provided that it could be shown to serve a worthwhile end. The positive arguments sketched in the previous subsection each identify worthwhile ends—fulfilment of positive duties, fulfilment of rectificatory duties, and ensuring that poor countries are not unduly burdened. Consequently, provided one can demonstrate that SDT is an effective means of achieving those ends, SDT would be justified.[14]

Economic Harm

As we saw above, it is sometimes claimed that SDT is counterproductive because it diminishes the bargaining power of the poor countries it is supposed to help. But SDT is also commonly criticized on the grounds that it harms the economies of poor countries in a more direct fashion. Many economists and policymakers believe that free trade promotes growth and development, and they criticize SDT because it permits poor countries to employ protectionist measures which undermine their development prospects. Instead of simply repeating the observation, made in chapter 4, that some eminent economists hold contrary views, and believe that protectionist policies can conduce to economic growth, what I want to do here is emphasize that SDT comes in many different varieties. Even if it is true that free trade promotes development, and that protectionist policies inhibit development, it does not follow that all conceivable forms of SDT are economically harmful, for not all forms of SDT permit developing countries to employ protectionist measures. As mentioned above, the GSP allows rich states to treat developing country imports more favourably than they treat those of their wealthier trading partners. This can be expected to expand, rather than contract, the amount of trade in which poor countries engage. Indeed, it is important to distinguish between the abstract idea or concept of granting special treatment to poor countries, and specific conceptions of that idea, which describe the form that special treatment should take. While particular conceptions of special treatment (e.g., those which permit the use of protectionist measures) might be economically harmful, the claim that the concept of special treatment must inevitably be expressed in policies that will hurt the interests of developing countries is implausible.

This concludes the first section of the chapter. We have explicated the idea of formal equality, identified several arguments for departing from formal

---

[14] When developing countries use SDT measures to restrict imports from countries at a comparable or lower level of development, such measures assume a more worrying character. Perhaps such uses should be proscribed. On this point see Peter Kleen and Sheila Page, 'Special and Differential Treatment of Developing Countries in the World Trade Organization', *Global Development Studies*, No. 2, 2005, p. 50.

equality, and seen how departures in the form of SDT can be defended against a number of objections. I do not claim to have offered a full vindication of SDT, but rather to have performed some of the philosophical groundwork that is necessary for the achievement of such a vindication. As we have seen, whether any particular conception of SDT can be fully vindicated depends upon the resolution of important economic questions regarding the efficacy of those conceptions.

II

The Principle of Reciprocity

The analysis in section I did not differentiate between the various expressions of formal equality found in the WTO (non-discrimination, reciprocity, etc.). In this section I focus on one particular expression of formal equality, namely, the principle of reciprocity. Whereas section I defended departures from formal equality by appealing to the needs of developing countries, this section reveals that some fairness-based demands for formal equality run into trouble even if we bracket those needs. I do, however, appeal to the needs of developing countries in order to defeat what I will call the 'special interest' conception of reciprocity.

Reciprocity means different things in different contexts and disciplines. In the study of world politics, reciprocity is a characteristic of interstate relations that is said to obtain when all parties make roughly equivalent contributions to a shared endeavour. A state behaves reciprocally when it acts in a way that is conducive to the achievement of reciprocity, i.e., by aiming to match the efforts of others.[15] It is this notion of reciprocity that I will be referring to throughout this section. This notion of reciprocity is often conceived as a strategy for achieving cooperation in an anarchic world order. But it is also sometimes said to be a requirement of fairness.

In the context of international trade, reciprocity is often regarded as a crucial value. As Andrew Brown and Robert Stern point out, in 'bilateral trade negotiations, negotiators have often directly compared, product by product, the size of the tariff cuts and the volume of trade in order to assure

---

[15] The idea of reciprocity as understood by scholars of international relations is actually more complex than this. In addition to equivalent contributions, it also requires that states make their behaviour conditional upon the behaviour of others. Moreover, reciprocity is not a characteristic of cooperative endeavours only; a state acts reciprocally when, for example, it fires a nuclear weapon at a state that has just fired a nuclear weapon at it. However, the definition given in the text is adequate for present purposes. See Robert Keohane, 'Reciprocity in International Relations', in Keohane (ed.), *International Institutions and State Power: Essays in International Relations Theory* (Boulder, CO: Westview Press, 1989).

themselves of equivalence.'[16] This insistence on what has been called *specific reciprocity* has been replaced in recent decades by an emphasis on *diffuse reciprocity*.[17] Brown and Stern observe that

> in recent negotiations among developed countries, *a rough* sense of equivalence could be perceived to have guided them even if there was no close accounting of the gains in market access. In each of the major areas of negotiation, the mutual concessions among these countries were roughly comparable.[18]

It is sometimes said that, in the absence of rough equivalence of concessions, unfairness obtains. Indeed, a number of US firms have insisted that fair trade requires nothing less than *strict* equivalence, or specific reciprocity.[19] But such claims are insensitive to a highly relevant consideration, namely, how liberal each country was at the start of negotiations. If Country A enters a round of negotiations with, say, very few tariff barriers, while Country B enters the round with very many tariff barriers, it hardly makes sense to say that the outcome of the negotiations is unfair simply by virtue of the fact that Country A agreed to fewer tariff reductions than Country B.

If A has a lower level of tariffs because it has made more reductions than B in the past, A can rightly insist that those reductions be taken into consideration when measuring each country's relative contribution and determining how many reductions each country should make in the future. Alternatively, if A has always maintained fewer tariff barriers than B, it can point out that, all along, it has offered B greater access to its market. Either way, expecting A to commit to the same number of future reductions as B is to demand more of A than of B. B might point out that by reducing tariffs by x per cent it will incur a certain level of costs, and that unfairness obtains unless A commits to reductions that entail costs of a comparable level. But A can maintain that it has borne such costs in the past. Moreover, given that B's market is currently more protected than A's, B has more to gain from liberalization—more precisely, B has more to gain from beginning the liberalization process than A does from further liberalization—and the costs B incurs can therefore be offset to a greater degree.

These points have not been lost on many US firms, who have been quick to advance an alternative conception of reciprocity according to which what

---

[16] Andrew G. Brown and Robert M. Stern, 'Concepts of Fairness in the Global Trading System', *Pacific Economic Review*, Vol. 12, No. 3, 2007, pp. 293–318, at p. 300.

[17] These terms were coined in Keohane, 'Reciprocity', p. 134. Specific reciprocity 'refer[s] to situations in which specified partners exchange items of equivalent value in a strictly delimited sequence.' Diffuse reciprocity, by contrast, refers to situations in which 'the definition of equivalence is less precise.'

[18] Brown and Stern, 'Concepts of Fairness', p. 300 (emphasis added).

[19] Kenneth W. Abbott, 'Defensive Unfairness: The Normative Structure of Section 301', in Jagdish Bhagwati and Robert E. Hudec (eds.), *Fair Trade and Harmonization: Volume 2—Legal Analysis* (Cambridge, Mass: MIT Press, 1996) pp. 425–8.

matters is not the level of concessions made during any given round of negotiations, but rather the relative openness of countries' markets. Proponents of this conception of reciprocity, which has been called the *equal access* conception,[20] allege that trade is fair when markets in all countries are equally accessible. The equal access conception of reciprocity comes in two varieties: *national* equal access reciprocity and *sectoral* equal access reciprocity.[21] According to the former, there must be equal access at the national level; the incidence of tariffs and other protectionist measures in one country must be no higher than the incidence of protectionist measures in other countries. On this view, the distribution of protectionist measures across different industries is unimportant. Country A may protect its agricultural industry to a greater extent that Country B, but, if Country B protects its textile industry to a greater extent than Country A, the demands of equal access reciprocity may nevertheless be satisfied. According to sectoral equal access reciprocity, by contrast, the distribution of market access must be the same in all countries. If Country B has few agricultural tariffs while Country A has many, unfairness obtains, irrespective of whether the incidence of protectionist measures employed by each country balances out at the national level.

National equal access reciprocity suffers from a fatal flaw, namely, it is insensitive to the fact that access to particular markets is valued differently by different countries. This insensitivity means that national equal access reciprocity generates perverse results. For example, it would regard as unfair a scenario in which Country A imposes a higher number of tariffs than Country B, even if none of the tariffs imposed by A protect markets of particular value to B, and none of the tariffs imposed by B protect markets of particular value to A. Conversely, it would regard as fair a scenario in which A and B impose the same number of tariffs, but in which A protects the markets of greatest value to B while B liberalizes the markets of greatest value to A. It is difficult to see how the second scenario could be fairer than the first. (Note that this argument does not appeal to the needs of developing countries.)

The same kinds of consideration that defeat national equal access reciprocity also reveal problems for sectoral equal access reciprocity. Suppose that Country A enjoys a comparative advantage in the production of Product P, and thus has a special interest in Country B ceasing to protect its market for P, while Country B enjoys a comparative advantage in the production of Product Q, and thus has a special interest in Country A ceasing to protect its market for Q. Now consider two scenarios. In the first scenario, both A and B cease to protect their market for P, while continuing to protect their market for Q. In the second scenario, by contrast, A ceases to protect its market for Q,

---

[20] Abbott, 'Defensive Unfairness', pp. 428.
[21] Abbott, 'Defensive Unfairness', pp. 428–35.

while continuing to protect its market for P, whereas B ceases to protect its market for P, while continuing to protect its market for Q. Sectoral equal access reciprocity tells us that the first scenario is fairer than the second. But this result is perplexing. In the first scenario, A gets what it wants, but B does not, while in the second scenario both countries get what they want. If either scenario is fairer than the other, it is surely the second. (This argument, like the argument offered in the previous paragraph against national equal access reciprocity, does not appeal to the needs of developing countries.)

Sectoral equal access reciprocity faces an additional problem. According to this form of reciprocity, if Country A liberalizes a particular industry, Country B is compelled by fairness to reciprocate by also liberalizing that industry. But B may have a strong interest in refraining from liberalizing that industry, while A might lack such an interest. For example, excessive subsidization of agriculture in developed countries has led to agricultural overproduction, while inadequate support for agriculture in developing countries has led to agricultural underproduction. Thus, developing countries have a strong interest, which developed countries lack, in subsidizing agriculture. But according to equal access reciprocity, if developed countries liberalize agriculture, fairness requires developing countries to follow suit. But this is bizarre. Why would fairness require two sets of countries to take the same course of action, when that course of action is economically sensible for one set but economically disastrous for the other?

These objections to national and sectoral equal access reciprocity suggest an alternative reciprocity principle. According to what we might call *special interest reciprocity*, if Country A liberalizes a market of special interest to Country B, fairness requires B to reciprocate by liberalizing a market of special interest to A. Against special interest reciprocity it might be argued that developed countries are required to liberalize markets of special value to developing (or, at least, least developed) countries even if developing countries continue to protect markets of special value to developed countries. Such an argument would appeal to one of the rationales for SDT that we encountered in section I. For example, it could invoke the widely endorsed normative premise that if one is in a position to alleviate severe deprivation at little cost to oneself then one ought to do so, along with the empirical premises that (i) severe deprivation can be alleviated when rich countries liberalize the markets in which poor countries enjoy a comparative advantage, and that (ii) rich countries can liberalize those markets without incurring large costs.

Premise (i) is widely accepted. Premise (ii) is slightly more controversial. As we saw in chapter 4, when rich countries liberalize an industry, workers employed in that industry suffer as a result of exposure to foreign competition. They may see their wages shrink, or they may lose their jobs. But, as economists have been keen to stress, and as we also saw in chapter 4, these workers can be compensated. The national income gains brought about by liberalization can, in principle, be redistributed so that everyone benefits.

In defence of developed countries liberalizing markets of special value to developing countries only on the condition that developing countries recip- rocate, one might argue that it is in developing countries' own interest to liberalize their markets, and then add that making liberalization conditional in the way described is an effective way of making them do so. But arguing that conditional liberalization by developed countries can be an effective tool for getting poor countries to help themselves is very different from arguing that there is unfairness when poor countries fail to reciprocate liberalizing efforts made by rich countries. Since it is the latter argument that would have to be made by proponents of special interest reciprocity, the former argument cannot play a role in vindicating special interest reciprocity.

Moreover, as was discussed in chapter 4, the claim that it is always in the interest of developing countries to liberalize their markets is controversial. By contrast, the claim that developing countries benefit in terms of poverty alleviation when developed countries liberalize the markets in which the former enjoy a comparative advantage is, as I have already noted, widely accepted. Thus, one might plausibly insist, against special interest reciprocity, that developed countries are required to cease protecting markets of special interest to developing (or, at least, least developed) countries, irrespective of whether or not those countries are willing to reciprocate, on the grounds that doing so is a low cost way of alleviating severe deprivation.

In this section I have argued that the principle of reciprocity should not be regarded as a requirement of fairness in trade. Moreover, I have shown that national and sectoral equal access conceptions of reciprocity are vulnerable to damaging objections even when the needs of developing countries are set aside.

III

Harmonization

So far we have focused on the claim that a just distribution of opportunities requires formal equality in the area of 'at-the-border policies' such as tariffs and quotas. In recent decades it has been claimed that a just distribution also requires formal equality in the area of 'behind-the-border policies'. It has become common to claim that, in order for trade to be just, some subset of the domestic laws or policies of trading countries (e.g., labour or environmen- tal laws) must be made more similar, or *harmonized*. The term 'harmonization' is somewhat misleading. As David Leebron has observed

[t]he term 'harmonization' is something of a misnomer insofar as it might be regarded as deriving from the musical notion of harmony, for it is difference, not sameness, that makes for musical harmony ... The claim for the harmonization of laws has come to mean something quite different—indeed almost the exact opposite of the musical notion of harmony—namely, that international trade relations will not run smoothly, or properly, unless the laws and policies of different jurisdictions are made more similar.[22]

Calls for harmonization are motivated by a variety of considerations. The claim, for example, might be that trade relations will not run 'properly' in the sense that they will not run *efficiently* in the absence of harmonization,[23] or the claim might be that trade relations will not run 'properly' in the sense that they will not be *just* or *fair* in the absence of harmonization. Of interest to us are harmonization claims motivated by a concern for justice or fairness. As Leebron points out, such claims are highly prevalent. He writes:

Recently, claims for harmonization of national laws and policies have been closely linked to claims for 'fair trade'. The scholarly literature has begun to embrace the notion that harmonization is the mechanism by which unfair differences in legal and other regimes are eliminated, and the level playing field, the metaphorical symbol of fairness, is restored.[24]

Leebron identifies three types of harmonization claim: 'pure normative' harmonization claims, 'pure non-normative' harmonization claims, and what we might call 'mixed' harmonization claims.[25] Pure normative harmonization claims maintain that all countries should adopt Policy P, because P is better, in some regard, than all alternative policies. Pure non-normative harmonization claims allege that all countries should adopt the same policy, because doing so is necessary to achieve some value (e.g., fairness or efficiency), but do not claim that any particular policy is better than any other. All that matters is that countries adopt the *same* policy; it does not matter *which* policy they adopt. Mixed harmonization claims incorporate both normative and non-normative elements. They call for all countries to adopt Policy

---

[22] David W. Leebron, 'Lying Down with Procrustes: An Analysis of Harmonization Claims', in Jagdish Bhagwati and Robert E. Hudec (eds.), *Fair Trade and Harmonization: Volume 1—Economic Analysis* (Cambridge, Mass: MIT Press, 1996), p. 43.

[23] For example, one might point out that the existence of different regulatory requirements in each country can deter producers from engaging in international trade. As Leebron writes: 'Even where the marginal compliance costs for different jurisdictional requirements are low ... legal information costs represent an additional fixed cost for each jurisdiction that must be recovered from the sales of products in that jurisdiction. In the face of ignorance and uncertainty, a producer might be unwilling to undertake the effort to engage in a small number of international transactions. In short, every separate legal system to some extent creates a barrier to trade.' Leebron, 'Lying Down with Procrustes', p. 62.

[24] Leebron, 'Lying Down with Procrustes', p. 41.

[25] Leebron, 'Lying Down with Procrustes', pp. 50–1.

P because (i) the realization of some value requires that all countries adopt the same policy, and (ii) P is the best policy.

Leebron notes that there is a sense in which pure normative harmonization claims are not bona fide harmonization claims. He observes that

> [t]he apparent harmonization claim results only from a truism: every nation should have a law or policy x; therefore, all nations should have the same policy. But here the only claim for harmonization is that all nations adopt policy x; there is no claim independent of policy x that all nations should have the same policy.[26]

I will not discuss pure normative harmonization claims in isolation, but I will discuss the normative aspect of mixed harmonization claims. Let us begin, though, by considering pure non-normative harmonization claims. To repeat, according to these claims, in order for a particular value—in our case, fairness—to be respected, all trading countries must adopt the same policy, but it does not matter which policy they adopt, because there is no policy the adoption of which is any better than any other. The upshot is that unfairness arises when Country A pursues policy P while Country B pursues policy Q, or vice versa, even if there is no unfairness inherent in A and B both pursuing P, or in A and B both pursuing Q.

This might be because fairness requires the realization of goal G, and G can be realized either by A and B both pursuing P, or by A and B both pursuing Q, but not by A pursuing P while B pursues Q, or vice versa. In the context of international trade, the goal ostensibly sought by those who advance fairness-based harmonization claims is invariably a 'level playing field'. The claim is that unless certain policies are harmonized, firms or workers in one country will enjoy an unfair advantage over firms or workers in another. A non-normative fairness-based harmonization claim might maintain, for example, that while it is acceptable for A and B to implement a set of environmental laws E, or to refrain from implementing E, if A implements E while B does not, and if this reduces the production costs faced by firms in B, firms in B are given an unfair advantage over firms in A.

Note that it does not make sense to say that, by virtue of its lower environmental standards, Country B *taken as a whole* enjoys an unfair advantage over Country A *taken as a whole*. This is because the latter can benefit from cheaper imports made possible by the former's lower standards. Nor does it make sense to say that *all* of the firms in A are unfairly disadvantaged by lower standards in B. This is because many firms can, and do, move production to where standards are lowest. The claim must be that (i) relatively immobile *workers* in A are unfairly disadvantaged when competition from B forces the firms that employ them to lower wages, make layoffs, or move their operations abroad, and (ii) *non-multinational* firms based in A are unfairly disadvantaged when

---

[26] Leebron, 'Lying Down with Procrustes', pp. 50–1.

competition from B reduces their profits or puts them out of business. But even these claims are problematical because, in theory, the national income gains resulting from cheaper imports could be redistributed so as to compensate workers and non-multinational firms for the losses they suffer.

Suppose that, while A enjoys national income gains as a result of B's lower standards (e.g., because it can purchase cheap imports), B's income gains are larger. Is this unfair? When attempting to answer this question it is important to notice that while B might benefit more in terms of national income, it does not follow that B benefits more overall, for B's lower standards may entail costs that, by virtue of its higher standards, A avoids. Indeed, if, as non-normative harmonization claims maintain, it is not impermissible for A to reduce its standards, there must be a reason why A chooses to maintain high standards. And one obvious reason is that the maintenance of high standards confers certain (non-income) benefits. Suppose the standards in question are environmental in character. By retaining high standards, A can benefit from a healthier and more pleasant environment. B might enjoy greater income gains, but only by sacrificing environmental quality. Thus, while we might be concerned about how much each country benefits in relative terms from the policies they pursue, it is not at all obvious that, overall, B is better-off.

Non-normative fairness-based harmonization claims suffer from an additional limitation. When workers and firms believe the playing field is uneven, they invariably call upon their governments to demand that other countries change their laws. But *non-normative* harmonization claims cannot support these demands, because, as we have seen, such claims do not identify one set of laws as superior to any other; they simply maintain that unfairness is a consequence of two or more countries adopting different, but equally acceptable, laws. Thus, if A calls upon B to change its laws in order to level the playing field, B can respond by insisting that if A is so concerned about levelling the playing field *it should change its own laws*.

Let us move on to mixed harmonization claims.[27] These claim that fairness requires all countries to pursue Policy P, rather than Policy Q, because (i) the latter is unjust and (ii) would give any country pursuing it an advantage over those who do not pursue it that, by virtue of the unjustness of Q, would be an unfair advantage. Pure normative (pseudo) harmonization claims would also recognize the injustice of a country pursuing Q, but they would not

---

[27] Leebron claims that all harmonization claims motivated by a concern for fairness seem to 'be based solely on the existence of difference' (i.e., are purely non-normative) (Leebron, 'Lying Down with Procrustes', p. 66). But, as I hope will become clear in the paragraphs that follow, fairness-based harmonization claims do not have to be construed in this way. Nor does it seem that those who have advanced fairness-based harmonization claims have understood themselves to be advancing purely non-normative claims; for, consider the reference to 'oppressive' working conditions in the Peace Conference memorandum quoted in the text below.

recognize the additional putative unfairness that arises when some countries pursue Q while others pursue P.

One of the most commonly advanced mixed harmonization claims asserts that unfairness occurs when workers and firms in developed countries have to compete with workers and firms in poor countries where labour standards and minimum wages are unjustly low or non-existent. The fairness of competitive advantages traceable to low labour standards and wages has long been challenged. A memorandum circulated at the 1919 Paris Peace Conference—which gave life to the International Labour Organization (ILO)—revealed a concern on the part of the British delegation that 'any state . . . which does not carry out a Convention designed to prevent oppressive [working] conditions is guilty of manufacturing under conditions which create a state of unfair competition in the international market.'[28]

Several of the points made in the discussion of non-normative harmonization claims apply here, too. It does not make sense to say that, by virtue of their lower labour standards and wages, developing *countries* enjoy an unfair advantage over developed *countries*. This is because the latter can benefit from cheaper imports made possible by the former's lower standards and wages.[29] Nor does it make sense to say that *all* rich-world firms are unfairly disadvantaged by lower standards in developing countries. This is because many rich-world firms can, and do, move production to where standards and wages are lowest. Indeed, the desire to attract multinational corporations is one of the things compelling poor countries to keep standards and wages low. As before, the claim must be that (i) relatively immobile *workers* in the developed world are unfairly disadvantaged when competition from developing countries forces the firms that employ them to lower wages, make layoffs, or move their operations abroad, and (ii) *non-multinational* firms based in the developed world are unfairly disadvantaged when competition from developing countries reduces their profits or puts them out of business. But, again, the national income gains resulting from cheaper imports could, in theory, be redistributed so as to compensate workers and non-multinational firms for the losses they suffer.[30]

Still, when addressing this kind of harmonization claim the fundamental question is whether the toleration of lower labour standards by developing-country governments, and their refusal to implement or enforce satisfactory (or any) minimum wage laws, are actually unjust. If they are not, the

---

[28] Quoted in Virginia A. Leary, 'Workers' Rights and International Trade: The Social Clause (GATT, ILO, NAFTA, U.S. Laws)', in Bhagwati and Hudec (eds.), *Fair Trade and Harmonization: Volume 2*, p. 186.
[29] Leebron, 'Lying Down with Procrustes', p. 60.
[30] Leebron, 'Lying Down with Procrustes', pp. 60–1.

harmonization claim collapses because one of its premises is revealed to be false. So, let us turn to this question.

Intuitively, the injustice of subsistence wages and miserable working conditions seems hard to deny. But one is given pause by the argument, often advanced by economists, that sweatshop labour can play a crucial role in an effective strategy of poverty alleviation.[31] No doubt this argument is often invoked disingenuously by reactionary apologists for the status quo, but that is no reason to dismiss it. The argument runs roughly as follows. The lower production costs that come with lower wages and standards enable developing-world firms to compete more effectively in the global market, and also to attract foreign direct investment (FDI). Foreign companies bring with them investment capital, cutting-edge technology, and advanced business, management, and marketing techniques. They provide their employees with valuable training, which they can take with them if they move to a different firm, and sometimes give technical and financial assistance to local contractors in order to enable them to meet the higher standards of foreign companies. This package of goods, it is argued, helps promote growth and reduce poverty.[32]

Let us assume that this argument, or some version of it, is empirically sound. If it is to stand any chance of vindicating the use of sweatshop labour it cannot simply claim that low wages and standards are one sufficient means among several for reducing poverty. Rather, the claim must be one of the following: (1) sweatshop labour is strictly necessary for poverty reduction, in the sense that poverty reduction would be literally impossible without it; (2) poverty reduction strategies that do not rely upon sweatshop labour are available, but they are morally inferior (because, say, they are much less effective, and would prolong the plight of the poor, or because they would violate the rights of others [imagine a government that seeks to alleviate domestic poverty by invading other countries and enslaving their citizens]); or (3) morally satisfactory alternatives exist, but the unjust behaviour of third parties renders them unavailable. (1) is undoubtedly false, but (2) and (3) are both much more plausible.

If it is reasonable for the governments of poor countries to believe that any of claims (1)–(3) is true, it is not obvious that it would be unjust for them to tolerate sweatshop labour. To be sure, patent injustices may have occurred along the way. It is possible to imagine a scenario in which (1) or (2) is true, but

---

[31] See, for example, Paul Krugman, 'In Praise of Cheap Labor: Bad Jobs at Bad Wages Are Better Than No Jobs at All', in Krugman (ed.), *The Accidental Theorist And Other Dispatches from the Dismal Science* (New York: Norton & Company, 1998).

[32] For a helpful review of the literature on the effects of FDI in developing countries see Stephen D. Cohen, *Multinational Corporations and Foreign Direct Investment: Avoiding Simplicity, Embracing Complexity* (New York: Oxford University Press, 2007), Ch. 8.

in which they were made true by unjust actions. And if (3) is true, it is unjust that others have acted in a way that has foreclosed the pursuit of strategies less burdensome to the global poor.

Nevertheless, if a government in the developing world reasonably believes that conditions (1), (2), or (3) hold, a strong case can be made for the claim that their toleration of sweatshop labour is permissible, and perhaps even required. It can be argued that, under such conditions, toleration of sweatshop labour is the least awful means with which developing-world governments can enable their severely poor citizens to acquire the resources needed to meet their most basic needs. Under such conditions, the argument continues, a developing-world government would do its poorest citizens no favours by prohibiting sweatshops. Such a prohibition would simply deny them an opportunity that they may find more appealing than the other options available to them, such as scavenging on landfill sites.[33]

One weakness of this argument is that some poor people in developing countries may well be better-off in a scenario in which sweatshops are outlawed, even if systematic poverty alleviation requires the toleration of sweatshops. For some individuals, working in a sweatshop might be their best option in a scenario in which sweatshops are tolerated, but, in a scenario in which sweatshops are prohibited, a better option might be available to them. It might then be argued that the rights of such individuals are violated by governments that tolerate sweatshops, even when sweatshops are tolerated only as a means to alleviating poverty; the rights of one set of poor people are violated in order to assist another set of poor people.

Powerful as it is, this line of argument cannot defeat the claim that, under certain conditions (which might well obtain), it is permissible for developing-world governments to tolerate sweatshops. This is because it is common to hold that measures that would undoubtedly constitute rights violations at a high level of economic development do not necessarily constitute rights violations at a lower level of development.[34] This thought might be cashed out by saying that the rights people possess differ depending on their country's level of development, or by saying (and this strikes me as the preferable formulation) that at a low level of development denying people the content of certain rights (which they do undoubtedly possess) can be permissible, and

---

[33] Debra Satz makes a similar point about child labour: 'bans on all child labor may drive families to choose even worse options for their children. Children … are presumably better off working in factories than as prostitutes or soldiers.' See Debra Satz, *Why Some Things Should Not Be for Sale: The Moral Limits of Markets* (Oxford: Oxford University Press, 2010), p. 163.

[34] As Rawls noted, 'when social circumstances do not allow the effective establishment of … basic rights … one can concede their limitation … [T]hese restrictions can be granted … to the extent that they are necessary to prepare the way for the time when they are no longer justified.' John Rawls, *A Theory of Justice*, Revised Edition (Cambridge, Mass: Harvard University Press, 1999), p. 132.

that such denial therefore constitutes a rights *infringement*, rather than a rights violation.[35] And if one holds this view, one can then argue that while poor individuals who are rendered worse-off by the toleration of sweatshops *are* regrettably denied the content of their rights, their rights are not violated. Their rights are not violated because the policies that deny them the content of their rights are permissible, and those policies are permissible because they can foster development and thereby alleviate a huge amount of severe suffering. Of course, it is often thought that the very point of rights is to constrain what can be done to individuals in the name of the greater good. But no one thinks that rights are absolute. If we were to conceive of rights as unbending rules that can block certain poverty-relief strategies and thereby condemn huge numbers of people to never-ending misery, then the appeal of rights would surely vanish.

Even if we accept what I have said so far, and even if conditions (2) or (3) are true (as I have already said, (1) is undoubtedly false), some forms of sweatshop labour will remain beyond the pale. For example, *forced* sweatshop labour is clearly indefensible, irrespective of its consequences for poverty alleviation.[36] Also, government regulations should ensure that employers fully inform their workers of any hazards to which they might be exposing themselves. Companies that fail to disclose such information should not be tolerated.[37] But if (2) or (3) hold, it is difficult to see how justice or fairness could impose upon the developing world a requirement to outlaw *all* forms of sweatshop labour.

Intuitively, what distinguishes offering people the opportunity to work in sweatshops, on the one hand, and forcing people to do so (or withholding relevant information, thereby denying the possibility of informed choice), on the other, is that the latter disrespects personal autonomy in a way that the former does not. But it might be objected that it is incredible to speak of autonomy in the kind of situations in which people are likely to accept offers to work in sweatshops. People who accept such offers in order to escape severe, debilitating poverty exercise no more autonomy—are no less *coerced*—than people who are forced into sweatshops at the barrel of a gun: they are coerced by the necessity of their situation.[38] I am sympathetic to this line of thought

---

[35] On the distinction between a rights infringement and a rights violation, see Judith Jarvis Thomson, *The Realm of Rights* (Cambridge, Mass: Harvard University Press, 1990), p. 122.

[36] Thus, nothing I say here contradicts Mathias Risse's claim that states have a *pro tanto* reason to prevent their citizens from purchasing goods that have been produced at the expense of workers who have been coerced into producing. See Mathias Risse, 'Fairness in trade I: obligations from trading and the pauper-labor argument', *Politics, Philosophy & Economics*, Vol. 6, No. 3, 2007, pp. 355–77, at p. 361–5.

[37] This point is stressed in Henry Shue, 'Exporting Hazards', *Ethics*, Vol. 91, No. 4, 1981, pp. 579–606, at pp. 593–5.

[38] On the notion of being coerced by the necessity of one's situation, see Michael Sandel, 'What Money Can't Buy: The Moral Limits of Markets', *The Tanner Lectures on Human Values*, 1998, pp. 87–122, at p. 94.

(or at least to an argument roughly along these lines), but I still maintain that there is a difference—even if it only one of degree—between the two cases. The important point to recognize is that one does not benefit the severely poor citizens of developing countries—and one certainly does not enhance their autonomy—by further reducing their options. Justice, in my view, imposes upon the affluent duties to alleviate severe poverty and thereby improve the range and quality of options available to the global poor. But, while severe poverty persists, forbidding the poor from making certain choices on the grounds that—given the nature of their situation—their choice cannot be genuine is difficult to justify. The situation is what it is, and denying people the freedom to take certain paths out of that situation for the reason that they would not take those paths if the situation were different simply exacerbates the injustice.[39] *Of course* people would not choose to work in sweatshops if they were not living in severe poverty, in the same way that people would not choose to undergo chemotherapy if they did not have cancer. But the point is that people *are* living in severe poverty, and they *do* choose to work in sweatshops, and that decision should not be disregarded.

In wealthier countries, labour regulations can be justified on the grounds that they enable the worker to defend her own conception of her interests against those with massively greater bargaining power. But in developing countries, where outlawing sweatshop labour might mean depriving the poor of what they regard as their least awful option, this argument looks much less plausible.

If, as things stand, sweatshops play a crucial role in the best poverty reduction strategy available to poor countries, it is unlikely to be unjust for those countries to tolerate sweatshop labour in some form. It might well be unjust that the parameters within which poor countries operate are such that sweatshop labour assumes this crucial importance—injustice obtains if rich countries possess the means to make available alternative development strategies, and if they could do so without imposing unreasonable costs upon their own citizens—but it does not follow that poor countries are required to eschew sweatshop labour.

Aaron James has suggested that the answer to the question of whether tolerating sweatshop labour is consistent with justice hinges on the speed at which sweatshops bring about wage increases, and also on the level of those increases. He writes:

---

[39] Richard Arneson makes the same argument in a different context. He writes: '[T]he idea that the narrow range of one's options unacceptably constrains one's choice is not a reason to limit further one's range of choice... [A] concern that some people are forced to choose their lives from an unfairly small menu of options is a reason to *expand not restrict* the range of options from which these people must choose.' Richard Arneson, 'Commodification and Commercial Surrogacy', *Philosophy & Public Affairs*, Vol. 21, No. 2, 1992, pp. 132–64, at pp. 158–9 (original emphasis).

You can't tell a sweatshop worker that her wage is not exploitative because, although *she* will never see more than modest benefit, her child will have a substantially better life. The benefit of rising wages must accrue to her, in a sufficiently short period of time, or at a sufficiently rapid rate of increase...[40]

The suggestion that sweatshops can be permissible only if they substantially improve the lives of their workers in a short period of time sounds appealing, but it is also incorrect. If (1), (2), or (3) is true, then the most we can say is that wages must rise *as quickly as possible*. If sweatshops do not facilitate substantial wage increases within the lifetime of a particular worker, but (1), (2), or (3) is true, it is hard to see how one can nevertheless insist that it is unjust for poor countries to permit sweatshop labour.[41] Outlawing sweatshops under such conditions would be to condemn the world's poor to crippling, life-threatening poverty for the foreseeable future; it would be to deny them the option of taking a course of action that they might regard as preferable to the alternatives, and which is essential to giving their descendants a better life.

If the toleration of sweatshop labour by developing countries is consistent with justice, the common mixed harmonization claim that we have been considering collapses. It does not follow from this that any costs imposed upon workers or firms in the developed world by global free markets are fair; the corollary is simply that one cannot defend the proposition that those costs are unfair by claiming that the toleration of sweatshop labour by poor countries is unjust.

IV

Conclusion

In this chapter I have sought to cast doubt on the claim that formal equality is a requirement of just or fair trade. Section I began by noting that the standard equity-based argument for formal equality does not fare well in the context of trade. I then moved on to show how preferential treatment for developing countries can be argued for and defended against a number of objections.

---

[40] Aaron James, *Fairness in Practice: A Social Contract for a Global Economy* (Oxford: Oxford University Press, 2012), p. 311 (original emphasis).

[41] This does not mean, of course, that if (3) is true, one cannot condemn as unjust the behaviour of those who force poor countries to rely upon sweatshop labour. One can condemn such behaviour *irrespective* of whether or not sweatshops facilitate substantial wage increases within the lifetime of a particular worker. Also, as mentioned in the text, one may be vulnerable to moral censure if one has acted in a way that makes (1) or (2) true.

Next, in section II, I argued that the principle of reciprocity should not be regarded as a requirement of fairness. Finally, in section III, I examined a more recent interpretation of formal equality in trade, according to which some subset of the laws or policies of trading countries should be harmonized. Three types of harmonization claim were identified and criticized.

6

The Gains from Trade

In chapter 5, I considered various accounts of how certain goods should be distributed within the trade regime. These goods were opportunities to reap the material benefits that trade makes available. In this chapter I consider whether a certain distributive principle ought to apply to those benefits themselves. By allowing states to restructure their economies according to comparative advantage—to specialize in producing the goods and services that they are relatively good at producing while importing everything else from abroad—trade enables states to augment their income. But how should these income gains be distributed? Are states permitted to keep everything that happens to accrue to them? Or are they required to share their gains with others? Conventional wisdom holds that states may retain whatever benefits they reap. In what follows, I challenge this view. More specifically, I argue that a variety of diverse accounts of distributive justice unexpectedly converge upon the conclusion that the gains from trade must be distributed in an egalitarian manner. This means either that the gains from trade should be distributed equally, or that they should be distributed in a way that conduces to the achievement of equality more broadly conceived (e.g., by offsetting other inequalities).

According to an influential school of thought—which I shall refer to as 'statism'—substantively egalitarian principles of distributive justice[1] are applicable only within states. This is said to be because egalitarian principles are grounded in particular kinds of relationship that exist only within state borders, and do not extend across them. One implication of this view is that egalitarian principles do not apply to the trade regime. My primary aim in what follows is to show that statist arguments do not support that conclusion.

---

[1] 'Substantively' egalitarian principles contrast with 'formally' egalitarian principles of the kind discussed in chapter 5. Throughout the present chapter, 'egalitarian' will mean 'substantively egalitarian'.

Statism contrasts with two forms of 'globalism': *relational* globalism and *non-relational* globalism.[2] Both forms of globalism contest the statist claim that egalitarian principles apply only within states, and maintain that egalitarianism actually has global reach, but they justify this claim in different ways. According to relational globalists, egalitarianism has global scope because, as a matter of contingent fact, there are global institutional relationships that ground global egalitarian principles. By contrast, non-relational globalists justify egalitarian duties by appealing directly to the unfairness of (certain kinds of) inequality: they argue that justice requires the mitigation of inequality irrespective of what kinds of global institution happen to exist.

The main claim of this chapter is that statists should convert to relational globalism, and that they should do so because the normatively relevant institutional relationships they identify within states also exist among members of the trade regime. In other words, I show that statist premises lead to the conclusion that the trade regime should be regarded as a subject of substantive egalitarian justice, and that the gains from trade should therefore be distributed in an egalitarian fashion. My arguments for this conclusion occupy sections III–VIII. In section IX I show how one set of relational globalist views generated by statist premises shares its conclusion with *non*-relational globalism.

I

The Limits of Statism

Before assessing statist arguments for the claim that principles of egalitarian justice apply exclusively within states, we should identify the limitations those arguments would impose, if successful, on normative evaluation of international trade. Statism is sometimes formulated in a way that suggests that there are no trade-related duties of justice whatsoever. Indeed, Thomas Nagel, an eminent proponent of the statist view, gives this impression when he expresses 'doubt that the rules of international trade rise to the level of collective action needed to trigger demands of justice, even in diluted form.'[3] But the statist view is more accommodating than Nagel's remark implies.

---

[2] These terms were coined in Andrea Sangiovanni, 'Global Justice, Reciprocity, and the State', *Philosophy & Public Affairs*, Vol. 35, No. 1, 2007, pp. 3–39, at pp. 5–6.

[3] Thomas Nagel, 'The Problem of Global Justice', *Philosophy & Public Affairs*, Vol. 33, No. 2, 2005, pp. 113–47, at p. 141.

To start with, it is important to distinguish between strong and modest forms of statism.[4] According to strong statists, like Nagel, the requirements of justice, or at least of 'socio-economic' justice, are exhausted by egalitarian concerns and, because egalitarian duties obtain only in the domestic realm, there are no duties of socio-economic justice whatsoever at the global level. Modest statists, by contrast, view distributive egalitarianism as one among several aspects of socio-economic justice, and maintain that while egalitarian duties apply exclusively at the domestic level, weaker duties of socio-economic justice, such as sufficientarian duties, exist at the global level. Moreover, while strong statists must deny that we have duties of *justice* to assist the global poor, they can accept that we have *humanitarian* duties to do so.[5] One implication of this is that statists could insist, on humanitarian or sufficientarian grounds, that the trade regime be designed in a way that affords 'special and differential treatment' to developing countries by, say, exempting them from rules requiring the removal of tariff barriers.

Similarly, statists could maintain that humanitarian or sufficientarian considerations should prompt us to condemn EU and US farm subsidies on the grounds that such subsidies exacerbate conditions of absolute deprivation. Writing in 2005, Nagel was supportive of the fact that 'WTO negotiations [had] finally begun to show some sense that it is indecent...when subsidies by wealthy nations to their own farmers cripple the market for agricultural products from developing countries.'[6]

Relatedly, statists recognize a negative duty borne by states to refrain from propping up regimes that are severely unjust. Nagel accepts that we should 'be concerned about the consequences of economic relations with states that are *internally* egregiously unjust.' He adds that '[e]ven if internal justice is the primary responsibility of each state, the complicity of other states in the active support or perpetuation of an unjust regime is a secondary offense against justice.'[7] An implication of this concession is that statists can recognize a duty

---

[4] Cf. the distinction made by Simon Caney between extreme and moderate versions of what he calls the *statist scope thesis* in his 'Global Distributive Justice and the State', *Political Studies*, Vol. 56, No. 3, 2008, pp. 487–518, at p. 488.

[5] Duties of humanity and duties of justice can be distinguished in different ways, and the nature of the relationship between strong and weak statism depends upon how they are distinguished. For example, humanitarian and justice-based duties might be distinguished by reference to their content—the former are concerned with the elimination of absolute deprivation whereas the latter are concerned with the reduction of relative deprivation—or by reference to their stringency—the former are charitable duties, the fulfilment of which is largely discretionary, while the latter may be coercively enforced. A strong statist who affirms the existence of global humanitarian duties, and who characterizes those duties solely in terms of their content, accepting that their stringency matches the stringency of duties of justice, occupies a position that is indistinguishable from the position endorsed by weak statists. By contrast, a strong statist who characterizes humanitarian duties in terms of their weaker stringency is committed to a position that is considerably more extreme.

[6] Nagel, 'The Problem', p. 143.   [7] Nagel, 'The Problem', p. 143 (original emphasis).

to refrain from engaging in certain types of trade with highly unjust states in cases where it is likely that such trade would exacerbate internal injustice.

Also, the statist view can acknowledge that governments have an obligation to alleviate harms that befall their own citizens as a result of exposure to the global market. As we saw in chapter 4, free trade poses a considerable threat to workers in import-competing industries, and statists can accept that governments have duties to either nullify that threat (via protective barriers or subsidies) or to compensate and retrain workers who lose their jobs. Similarly, it is consistent with statism to think that governments are required to reduce or eliminate any domestic inequalities generated by trade. Nagel himself observes that, on the statist view, governments 'that establish the framework within which [international] transactions can be undertaken will be guided by the interests of their own members, including their interests in domestic social justice.'[8]

An upshot of the preceding comments is that statists can accept that states have non-negligible trade-related duties of justice. Affirmation of the statist view is compatible with accepting that states have duties to compensate and retrain workers displaced by foreign competition; to demand special and differential treatment for poor countries; to oppose the use of agricultural subsidies by wealthy states; and to refrain from engaging in certain types of trade with internally unjust regimes. But we should be clear about the limits of the statist view. Principal among these limits is the fact that statist conclusions are incompatible with the claim that egalitarian duties exist among trading countries. In order to assess the statist view on this matter, we must examine the arguments by which it is underpinned.

II

The Varieties of Statism

Statists are usually divided into two main camps: the coercion camp and the cooperation camp. The central claim of the former is that the state's uniqueness is a function of its coerciveness; it is the coercive relationship between the state and its subjects that gives rise to the egalitarian duties that exist within state borders but not beyond them. One prominent variant of the coercion account adds that the laws that the state coercively enforces are imposed in the name of, or jointly authored by, the state's citizens, and places this fact at the centre of its account of the state's normative particularity. The central

---

[8] Nagel, 'The Problem', p. 142.

claim made by statists in the cooperation camp is that the state is a locus of a unique form of social cooperation that is necessary to trigger egalitarian duties. Some statists appeal to both the state's coerciveness and its status as a site of social cooperation in order to explain why it must be regulated by egalitarian principles.[9] While different statist theories are usually characterized by reference to whether they focus on coercive or cooperative relations, such theories also regard as pertinent a variety of other features of the state. They point out that membership in a state is non-voluntary, and that the state imposes rules that have a profound and pervasive impact upon the lives of those who are governed by them. In summary, we can say that statist theories provide an account of the state's alleged quiddity by appealing to (some combination of) the following: coercion; joint authorship; social cooperation; non-voluntariness; and profound and pervasive impact. In what follows, I examine each of these statist ideas.

I aim to show that (the best interpretation of) statist premises support the claim that the gains from trade should be distributed in an egalitarian fashion. This is because statists are mistaken when they say that the relationships that they claim ground egalitarian duties exist only within states: those relationships also obtain among members of the trade regime. Thus, we can embrace key normative premises affirmed by statist thinkers while rejecting their conclusions. To be sure, some interpretations of statist premises are not compatible with the view that the trade regime should be regarded as a subject of egalitarian justice, but, as I will show, those interpretations must be rejected.

One clarificatory point is worth emphasizing before we proceed. My aim is to show that (the best interpretation of) key normative premises affirmed by statist thinkers support the conclusion that the trade regime is to be regulated by *some* egalitarian conception of justice; my claim is not that normative statist premises are compatible with the conclusion that the trade regime should be regulated by the *same* egalitarian conception. The substantive content of any conception of justice will be shaped by the specific grounding rationale upon which the conception relies. Accordingly, the content of any egalitarian conception of trade justice may vary depending upon which of the various statist premises is employed.

Whenever distributive equality is proposed, at the international or domestic level, we can ask (i) what is to be equalized?, and (ii) among whom? Regarding the first question, one might argue that we should aim for an egalitarian distribution of the social product generated by certain cooperative enterprises. (Call this 'social product egalitarianism'.) On this view, the metric of egalitarian justice is conceived relatively narrowly. Alternatively, one might define

---

[9] Mathias Risse, *On Global Justice* (Princeton, NJ: Princeton University Press, 2012), Chs. 2 and 3.

the metric of egalitarian justice more broadly, and argue that we should aim to ensure that people are equally well-off in a more general and comprehensive sense. (Call this 'general egalitarianism'.) One might insist, for example, upon an egalitarian distribution of (access to) welfare, or advantage, or well-being. Some of the arguments I consider support a version of social product egalitarianism that mandates an equal distribution of the national income gains created by trade. Others support a version of general egalitarianism, the upshot being that we should aim not for an equal distribution of the gains from trade, but rather for a distribution of those gains that conduces to the realization of equality more broadly conceived. I elaborate on these ideas in sections VII, VIII, and IX.[10]

One might answer the second question by saying that inequalities (in some set of goods) should be reduced among states, or individuals, or some subset of states (e.g., trading states), or some subset of individuals (e.g., individuals living in trading states). Again, different arguments will likely vindicate different answers. Some of the arguments I consider are best interpreted as supporting the conclusion that there should be distributive equality among trading states, while others are best interpreted as supporting the conclusion that there should be distributive equality among the individuals who comprise those states. I will not try to identify the precise nature of the answers suggested by the arguments I discuss, but this point should be borne in mind throughout.

It might be thought that the clarificatory point I have just made reduces the significance of my conclusions, for it might be argued that what statists oppose is the claim that justice at the international level requires what I have called general egalitarianism, and that they might happily accept an international version of social product egalitarianism according to which the gains from trade should be distributed equally. In response, two points should be noted. First, some statists have been explicit in their rejection of the claim that justice requires an egalitarian distribution of the gains created by trade.[11] Second, even if some statists are willing to accept that the gains from trade should be distributed equally among states, they have not made that clear. On the contrary, they have written as though their arguments provide grounds

---

[10] There is an ongoing debate, which I shall not enter into here, around the question of how we can distinguish between gains from trade, on the one hand, and the income a country could generate under autarky, on the other. The question is made more difficult by the fact that the productive capacities a country currently possesses, and could utilize under autarky, were shaped by past trading. See, for example, Mathias Risse and Gabriel Wollner, 'Three Images of Trade: On the Place of Trade in a Theory of Global Justice', *Moral Philosophy and Politics*, Vol. 1, No. 2, 2014, pp. 201–25. For a response to the concerns raised by Risse and Wollner, see Aaron James, 'A Theory of Fairness in Trade', *Moral Philosophy and Politics*, Vol. 1, No. 2, 2014, pp. 177–200.

[11] Risse, *Global Justice*, pp. 273–4; Michael Blake, *Justice and Foreign Policy* (Oxford: Oxford University Press, 2013), pp. 99–100.

for rejecting all conceptions of egalitarian justice with international scope; it is therefore important to show that they do not. With these preliminary matters taken care of, let us proceed to examine statist arguments.

III

Coercion

According to an influential argument formulated by Michael Blake, the state must maintain an egalitarian distribution of benefits and burdens among its citizens in order to compensate for subjecting them to coercive institutions.[12] Coercion is prima facie objectionable, Blake says, because it encroaches upon individual autonomy. However, we cannot simply abolish state coercion, because, in addition to compromising autonomy to some degree, state coercion is also necessary to provide citizens with the conditions needed to live autonomous lives. Given that we cannot abolish state coercion, measures must be implemented which ensure that it can be justified to all citizens, including those who are least advantaged by the institutions it sustains. Blake suggests that justifying state coercion to all citizens requires implementing policies that guarantee distributive equality. Unless distributive equality obtains, the least advantaged can reasonably reject state coercion.[13]

Blake adds that while some international institutions also exercise coercion, they are not coercive in the relevant sense, and thus do not give rise to egalitarian obligations. I will return to this claim shortly, but let us first consider Blake's justification of egalitarianism within the state. There are good reasons to be sceptical about Blake's account. Crucially, it is not at all obvious that distributive equality is necessary to justify state coercion. A number of commentators have argued that state coercion can be defended by reference to the fact that it often makes individuals better-off than they would otherwise be.[14] Indeed, it seems plausible to think that state coercion can be justified by appealing to the value at the heart of Blake's argument,

[12] Michael Blake 'Distributive Justice, State Coercion, and Autonomy', *Philosophy & Public Affairs*, Vol. 30, No. 3, 2001, pp. 257–96. Andrea Sangiovanni points out that Blake equivocates between the claim that egalitarian redistribution *compensates* for the wrong of state coercion, and the claim that egalitarian redistribution *outweighs* the wrong of state coercion. I shall not pursue this point here. See Sangiovanni, 'The Irrelevance of Coercion, Imposition, and Framing to Distributive Justice', *Philosophy & Public Affairs*, Vol. 40, No. 2, 2012, pp. 79–110, at p. 88.

[13] For an alternative formulation of the coercion view, see Laura Valentini, *Justice in a Globalized World: A Normative Framework* (New York: Oxford University Press, 2011).

[14] Sangiovanni, 'Global Justice', pp. 12–13, 14, 20; Ryan Pevnick, 'Political Coercion and the Scope of Distributive Justice', *Political Studies*, Vol. 56, 2008, pp. 399–413, at pp. pp. 401–3; Gabriel Wollner, 'Equality and the Significance of Coercion', *Journal Of Social Philosophy*, Vol. 42, No. 4, 2011, pp. 363–81, at p. 369; Sangiovanni, 'Coercion, Imposition, and Framing', p. 91.

namely, the value of autonomy.[15] State coercion often grants individuals a greater degree of autonomy than they would enjoy in the absence of state coercion. It does this by increasing the number and quality of options available, thereby facilitating the formation and pursuit of a conception of the good. As we saw, Blake explicitly acknowledges that state coercion is necessary for the provision of an environment in which individuals can live as autonomous agents. But, if this is so, why is that fact not sufficient to justify state coercion? Why does a demand for distributive equality arise?

Let us suppose that this question can be answered. Even if Blake's account of the grounds of egalitarian justice could somehow be vindicated, his theory would not be out of the woods, for doubts would persist about his claim that only states are coercive in the relevant sense, and thus about his conclusion that egalitarian principles arise only in the context of state coercion. Importantly, as will now be shown, there is good reason to think that Blake's account of the grounds of egalitarian justice leads to the conclusion that the WTO is an appropriate subject of egalitarian justice.

Blake does not provide a definition of coercion, but, following Mathias Risse, another theorist who emphasizes the importance of coercive relationships, we can say that coercion is the use of a threat to ensure that a person or group has no reasonable alternative to performing a particular (set of) action(s).[16] On this definition of coercion, the WTO is clearly a coercive institution.[17] Under the WTO's Dispute Settlement Understanding, if a member state is found by the General Council to be in breach of WTO rules, injured parties may be permitted to take retaliatory action. More specifically, injured parties may be permitted to deny Most Favoured Nation treatment to the recalcitrant state, and to impose tariffs that they would usually be forbidden from imposing.[18]

The costs inflicted by such retaliatory measures can be considerable. For example, when the Council ruled that the EU's banana import regime violated WTO rules, it granted Ecuador the right to impose sanctions worth US $201.6 million per annum on EU exports; and it granted the US the right to impose sanctions worth US$191.4 million per annum.[19] Moreover, states have devised ways to maximize the harm inflicted by retaliatory measures. For example, the US has employed a method known as 'carouseling' whereby

---

[15] Sangiovanni, 'Coercion, Imposition, and Framing'; Pevnick, 'Political Coercion'; Wollner, 'Equality'.

[16] Risse, *Global Justice*, p. 25. This definition coheres with Blake's claim that coercion 'replace[s] our own agency with the agency of another.' Blake, 'Distributive Justice', p. 272.

[17] Sangiovanni, 'Global Justice', p. 9; Risse, *Global Justice*, p. 50.

[18] On the WTO's Dispute Settlement Understanding see, for example, Michael J. Trebilcock and Robert Howse, *The Regulation of International Trade 3rd Edition* (New York: Routledge, 2005), Ch. 4.

[19] WTO, 'Bananas: Discussions Continue on a Long Standing Issue' (available at: http://www.wto.org/english/thewto_e/minist_e/min05_e/brief_e/brief22_e.htm.)

the target of retaliatory tariffs alternates periodically. This increases the uncertainty faced by those wishing to export targeted products.[20] To take another example, during the EU/US steel dispute, the EU threatened to aim retaliatory tariffs at goods produced primarily in Southern US states whose support was relied upon by George W. Bush, who was president at the time. This threat surely influenced the US's decision to repeal the offending tariffs.[21]

In light of these considerations, it is hard to deny that the WTO is coercive. The WTO can sanction the use of measures that leave member states with no reasonable alternative but to comply with WTO rules. Blake acknowledges that some international institutions are coercive, but he maintains that they are not coercive in the relevant sense. State coercion and WTO coercion are asymmetrical in one respect that Blake thinks is crucial. Whereas states engage in direct coercion against individuals, WTO coercion is mediated: it targets governments, not individuals.[22] But how could this matter? Blake's central claim, recall, is that coercion is normatively relevant because it restricts autonomy, and the fact that the subjects of trade-regime coercion are governments, rather than individuals, does not render it non-autonomy-restricting.[23] Trade-regime coercion restricts autonomy by lowering the number and/or quality of options available, thereby reducing the capacity of individuals to act as authors of their lives. It also forces governments to enact certain measures, and thereby reduces the autonomy of individuals by diminishing their ability to pursue their ends by influencing their government. Trade-regime coercion binds the hands of governments, and makes them less amenable to persuasion by their citizens.

In a response to his critics, Blake argues that there is another crucial asymmetry between domestic and international coercion, namely, the former can be justified by egalitarian redistribution, but the latter cannot. Moreover, while state coercion at the domestic level is something we should want to preserve—because, as we have already noted, such coercion enables individuals to lead autonomous lives—there is no good reason to preserve the coercive practices that exist at the international level. This is because those practices involve powerful states coercing weaker states in morally

---

[20] Robert Read, 'Dispute Settlement, Compensation and Retaliation Under the WTO', in Kerr and Gaisford (eds.), *Handbook on International Trade Policy* (Northampton, MA: Edward Elgar Publishing, 2007).

[21] BBC, 'Q&A: The US-EU Steel Dispute' (available at: http://news.bbc.co.uk/1/hi/business/3291675.stm).

[22] Blake, 'Distributive Justice', p. 80.

[23] Cf. Risse, 'What to Say about the State', *Social Theory and Practice*, Vol. 32, No. 4, 2006, pp. 671–98, at p. 681.

objectionable ways. Thus, instead of trying in vain to justify international coercion through redistributive transfers, we should strive for its elimination.[24]

There are two things to note about this argument. First, preventing strong states from coercing weaker ones will almost undoubtedly require egalitarian redistribution. This is because large disparities in wealth are what make such coercion possible. It is often pointed out, for example, that inequalities between rich and poor countries undermine the bargaining power that the latter can wield in negotiations within the WTO and other international fora, and that such asymmetric bargaining power inevitably results in outcomes that are disadvantageous to the poor.[25] Rich countries can afford to walk away from the bargaining table if they do not get what they want, and the threat that they will do so (whether or not it is explicitly made) is often sufficient to keep poor countries compliant. Blake explicitly acknowledges this point, conceding that eliminating international coercion will probably require the kinds of measures demanded by proponents of global equality.[26]

Second, it is not at all obvious that we should want to eliminate all forms of international coercion. Blake grants that the WTO and other international organizations are coercive, but when he defends the claim that international coercion must be abolished rather than justified, the one example of international coercion he gives is the US invasion of Iraq in 2003. But the kind of coercion exercised by the US when it invaded Iraq is hardly comparable to the kind of coercion exercised by the WTO. As we saw above, WTO coercion is economic (rather than military) in nature, and its aim is to ensure compliance with WTO rules, an aim which is surely at least potentially justifiable. I say 'at least potentially' because, in its present form, WTO coercion might well be morally defective. Note that the WTO does not administer coercive penalties itself, but rather delegates coercive power to individual states, permitting them to impose sanctions upon those that have violated trade agreements. The problem with this is that the ability to make effective use of this permission is distributed unequally among states. Wealthy states can easily keep others in line by threatening to impede market access, but analogous threats made by poorer states have little force: the costs imposed on wealthy states when poor countries erect tariff barriers are usually too small to compel the former to change their policies.

However, it does not follow from the fact that WTO coercion is defective in its present form that it ought to be eliminated. Rather, we might seek to

[24] Michael Blake, 'Coercion and Egalitarian Justice', *The Monist*, Vol. 94, No. 4, pp. 555–70, at pp. 566–9.
[25] Thomas Pogge, *Realizing Rawls* (Ithaca, NY: Cornell University Press, 1989), pp. 248–9; Charles R. Beitz, 'Does Global Inequality Matter?', *Metaphilosophy*, Vol. 32, Nos. 1/2, 2001, pp. 95–112.
[26] Blake, 'Egalitarian Justice', pp. 567, 569.

correct its deficiencies. We could do this by, for example, allowing collective punishment, whereby multiple parties are permitted to deny market access to recalcitrant wealthy states, or by allowing poor states to nominate other, more powerful, states with more valuable markets to punish wealthy rule-breakers on their behalf.[27] Now, it might seem that this argument proves too much, namely, that while there may actually be good reasons for preserving WTO coercion in some form, it can be justified without egalitarian redistribution. But, if we follow the logic of Blake's argument, this is not the case. If there are good reasons for preserving WTO coercion, that fact puts it in the same boat as domestic state coercion, which, recall, should be preserved because it promotes autonomy. But, in Blake's opinion, the fact that there is a good reason to preserve state coercion is not sufficient to justify it: state coercion remains *pro tanto* wrongful because, in addition to guaranteeing autonomy, it also restricts it, and that wrongfulness can be outweighed or compensated for only by promoting distributive equality. Analogously, we should say that, while there may be a good reason to preserve WTO coercion—namely, it serves the legitimate end of promoting compliance with WTO rules—it is still autonomy-curtailing (in the sense discussed above), and it therefore requires justification through egalitarian redistribution.

The preceding considerations lead us to the following, anti-statist, conclusion: the coercive, autonomy-restricting nature of state institutions does not distinguish them from the WTO. If the coercive, autonomy-restricting character of state institutions grounds, or contributes to grounding, a case for distributive equality within the state, the comparable character of the WTO grounds, or contributes to grounding, an analogous case for distributive equality among WTO member states.

IV

Joint Authorship

I have suggested that Blake's version of coercion-based statism struggles to establish a morally relevant asymmetry between states and the trade regime, and thus to justify the claim that principles of egalitarian justice apply to the former but not to the latter. Let us now consider a well-known variant of the coercion view developed by Thomas Nagel. Nagel argues that in addition to

---

[27] See, for example, Giovanni Maggi, 'The Role of Multilateral Institutions in International Trade Cooperation', *The American Economic Review*, Vol. 89, No. 1, 1999, pp. 190–214; Robert E. Hudec, 'Broadening the Scope of Remedies in WTO Dispute Settlement', in Friedl Weiss and Jochem Wiers (eds.), *Improving WTO Dispute Settlement Procedures* (Folkestone: Cameron May Publishers, 2000).

imposing coercive practices, states give their citizens a part to play in the maintenance of those practices, and that this fact distinguishes states from international institutions. According to Nagel, citizens are assigned by their state a

> dual role ... both as one of the society's subjects and as one of those in whose name its authority is exercised ... [W]e are both putative joint authors of the coercively imposed system, and subject to its norms ... [S]ociety makes us responsible for its acts, which are taken in our name ... and it holds us responsible for obeying its laws and conforming to its norms, thereby supporting the institutions through which advantages and disadvantages are created and distributed.[28]

Nagel infers from these facts that states must ensure that distributive equality prevails among their citizens. 'Insofar as [state] institutions admit arbitrary inequalities, we are, even though the responsibility has been simply handed to us, responsible for them, and we therefore have standing to ask why we should accept them.'[29] Because we are asked to maintain the coercive institutions that determine our prospects, those institutions must satisfy an important condition; they must not allow us to be disadvantaged by factors that are morally arbitrary. We cannot reasonably be asked to uphold state institutions unless that condition is met.

Some commentators have objected to Nagel's argument on the grounds that it has absurd implications for how we should assess states that clearly do *not* assign to their subjects a role as joint authors. The thought is that those who accept Nagel's reasoning must surrender the right to criticize non-democratic regimes on justice-based grounds, for such regimes cannot be regarded as amenable to justice-based evaluation. According to Arash Abizadeh, it follows from Nagel's view that '[t]he closer a tyrant's rule approaches pure slavery, the less it can be criticized for being unjust.'[30]

This kind of objection should not be overstated. In Nagel's view, only principles of *socio-economic* justice require joint authorship as a trigger. Given that one does not have to invoke the dictates of socio-economic justice in order to condemn slavery, or regimes approaching it, one can subscribe to Nagel's position without completely immunizing malevolent regimes from justice-based criticism. As Nagel remarks:

> The normative force of the most basic human rights against violence, enslavement, and coercion ... depends only on our capacity to put ourselves in other people's shoes. The interests protected by such moral requirements are so fundamental, and the burdens they impose, considered statistically, so much slighter

---

[28] Nagel, 'The Problem', pp. 128–9.   [29] Nagel, 'The Problem', p. 129.
[30] Arash Abizadeh, 'Cooperation, Pervasive Impact, and Coercion: On the Scope (not Site) of Distributive Justice', *Philosophy & Public Affairs*, Vol. 35, No. 4, 2007, pp. 318–58, at p. 352.

[than the burdens imposed by requirements of socioeconomic justice], that a criterion of universalizability of the Kantian type clearly supports them.[31]

Moreover, Abizadeh's objection would have less force if applied to a weak statist who appealed to joint authorship, for such a statist would claim that only a subset of socio-economic principles—namely, principles of distributive equality—require joint authorship as a trigger.

While Nagelians, and, a fortiori, weak joint-authorship statists, retain some justice-based resources with which to criticize egregious states, it remains true that both groups are committed to the unpalatable and counter-intuitive conclusion that while democratic states are required to promote economic equality among their citizens, dictatorships are not. Nagel discusses an objection of this kind, and responds by insisting upon a 'broad interpretation' of the notion of joint authorship.[32] He writes:

> If [for example] a colonial or occupying power claims political authority over a population, it purports not to rule by force alone. It is providing and enforcing a system of law that those subject to it are expected to uphold as participants, and which is intended to serve their interests even if they are not its legislators. Since their normative engagement is required, there is a sense in which it is being imposed in their name.[33]

In other words, Nagel's response to the kind of objection being advanced is that the subjects of non-democratic regimes can be regarded as joint authors, and thus as entitled to egalitarian shares. If this move is viable, it allows Nagel and other joint-authorship statists to reject the unpalatable claims that critics have claimed they are committed to endorsing. But this move also creates a new, and even more serious, problem: it jeopardizes the statist thesis that egalitarian principles are applicable only within the state. For if the subjects of colonial regimes and occupying powers can be regarded as joint authors, then it is surely the case that citizens of trading states can be regarded as joint authors of the rules and regulations imposed by the WTO.[34] The WTO's mission to liberalize trade is justified by the claim that free trade is mutually beneficial, and the WTO sometimes attempts to accommodate the interests of those states that might not benefit from opening their markets by exempting them from rules that apply to other members. The WTO is thus ostensibly designed to serve the interests of its participants. And it is hard to see how one could deny that WTO members are expected to comply with WTO rules.

---

[31] Nagel, 'The Problem', p. 131.   [32] Nagel, 'The Problem', p. 129, n. 14.
[33] Nagel, 'The Problem', p. 129, n. 14.
[34] Cf. Joshua Cohen & Charles Sabel, 'Extra Rempublicam Nulla Justitia?', *Philosophy & Public Affairs*, Vol. 34, No. 2, 2006, pp. 147–75, at pp. 167–8.

Joint-authorship statists thus appear to be caught in a dilemma.[35] They can either adopt an interpretation of joint authorship that commits them to the unattractive claim that dictators are not bound by the requirements of economic egalitarianism, or they can adopt Nagel's broader interpretation, which allows them to avoid that particular implication, but which also prevents them from drawing a sharp normative distinction between states and the trade regime.

Joint-authorship statists may choose to take the first horn of this dilemma, and deny that it is obviously absurd to think that, while the requirements of economic egalitarianism apply to democracies, they do not apply to dictatorships. They might argue that while justice does not require dictatorships to conform to distributive egalitarian demands, it does require the *dissolution* of dictatorships, and that once a dictatorship is dissolved, and a democratic state established, the demands of distributive equality kick in. This response is not available to Nagel, who maintains that *all* socio-economic requirements—including a right to democracy[36]—need joint authorship as a trigger, but it is available to weak statists.

This response is unpersuasive, however. It is unpersuasive because it prevents one from differentiating between economically egalitarian dictatorships, on the one hand, and economically *in*egalitarian dictatorships, on the other. It commits one to holding that a dictatorship that permits massive economic inequalities is no less just than a dictatorship that employs distributive measures to maintain some degree of economic equality. And that is surely unacceptable. Joint-authorship statists must therefore take the second horn; they must adopt Nagel's broad interpretation of joint authorship, and accept that the trade regime is an appropriate subject of egalitarian justice.

V

Non-Voluntariness

A number of statist thinkers claim that membership in states, unlike membership in international institutions, is non-voluntary, and that this fact contributes to explaining why egalitarian requirements apply to the former but not to the latter. Participation in an association can be non-voluntary in two distinct ways.[37] Firstly, participation in an association is non-voluntary if it is coerced. Note that an association can be coercive even if participation in it is not.

---

[35] Chris Armstong, 'Coercion, Reciprocity, and Equality Beyond the State', *Journal of Social Philosophy*, Vol. 40, No. 3, 2009, pp. 297–316, at pp. 301–2.

[36] It is somewhat strange to define the right to democracy as a *socio-economic* right, but that is what Nagel does. See Nagel, 'The Problem', p. 127.

[37] Sangiovanni, 'Global Justice', pp. 11–13.

One can be subject to coercion for as long as one remains a member of a given association, without having been coerced into joining, and without being coercively prevented from leaving. Thus, claiming that an association is coercive *and* that membership is non-voluntary because members are coerced into participating need not be tautological. Secondly, participation in an association is non-voluntary if the costs of leaving are excessively high. Adequate formulation of this second sense of non-voluntariness requires a greater degree of care than has previously been appreciated. As we shall see, we have to be quite precise in our specification of what constitutes a voluntariness-vitiating exit cost.

Exit costs can be measured in different ways. One method compares how well-off an individual is, according to some metric and in some dimension (wealth, health, reputation, etc.), while belonging to an association with how well-off she would be if she left the association, and defines the exit cost as the difference between the two conditions. For example, if P has a material welfare level of 50 while belonging to association X, and if that welfare level would be reduced to 20 if P leaves X, the exit cost P incurs by leaving X is 30. On this approach, exit costs are relative in nature; they are defined by reference to how well-off an individual would be after leaving an association relative to how well-off she would be if she remained a member. It is difficult to see how one could develop a satisfactory account of non-voluntary participation that appeals to the size of exit costs measured in this way. To see why, note that one individual, P, could incur a large cost (in one dimension) by leaving association X, and yet remain well-off (in that same dimension), while another individual, Q, could incur a smaller exit cost by leaving a different association, Y, and yet consequently become badly-off. In such a case, we would presumably want to say that Q's participation in Y is non-voluntary, without committing ourselves to the claim that P's participation in X is also non-voluntary. But if we were to justify the claim that Q's participation in Y is non-voluntary by pointing to the relative exit cost Q incurs by leaving, we would also have to accept that P's participation in X is non-voluntary, for the relative exit cost incurred by P is larger than the relative exit cost incurred by Q.

Therefore, we should reject this approach and adopt an account of voluntary participation that invokes considerations about how well-off an individual would be in *absolute* terms (according to some metric and in some dimension) if she left a particular association. This account would say that association X is non-voluntary for a given individual, P, when (i) P would be rendered badly-off in absolute terms—when P's well-being (according to some metric) would be reduced to below some minimal threshold—if she left X; or, if P is already badly-off in absolute terms, (ii) P would be made even worse-off by leaving X; or (iii) P would be denied an opportunity to escape absolute deprivation if she left X.

I said that we have to be quite precise when specifying when an exit cost undermines the voluntariness of an association, but it is not necessary to be more precise than this. It is not my intention to specify where the minimal threshold lies. For present purposes an intuitive grasp of what it means to be badly-off in absolute terms—to be below a minimal well-being threshold— will suffice. This is because it is obviously true that developing countries suffer absolute material deprivation, and it is uncontroversial to think that by leaving the WTO trade system developing countries would thereby deepen their plight and close off one of the most promising routes out of their current predicament. Thus, for developing countries at least, and especially for the least developed countries, the WTO trade system is non-voluntary in the second way that an association can be non-voluntary.[38]

Of course, it is not the case that the only alternative to membership in the WTO is autarky. States can and do form bilateral and regional trade groups which exist alongside the WTO regime. Examples of existing regional trade groups include The Association of South East Asian Nations (ASEAN), the Common Market of the South (MERCOSUR), and the North American Free Trade Agreement (NAFTA). But it is a mistake to think of participation in regional groups as something that can substitute for participation in the multilateral WTO regime. As Ngaire Woods notes, 'no country has a clearcut choice between regional trade and international trade. All regions depend heavily on other markets'. Elaborating, she adds: 'No regional unit seems to be inward-looking. Indeed, no regional unit can afford to be so, nor to grow apart from others.'[39]

What follows from the preceding considerations? The implications are somewhat obscure. Given that participation in the trade regime is arguably non-voluntary for developing countries, but voluntary for developed countries, perhaps we should conclude that egalitarian concern is owed to the former but not to the latter. But what would that mean? That inequalities among developed countries are permissible, but inequalities among developing countries are not? That developing countries must do as well out of trade as developed countries? But if inequalities between developed countries are permissible, which developed countries must developing countries do as well as?

A more straightforward and defensible path to egalitarian conclusions is cleared if we focus not on countries but rather on individuals. For individuals,

---

[38] The claim that state participation in the trade regime is non-voluntary in made by a variety of thinkers, including Charles R. Beitz, *Political Theory and International Relations* (Princeton, NJ: Princeton University Press, 1999), pp. 160–1; Cohen & Sabel, 'Extra Rempublicam Nulla Justitia?', p. 161; Sangiovanni, 'Global Justice', p. 18; and Aaron James, *Fairness in Practice: A Social Contract for a Global Economy* (Oxford: Oxford University Press, 2012), p. 173.

[39] Ngaire Woods, 'Trade, Regionalism, and the Threat to Multilateralism', in Woods (ed.), *The Political Economy of Globalization* (London: MacMillan Press, 2000), pp. 70–2.

the WTO trade regime is non-voluntary in the first way that I said an associ-ation can be non-voluntary. That is, the participation of individuals in the WTO is *coerced*. The decision to join and remain a member of the WTO is made by a country's ruling elite. That decision, as we have seen, may be non-voluntary because the costs attached to the opposite decision are excessively high. But even if this is not the case, and political rulers voluntarily decide that the country they represent will join and remain a member of the WTO, it does not follow that the *citizens* of that country voluntarily submit to the WTO; WTO rules are simply imposed upon them, and they have no choice regarding whether or not to comply.[40] Note that I am not simply repeating the claim, made in section III, that the WTO is coercive. The claim there was that the WTO sanctions the use of coercion against those who have decided to become members. The claim here is that the decision to join and remain part of the WTO is itself coerced, and that participation is thus non-voluntary.

VI

Profundity and Pervasiveness

A fourth version of the statist view suggests that the subjects of egalitarian justice are identified by reference to the profundity and pervasiveness of their effects. Rawls pointed to the profundity and pervasiveness of the basic struc-ture of domestic society in order to justify singling out the basic structure as the primary subject of justice and the sole target of his two principles.[41] It might be argued, then, that egalitarian evaluation is appropriate only when applied to the state because the basic structure extends no further than the borders of the state, and there is nothing beyond the state that has similarly profound or pervasive effects.

The first thing to note here is that Rawls' claim that the basic structure is the *primary* subject of justice is not the same as the claim that the basic structure is the *exclusive* subject of justice. Taking the primary subject of justice to be the basic structure is consistent with regarding the WTO trade regime as, say, a secondary or tertiary subject of justice. Similarly, thinking that Rawls' two principles of justice apply exclusively to the basic structure is consistent with thinking that *different* (and possibly egalitarian) principles regulate other subjects of justice. Rawls himself claimed that institutions within and beyond

---

[40] Cf. Christian Barry and Laura Valentini, 'Egalitarian Challenges to Global Egalitarianism: A Critique', *Review of International Studies*, Vol. 35, No. 3, 2009, pp. 485–512, at p. 495.
[41] John Rawls, *A Theory of Justice* (Cambridge, Mass: Harvard University Press, 1999), pp. 7, 82.

the basic structure are to be regulated by principles of *local* and *global* justice, respectively.[42]

While secondary and tertiary subjects of justice might be identified by reference to something other than the profundity and pervasiveness of their effects, it is worth emphasizing just how profound and pervasive the effects of the WTO trade regime are.[43] The effects I describe will be familiar from discussions in earlier chapters. Notice, first, that by determining the degree to which countries can protect domestic industries (e.g., with the use of tariffs, quotas, and subsidies), the trade regime affects the career options available to people. If a country is not permitted to grant (a particular degree of) protection to a particular industry, that industry may collapse, and certain types of jobs may disappear. Even if lack of protection does not lead to the collapse of an industry, the industry may contract, and the number of certain types of jobs will decline. Thus, the trade regime affects people's freedom to pursue a career of their choosing.

Second, by determining the degree to which countries can protect domestic industries, the trade regime affects employment security. If a country is not permitted to grant (a particular degree of) protection to a particular industry, certain individuals will lose their jobs. The costs associated with losing one's job, and the threat of losing one's job, extend beyond the loss (or absence) of freedom to pursue a career of one's own choosing. Third, by determining the degree to which countries can protect domestic industries, the trade regime influences the level of income an individual can attain. While workers displaced by free trade will often be able to find alternative employment in expanding export industries, their new jobs will often pay lower wages.

Fourth, the trade regime can affect a government's ability to protect its country's cultural distinctiveness. If a government is prevented from restricting the importation of certain goods, aspects of its country's cultural heritage, which may be highly valued by the citizenry, might be degraded. Fifth, the trade regime has the capacity to limit a government's ability to act in accordance with the ethical convictions of its citizens. For example, the trade regime has the capacity to license retaliation against policies banning the importation of animal-based products, the production of which the citizens of a particular state may regard as unjust. Sixth, the trade regime has the capacity to limit access to essential goods. For example, the trade regime can ban trade in cheap, generic versions of patented pharmaceutical products needed to treat life-threatening diseases such as HIV/AIDS. Restrictions on such products,

---

[42] John Rawls, *Justice as Fairness: A Restatement* (Cambridge, Mass: Harvard University Press, 2001), p. 11.

[43] Darrel Moellendorf suggests that the trade regime is amenable to egalitarian evaluation because it exerts a profound and pervasive effect on its members. See his 'The World Trade Organization and Egalitarian Justice', *Metaphilosophy*, Vol. 36, No. 1, 2005, pp. 145–62.

combined with the high price of branded versions, may result in poor people lacking access to *any* version of those products.

Seventh, the trade regime can affect, either positively or negatively, countries' development prospects. It is widely acknowledged that the GATT–WTO regime has inhibited the development of poor countries by (i) permitting rich countries to use tariffs and quotas to protect markets in which poor countries enjoy a comparative advantage (e.g., labour intensive manufactures such as textiles and food processing); (ii) permitting rich countries to subsidize domestic agriculture; and (iii) globalizing intellectual property protection. Imitation and reverse engineering were methods frequently employed by developed countries in the early years of their development period. As Robert Wade observes, 'Japan, Taiwan, and South Korea were each known as "the counterfeit capital" of the world in their time. And the US in the nineteenth century, then a rapidly industrializing country was known—to Charles Dickens, among many other aggrieved foreign authors—as a bold pirate of intellectual property.'[44] But many of the methods employed by these countries are prohibited by the WTO Agreement on Trade Related aspects of Intellectual Property (TRIPs), and are thus unavailable to today's developing countries.

In an attempt to show that the state exerts a uniquely profound effect on the lives of its members, Risse claims that 'in well-functioning states, it is the state in which individuals live that guarantees their basic rights.'[45] But this kind of argument is vulnerable to a serious objection, namely, whether a state can be well functioning is affected by aspects of the international system in which it exists, including aspects of the trade regime. Specifically, whether a state can be well functioning is affected by the 'resource privilege', the trade regime's customary rule for establishing who has the right to sell a country's resources. According to the resource privilege

> all that is necessary for a group to acquire the legal right to sell off a territory's resources is the power to inflict violence on the territory's people. Whoever can maintain coercive control over a country's population (or in the case of civil warriors, over part of a population) is recognized internationally as legally authorized to sell off that country's resources.[46]

The resource privilege contributes to what is known as the 'resource curse', a phenomenon which hobbles the development prospects of resource-rich

---

[44] Robert Hunter Wade, 'What Strategies are Viable for Poor Countries Today? The World Trade Organization and the Shrinking of "Development Space"', *Review of International Political Economy*, Vol. 10, No. 4, 2003, pp. 621–44, at p. 626. Cf. Dani Rodrik, 'The Global Governance of Trade as if Development Really Mattered', background paper to the United Nations Development Programme's Project on Trade and Sustainable Human Development, 2001.

[45] Risse, *Global Justice*, p. 28.

[46] Leif Wenar, 'Property Rights and the Resource Curse', *Philosophy & Public Affairs*, Vol. 36, No. 1, 2008, pp. 2–32, at p. 12.

countries. Economists have long recognized that countries that are rich in natural resources, such as oil, gas, and diamonds, are more likely to be plagued by authoritarianism, civil war, and coup attempts, and are, consequently, more likely to have a poor citizenry. This fact is explained by the resource privilege: it enables oppressive regimes to consolidate their power by using the revenues derived from resource sales to purchase weapons and security forces, and to buy off opposition, and it provides rival armed groups with a strong incentive to violently seize power. These groups know that if they can manage to topple the government and install themselves as rulers, the resource privilege will grant them access to the country's resource wealth.[47]

In each of the ways described above, the WTO trade regime exerts profound and pervasive effects on the lives of its members. Thus, if the subjects of egalitarian justice are identified by reference to the profundity and pervasiveness of their effects, the WTO trade regime should be regarded as a subject of egalitarian justice.

VII

Social Cooperation

According to another form of statism, defended by, among others, the Rawlsian political philosopher Samuel Freeman, the basic structure of domestic society is an appropriate subject of egalitarian justice, whereas international institutions are not, because the former, unlike the latter, is a locus of social cooperation.[48] Rawlsians distinguish between social *cooperation* and mere social *production*. The two concepts are importantly different in three respects. First, social cooperation is voluntary, whereas one may be forced to engage in social production by a coercive authority. Second, the aim of social cooperation is to realize the good of its participants, whereas social production may aim to achieve an end with which none of the participants identify. And, third, social cooperation incorporates the idea of 'fair terms of cooperation'. Social cooperation is social production governed by terms that all reasonable participants can accept.[49]

Defining the idea of social cooperation in this moralized way creates difficulties for anyone who wishes to invoke the fact of social cooperation in order to identify the correct subjects of justice. As Abizadeh has argued, restricting justice-based evaluation to institutions that comprise a scheme of social

---

[47] Wenar, 'Property Rights and the Resource Curse', pp. 2–32.
[48] Samuel Freeman, 'The Law of Peoples, Social Cooperation, Human Rights, and Distributive Justice', in Freeman *Justice and the Social Contract* (New York: Oxford University Press, 2007).
[49] Freeman, 'The Law of Peoples', p. 266; John Rawls, *Political Liberalism* (New York: Columbia University Press, 1993), p. 16.

cooperation has the perverse consequence of limiting justice-based evaluation to those institutions that are regulated by fair terms, that is, to institutions that are *already* (at least partially) just.[50] On this view, schemes of mere social production—which may be involuntary, regulated by unfair rules, and aim to achieve an end that their participants renounce—are not amenable to justice-based evaluation. Abizadeh concludes that social cooperation is not an *existence* condition of justice, but rather a *constitutive* feature of justice.[51] That is, it is not necessary for social cooperation to obtain before principles of justice become applicable; rather, the existence of social cooperation indicates that principles of justice are (at least partially) satisfied.[52]

If Rawlsians such as Freeman can be convinced to abandon the view that only schemes of social cooperation are appropriate sites of egalitarian distributive justice, they may be inclined to fall back on the view that mere social *production* is relevant to establishing whether distributive principles are applicable in any given context. Support for this view can be motivated by reflecting on the way that it allows one to sidestep Robert Nozick's well-known complaint that distributive justice 'treat[s] objects as if they appeared from nowhere, out of nothing.'[53] Rawls' own egalitarian account of distributive justice was never vulnerable to this objection, because, for Rawls, distributive justice was, by definition, about how socially produced goods should be shared among those who contribute to their production. Individuals who participate in a productive process were deemed to have a claim to a fair share of the output of that process because it would not have existed without their efforts. Rawls could thus agree, to an extent, with Nozick's claim that many things 'come into the world already attached to people having entitlements over them.'[54]

A theorist eager to escape Nozick's criticism might argue, then, that the fact of social production plays an important role in any argument for the claim that a particular institution should be regulated by egalitarian principles. Unless the institution in question can be regarded as a scheme of social production, it might be argued, egalitarian principles cannot apply. Does the trade regime constitute a system of social production? A strong case can be made for an affirmative answer to this question. As Aaron James has argued, WTO member states can be conceived as engaging in a kind of social

[50] Abizadeh, 'Cooperation, Pervasive Impact, and Coercion', p. 230.
[51] Abizadeh, 'Cooperation, Pervasive Impact, and Coercion', pp. 230–3.
[52] Charles Beitz writes: 'To say that society is a "cooperative venture for mutual advantage" is to add certain elements of a social ideal to a description of the circumstances to which justice applies. These additional elements unnecessarily narrow the description of these circumstances. It would be better to say that the requirements of justice apply to institutions and practices (whether or not they are genuinely cooperative) in which social activity produces relative or absolute benefits or burdens that would not exist if the social activity did not take place.' *Political Theory and International Relations*, p. 131ff; p. 150 (n. 52).
[53] Robert Nozick, *Anarchy, State, and Utopia* (New York: Basic Books, 1974), p. 160.
[54] Nozick, *Anarchy, State, and Utopia*, p. 160.

production when they reduce barriers to trade and construct a global market. The fruit of this production is the greater national income made possible by a refined division of labour. These income gains exist only by virtue of the efforts made by WTO member states, and it can therefore be argued that these states have a claim to an equal share of the gains.[55]

As I mentioned in section II, my central aim in this chapter is to show that statist premises support the claim that the trade regime should be regulated by *some* conception of egalitarian justice, and that the gains from trade should therefore be distributed in a manner that is in some sense egalitarian. Not all statist premises will converge upon the *same* conception, and the various conceptions with which different statist premises are compatible will not necessarily have the same content as the conceptions that egalitarians have endorsed at the domestic level. This point is well illustrated by James's view. James's view is that the fact of international social production can be used to justify an equal distribution of the goods that international social production yields—namely, the gains from trade—not that those goods should be distributed in a way that conduces to the achievement, at the global level, of the kind of comprehensive socio-economic equality that many egalitarians defend domestically.

VIII

Social Cooperation (Continued): Reciprocity

An alternative version of cooperation-based statism is defended by Andrea Sangiovanni. Sangiovanni, who refers to his theory as a 'reciprocity-based' account, suggests that we have a special relationship with our fellow citizens because, unlike members of other states, they contribute to the provision of the basic collective goods that enable us 'to develop and act on a plan of life'.[56] By complying with laws, providing resources (in the form of taxes), and participating in various forms of political activity, our fellow citizens maintain and reproduce the state, which, in turn, provides us with security, guarantees access to a legally regulated market, and defines and upholds property rights.[57] By contributing to the provision of these goods, our fellow citizens ensure that we possess 'the individual capabilities to function as citizens, producers, and biological beings.'[58] It is by virtue of the fact that our fellow citizens supply us with basic collective goods that we have egalitarian duties toward them. By eliminating morally arbitrary inequalities—that is, inequalities attributable to

---

[55] James, *Fairness in Practice*, Chs. 6 and 7.   [56] Sangiovanni, 'Global Justice', p. 20.
[57] Sangiovanni, 'Global Justice', p. 20.   [58] Sangiovanni, 'Global Justice', p. 21.

natural fortune and social contingencies—we give our fellow citizens a fair return for what they have given us.[59]

Notice that Sangiovanni's account appeals to two distinct forms of reciprocity, the first of which, to reuse Abizadeh's terminology, is treated as an existence condition of justice, and the second of which is treated as a constitutive condition of justice. Members of a state contribute to the production of basic collective goods, thereby engaging in the first form of reciprocity, and this then triggers egalitarian duties of distributive justice, the fulfilment of which constitutes the second form of reciprocity.[60] Sangiovanni thus sidesteps the criticism that was levelled at the version of social cooperation statism discussed in section VII: he does not confuse existence and constitutive conditions of justice.

Nevertheless, Sangiovanni's account is undermined by different considerations. As noted above, Sangiovanni claims that our fellow citizens play an important role in the provision of basic collective goods, and that it is by virtue of this that we owe our fellow citizens comprehensive distributive equality. Now, it is important to be clear about the ways in which the collective goods Sangiovanni identifies are valuable. Implicit in Sangiovanni's account is the idea that these goods are instrumentally, and not just intrinsically, valuable. Consider the first collective good Sangiovanni mentions, namely, security. Sangiovanni clearly holds that security is valuable as a means to an end, and not just as an end in itself. Jeremy Waldron has explicated the instrumental value of security in the following terms: '[W]e want not only to *have* our lives and limbs but to *do* things with them, make plans and pursue long-term activities . . . Our safety is not just an end in itself, but an indispensable platform or basis on which we will enjoy other values and activities.'[61] In Sangiovanni's account of domestic social cooperation as a ground of egalitarian justice, security is valued for the instrumental role it plays in enabling us to acquire income. The well-off have distributive obligations to the less advantaged because the latter have contributed to their wealth, and one of the ways in which they have contributed to their wealth is through the provision of security: security provides the talented with an environment in which they can exercise their talents and acquire income.

Suppose a wealthy individual responds to Sangiovanni's argument in the following way: 'it is true that my fellow citizens have contributed to the provision of basic collective goods, but I have also contributed to the provision of those goods. Why is this *in kind* reciprocity not sufficient to repay my debt? Why, in order to fully reciprocate their efforts, am I also required to

---

[59] Sangiovanni, 'Global Justice', pp. 25–7.   [60] Cf. Risse, *Global Justice*, p. 30.
[61] Jeremy Waldron, *Torture, Terror, and Trade-Offs: Philosophy for the White House* (New York: Oxford University Press, 2010), p. 127.

share my wealth with them in a manner dictated by distributive egalitarianism?' I presume that Sangiovanni would answer this question by pointing out that the instrumental value of basic collective goods is not distributed equally. As we have just noted, security has exceptionally high value to the talented, because it enables them to exercise their talents and thereby acquire wealth. Security also has value for the less talented, of course, but it does not have as much value. The less talented can say that, by contributing to the provision of security, they have given more to the talented than the talented have given to them: they have contributed to the creation of the considerable wealth that the talented have been able to amass, and they thus have a claim to a share of that wealth. This idea is at the core of Sangiovanni's argument.

A question that must now be asked is this: why should Sangiovanni's core idea apply only when people have participated in the creation of wealth by contributing to the provision of the basic collective goods that Sangiovanni identifies? Why does the idea not apply to other forms of participation in wealth creation, such as those forms engaged in by members of the trade regime? Through international trade each country can reap substantial income gains. These gains depend for their existence upon members of other countries reducing trade barriers, buying our produce, selling us their goods, and enabling us to restructure our economy in order to specialize according to comparative advantage. But if the basic collective goods that our fellow citizens contribute to producing are valued as instruments for generating income, and if we have egalitarian obligations to share our wealth with our fellow citizens because they contribute to producing those goods, and thus to producing our wealth, why do we not also have egalitarian obligations to share our wealth with the foreigners who have contributed to producing our wealth in different ways? It seems to me that Sangiovanni's theory supports the same conclusion reached by Aaron James, namely, that the gains from trade are the fruit of international cooperation, and should therefore be distributed equally among trading countries. Sangiovanni's denial that his theory has this implication—his insistence that his argument vindicates the claim that egalitarian justice applies exclusively at the level of the state—appears to be misguided.

So, we might accept Sangiovanni's claim that members of other countries do not contribute to the provision of the basic collective goods he identifies, but reject his conclusion on the grounds that members of other countries contribute to the achievement of the ends that those goods are instruments for realizing. We could accept that members of other countries do not contribute on the same scale as our fellow citizens—that they contribute only to the creation of a portion of our national wealth (i.e., that portion attributable to international trade)—while insisting that this is sufficient to ground a type of global equality (i.e., a form of social product egalitarianism that mandates an equal distribution of the gains from trade).

But Sangiovanni's argument can also be challenged more directly, for, as I will now show, it can plausibly be argued that members of other states *do* contribute to the provision of the basic collective goods that Sangiovanni identifies. Consider security again. There is a large body of work—the literature on 'commercial liberalism'—that aims to show that international trade reduces the likelihood of military conflict among states, and thus enhances our security. International trade is said to promote peace among countries through a variety of channels. Consider three examples. First, when trading relations are established between countries, the use of military force becomes less attractive. This is because military conflict disrupts international commerce and thereby produces sizable economic costs. Second, relative to international trade, conquest and plunder are inefficient means of generating economic growth, so as international trade increases, the incentives to engage in such practices are reduced. Third, international trade fosters the creation of cosmopolitan identities, and thus reduces the nationalistic sentiments and antagonistic relations among states that encourage military conflict.[62]

The important point to recognize here is this: to the degree that international trade enhances our security, the citizens and residents of other countries enhance our security. As noted above, the economic gains that trade produces—the prospect of which disincentivizes the use of military force—depend for their existence upon members of other countries reducing trade barriers, buying our produce, and selling us their goods. These observations create a larger breach in Sangiovanni's theory. If members of other countries contribute to the provision of basic collective goods, and if contribution to the provision of basic collective goods grounds general egalitarian entitlements, it follows that we have general egalitarian duties to members of other countries. These are not merely duties to share the international social product, but rather duties to realize a more comprehensive form of distributive equality. Thus, the upshot of Sangiovanni's view is not that the gains from trade should be divided equally, but that they should be distributed in a manner that conduces to the achievement of equality broadly conceived.

Notice that Sangiovanni envisions our fellow citizens contributing to the production of basic collective goods in quite minimal ways. The three modes of contribution he mentions—compliance, provision of resources, and political participation—are conceived as individually sufficient to trigger egalitarian duties. About people who are able but unwilling to work, Sangiovanni writes: 'If they continue to comply with the laws (and if they continue to pay taxes, assuming they have any to pay), they are participating and contributing to the maintenance of the state . . . They are, therefore, rightful beneficiaries

---

[62] Patrick J. McDonald, 'Peace through Trade or Free Trade?', *Journal of Conflict Resolution*, Vol. 48, No. 4, 2004, pp. 547–72.

of equality as a demand of justice.'[63] In other words, our fellow citizens are owed distributive equality (protection against morally arbitrary disadvantage) even if their only form of contribution to the provision of collective goods is compliance with the law. But if our fellow citizens are entitled to distributive equality provided that their productive contributions cross such a minimal threshold, on what grounds could Sangiovanni consistently reject a form of global egalitarianism that grounds egalitarian duties in the fact that foreigners contribute to our security in the ways I have described?

A statist like Blake might claim that complying with laws is especially burdensome, for laws constrain our autonomy, and that it is this fact that distinguishes the contributions of our fellow citizens from the contributions of foreigners. But this argument is unavailable to Sangiovanni, because, as was recorded above, he is among the critics of coercion-based statism who stress how coercive laws make us better off by *enhancing* our autonomy.

So, Sangiovanni's social-cooperation view, like the other forms of statism we have considered, leads to the conclusion that the trade regime should be regulated by principles of egalitarian justice.

IX

Non-Relational Globalism

This brings my discussion of statism to an end. I have tried to show that statists should convert to relational globalism, and that they should do so because the normatively relevant institutional relationships they identify within states also exist among members of the trade regime. Statist premises support the view that the trade regime should be regulated by substantive egalitarian principles. This might mean that (i) the gains from trade should be distributed equally, or it might mean that (ii) the gains from trade should be distributed in a way that conduces to the achievement of equality broadly conceived. Statist premises, then, can justify one of two relational-globalist conclusions. I want to finish by showing how the second relational-globalist conclusion generated by statist premises converges with the conclusion of *non*-relational globalism.

Non-relational globalism, recall, is the view that justice requires the reduction or elimination of inequality at the global level, regardless of the kinds of global institutions that actually exist. Non-relational globalism often invokes the fact that many inequalities are a product of luck. Lots of people enjoy advantages that are attributable to their genes, their upbringing, their place

---

[63] Sangiovanni, 'Global Justice', p. 28, n. 45.

of birth, and to a variety of other sources for which they cannot plausibly take credit. According to non-relational globalists, justice requires us to distribute these unearned advantages equally. The rationale for this conclusion is that it is not fair for some people to be worse-off than others through no fault of their own. This is the 'luck egalitarian' formulation of non-relational globalism. Luck egalitarianism aims for a distribution that is egalitarian but also 'choice sensitive': inequalities attributable to luck should be eliminated, but those traceable to choices made by the less advantaged may be tolerated.

This chapter has identified the national income gains generated by trade as a distinct distribuendum of egalitarian justice. What would a luck egalitarian distribution of these gains look like? Luck egalitarianism might seem to entail a commitment to neutralizing the distributive effects of certain national endowments. This would be in sharp contrast to the distributive principles defended by Aaron James. James holds that departures from equality that track differential national endowments are permissible.[64] But some national endowments—such as a country's resource base—are a product of luck, and it might seem that a luck egalitarian could not regard as just a situation in which some states or individuals get more from trade simply because they were born into a country with a particular resource profile.

However, it is important to note that luck egalitarians typically aim not for an egalitarian distribution of each and every good, but rather for a situation that can be regarded as egalitarian when assessed holistically. To use the terminology introduced earlier, they are *general* egalitarians. Luck might grant to Person P a larger share of Good X than to Person Q, but if luck also grants to Q a larger share of Good Y than to P, there may be no objectionable inequality between P and Q. P's surfeit of X may compensate for her lack of Y, while Q's surfeit of Y may compensate for his lack of X. In other words, the two inequalities might cancel each other out. Consequently, redistributing X from P to Q (or Y from Q to P) could actually frustrate egalitarian objectives.

One upshot of these reflections is that non-relational globalists should not necessarily aim to eliminate luck-generated inequalities in the gains from trade. Redistributive measures that neutralize the effects of luck on the distribution of these gains might actually result in advantages being taken away from states or individuals who, viewed from a holistic perspective, are victims of bad luck. An unequal share of the gains from trade might compensate for a shortfall in some other good, and cancel out an existing unjust inequality.[65]

---

[64] James, *Fairness in Practice*, p. 222.
[65] Analogous arguments against equal distributions of natural resources and rights to emit greenhouse gases appear, respectively, in Chris Armstrong, 'Natural Resources: The Demands of Equality', *Journal of Social Philosophy*, Vol. 44, No. 4, 2013, pp. 331–47, and Simon Caney, 'Just Emissions', *Philosophy & Public Affairs*, Vol. 40, No. 4, 2012, pp. 255–300.

In addition to noting that luck egalitarians should not necessarily recommend eliminating luck-generated inequalities in the gains from trade, we should also observe that they should not necessarily reject proposals to rectify *choice*-generated inequalities in the gains from trade. This is again because luck egalitarians should adopt an inclusive perspective, rather than one that focuses narrowly on the gains from trade. State A's larger share of the gains from trade might be attributable to choice, but its overall level of advantage may be greater than State B's as a result of luck. A's gains from trade may sit atop a pile of other goods that it accumulated through good fortune. Where this is true, redistributing those gains from A to B would move us closer to justice, not further away. There is, of course, no reason why efforts to correct the unjust disparity between A and B should focus on redistributing gains from trade, as opposed to some other (set of) good(s), but nor is there any reason why they should not. If an opportunity arises to correct the disparity, and that opportunity comes in the form of a chance to redesign the trade regime in a way that will facilitate redistribution of gains from A to B, that is an opportunity that luck egalitarians should embrace. The fact that A's larger share of those gains is not, in itself, unjust, is immaterial. What matters is that those gains form part of an inequality that is unjust when viewed from a suitably holistic perspective.

Luck egalitarians should not focus on the gains from trade in isolation. Rather, they should concern themselves with how states and individuals fare in more holistic terms. They should acknowledge that luck-generated inequalities in the gains from trade may sometimes offset unjust inequalities in other goods, and that choice-generated inequalities in the gains from trade may sometimes supplement unjust inequalities in other goods. They should infer from this that inequalities in the gains from trade should not be opposed simply because they are a product of luck, nor tolerated simply because they are a product of choice. For the luck egalitarian globalist, an egalitarian distribution of the gains from trade must be conceived as one that conduces to the realization of equality holistically conceived, irrespective of whether that distribution conforms, in itself, to an egalitarian pattern.

X

Conclusion

We began this chapter by describing a limited, 'statist', conception of trade justice. We saw that this conception recognizes certain trade-related duties, but that it opposes the application of egalitarian principles to the trade regime. We have seen that statist premises cannot vindicate this opposition. When statist premises are suitably refined, and employed in conjunction with relevant empirical facts, they yield the conclusion that the trade regime must be regulated by principles of substantive equality. In this sense, statist views collapse into a form of relational globalism, and can converge upon the same conception of trade justice supported by non-relational globalism. This outcome has significant implications for how the gains from trade should be shared. Either these gains must be shared equally, or they must be distributed in a manner that conduces to the realization of a more comprehensive egalitarianism.

We have travelled a considerable distance not only from the ideas discussed at the beginning of this chapter, but also from those that commanded our attention at the start of the book. In the opening chapters we were concerned to address the most serious physical harms with which international trade is associated. Our discussion of those harms was motivated by the aspiration to ensure that trade works for, and not against, those whom it encircles. That same aspiration has led us to the bolder proposals advanced here. Achievement of the egalitarian ends defended in this chapter may seem remote, but that is no reason to dismiss them. Unless we have an idea of where we are heading, we can make only limited progress. Political theory must help us to navigate the difficult terrain in which we currently find ourselves, but it must also keep one eye on the horizon.

7

Conclusion

In recent decades, notions of fair and just trade have become increasingly widespread. But what does the achievement of these ideals demand of us? One conclusion that can be drawn from the discussions in this book is that our question cannot be reduced to the common one of whether trade should be 'free'. The latter question obscures too much complexity. Firstly, it obscures the fact that we can endorse free trade in a wide range of goods, and among a wide range of states, while also believing that the scope of free trade should be limited, that certain goods should not be traded with certain states. We can believe this even if we think that trade in these goods should not be forbidden altogether, and that the states in question are legitimate partners in other forms of trade. To illustrate, it may be permissible to sell pentobarbital to a variety of buyers, and Texas may be a legitimate trading partner, but it may be impermissible to sell pentobarbital to Texas, given that the death penalty is practised in Texas, and that pentobarbital is used to administer the death penalty.

Secondly, even if we bracket the fact that certain goods cannot legitimately be traded with certain states, the permissibility of restricting trade will still depend on who is imposing restrictions upon whom. Developing states can be justified in restricting trade with developed states (e.g., in order to prevent the destruction of infant industries), and developed states can be justified in restricting trade with other developed states (e.g., in order to guard against cultural degradation), but a developed state may not permissibly restrict trade with a developing state when doing so will undermine the latter's ability to escape from poverty.

Thirdly, a narrow focus on free trade overlooks questions about fairness that arise in conditions that fall short of free trade. As we have seen, some people believe that making unfree trade fair (or as fair as it can be) involves ensuring that markets in all countries are equally accessible. Relatedly, even when trade is formally free, some people argue that market access can be unfairly impeded by the existence of different laws and policies in different countries. These are claims that demand responses, and, in chapter 5, I offered my own.

Finally, while there are cases where free trade is necessary for justice, it is often not sufficient. For example, while developed states may not restrict trade with the developing world in order to protect the jobs of their workers, they must supplement free trade with compensatory transfer payments. If they do not, the domestic working class is required, unreasonably, to bear an excessive amount of the burden of discharging our duties to the world's poor. Similarly, free trade will be regarded as insufficient for justice if we believe that the gains from trade must be distributed in a certain way. I have argued that trade justice requires ensuring that these gains are distributed in an egalitarian manner.

In short, a narrow focus on free trade overlooks important demands of justice, demands that, I should add, are not currently being met. International trade relations currently fall considerably short of satisfying the requirements of justice. In one respect, actually existing global capitalism resembles the 'actually existing socialism' of the previous century. It projects an alluring vision of an emancipated human future, but seems singularly incapable of realizing that vision. Consequently, it is a system in which many have lost faith. Moving beyond the status quo to a more satisfactory alternative will require hard work, of both an intellectual and a more practical kind. Justifying the machinery of global commerce will involve ensuring, as a matter of urgency, that the vulnerable are no longer crushed between its gears. But more will be required. We must ensure that the goods this machinery produces are shared equitably among those who keep its gears turning. We must ensure that a preoccupation with free trade does not overshadow the demand for trade justice.

Bibliography

Abbott, K. W., 'Defensive Unfairness: The Normative Structure of Section 301', in Bhagwati, J. and Hudec, R. E. (eds.), (1996b).

Abizadeh, A., 'Cooperation, Pervasive Impact, and Coercion: On the Scope (not Site) of Distributive Justice', *Philosophy & Public Affairs*, Vol. 35, No. 4, 2007, pp. 318–58.

Appellate Body Report, *European Communities—Measures Prohibiting the Importation and Marketing of Seal Products*, WT/DS400/AB/R and WT/DS401/AB/R (22 May 2014).

Armstrong, C., 'Coercion, Reciprocity, and Equality Beyond the State', *Journal of Social Philosophy*, Vol. 40, No. 3, 2009, pp. 297–316.

Armstrong, C., 'Natural Resources: The Demands of Equality', *Journal of Social Philosophy*, Vol. 44, No. 4, 2013, pp. 331–47.

Arneson, R. J., 'Commodification and Commercial Surrogacy', *Philosophy & Public Affairs*, Vol. 21, No. 2, 1992, pp. 132–64.

Barnard, C. and Hepple, B., 'Substantive Equality', *Cambridge Law Journal*, Vol. 59, No. 3, 2000, pp. 562–85.

Barry, C. and Valentini, L., 'Egalitarian Challenges to Global Egalitarianism: A Critique', *Review of International Studies*, Vol. 35, No. 3, 2009, pp. 485–512.

Bazargan, S. and Rickless, S. C. (eds.), *The Ethics of War: Essays* (New York: Oxford University Press, 2017).

BBC, 'Q&A: The US-EU Steel Dispute' (available at: http://news.bbc.co.uk/1/hi/business/3291675.stm).

Beitz, C. R., *Political Theory and International Relations* (Princeton, NJ: Princeton University Press, 1979).

Beitz, C. R., 'Does Global Inequality Matter?', *Metaphilosophy*, Vol. 32, Nos. 1/2, 2001, pp. 95–112.

Bhagwati, J. and Hudec, R. E. (eds.), *Fair Trade and Harmonization: Volume 1—Economic Analysis*, (Cambridge, Mass: MIT Press, 1996a).

Bhagwati, J. and Hudec, R. E. (eds.), *Fair Trade and Harmonization: Volume 2—Legal Analysis* (Cambridge, Mass: MIT Press, 1996b).

Birnie, P. et al., *International Law and the Environment: Third Edition* (New York: Oxford University Press, 2009).

Bishop, T., 'France and the Need For Cultural Exception', *New York University Journal of International Law and Politics*, Vol. 29, 1996–7, pp. 187–92.

Blake, M., 'Distributive Justice, State Coercion, and Autonomy', *Philosophy & Public Affairs*, Vol. 30, No. 3, 2001, pp. 257–96.

Blake, M., 'Coercion and Egalitarian Justice', *The Monist*, Vol. 94, No. 4, 2011, pp. 555–70.

Blake, M., *Justice and Foreign Policy* (Oxford: Oxford University Press, 2013).

Bodansky, D. et al. (eds.), *The Oxford Handbook of International Environmental Law* (New York: Oxford University Press, 2007).

Bowman, M. et al., *Lyster's International Wildlife Law: Second Edition* (New York: Cambridge University Press, 2010).

Brown, A. G. and Stern R. M., 'Concepts of Fairness in the Global Trading System', *Pacific Economic Review*, Vol. 12, No. 3, 2007, pp. 293–318.

Buchanan, A., 'The Ethics of Revolution and its Implications for the Ethics of Intervention', *Philosophy & Public Affairs*, Vol. 41, No. 4, 2013, pp. 291–323.

Caney, S., *Justice Beyond Borders: A Global Political Theory* (Oxford: Oxford University Press, 2005).

Caney, S., 'Global Distributive Justice and the State', *Political Studies*, Vol. 56, No. 3, 2008, pp. 487–518.

Caney, S., 'Just Emissions', *Philosophy & Public Affairs*, Vol. 40, No. 4, 2012, pp. 255–300.

Caney, S., 'Global Justice, Climate Change, and Human Rights', in Hicks, D. A. and Williamson, T. (eds.) (2012).

Carmody, C. et al. (eds.), *Global Justice and International Economic Law: Opportunities and Prospects* (New York: Cambridge University Press, 2012).

CAAT, 'About CAAT: Ending the Arms Trade' (available at: http://www.caat.org.uk/).

Chang, H., *Bad Samaritans: The Myth of Free Trade and the Secret History of Capitalism* (New York: Bloomsbury Press, 2008).

Charnovitz, S., 'The WTO's Environmental Progress', *Journal of International Economic Law*, Vol. 10, No. 3, 2007, pp. 685–706.

Convention on International Trade in Endangered Species of Wild Fauna and Flora (CITES) (available at: http://www.cites.org/sites/default/files/eng/disc/E-Text.pdf).

Coughlin, C. C., 'The Controversy Over Free Trade: The Gap Between Economists and the General Public', *The Federal Reserve Bank of St. Louis*, January/February, 2002, pp. 1–22.

Cohen, G. A., *Self-Ownership, Freedom, and Equality* (Cambridge: Cambridge University Press, 1995).

Cohen, G. A., *Rescuing Justice & Equality* (Cambridge, Mass: Harvard University Press, 2008).

Cohen, G. A., 'On the Currency of Egalitarian Justice', *Ethics*, Vol. 99, No. 4, 1989, pp. 906–44.

Cohen, J. and Sabel, C., 'Extra Rempublicam Nulla Justitia?', *Philosophy & Public Affairs*, Vol. 34, No. 2, 2006, pp. 167–8.

Cohen, S. D., *Multinational Corporations and Foreign Direct Investment: Avoiding Simplicity, Embracing Complexity* (New York: Oxford University Press, 2007).

Crelinsten, R. D., *Counterterrorism* (Cambridge: Polity Press, 2009).

Critharis, M., 'Third World Nations are Down in the Dumps: The Exportation of Hazardous Waste', *Brooklyn Journal of International Law*, Vol. XVI, No. 2, 1990, pp. 311–19.

Dart, T. and Pilkington, E., 'States subjecting death row inmates to longer deaths amid scramble for drugs', *The Guardian*, 30 January 2014 (available at: http://www.theguardian.com/world/2014/jan/30/death-row-inmates-longer-deaths-scramble-drugs/print).

Davis, N. A., Keshen, R. and McMahan, J. (eds.), *Ethics and Humanity: Themes from the Philosophy of Jonathan Glover* (New York: Oxford University Press, 2010).

Donaldson, S. and Kymlicka, W., *Zoopolis: A Political Theory of Animal Rights* (New York: Oxford University Press, 2011).

Dworkin, R., *A Matter of Principle* (Oxford: Oxford University Press, 1985).

Dworkin, R., *Sovereign Virtue: The Theory and Practice of Equality* (Cambridge, Mass: Harvard University Press, 2000).

Evenett, S. and Hoekman, B. M. (eds.), *Economic Development and Multilateral Trade Cooperation* (New York: Palgrave Macmillan, 2006).

Freeman, S., 'The Law of Peoples, Social Cooperation, Human Rights, and Distributive Justice', in Freeman *Justice and the Social Contract* (New York: Oxford University Press, 2007).

General Agreement on Tariffs and Trade, The, (available at: http://www.wto.org/english/docs_e/legal_e/gatt47_e.pdf).

Gabbatt, A. and Batty, D., 'Danish firm Lundbeck to stop US jails using drug for lethal injections', *The Guardian*, 1 July 2011 (available at: http://www.theguardian.com/world/2011/jul/01/lundbeck-us-pentobarbital-death-row/print).

Gardiner, S. M., 'Ethics and Global Climate Change', *Ethics*, Vol. 114, No. 3, 2004, pp. 555–600.

GATT, *United States—Restrictions on Imports of Tuna: Report of the Panel (DS21/R - 39S/155)*, 3rd September 1991 (available at: http://www.worldtradelaw.net/reports/gattpanels/tunadolphinI.pdf);

United States—Restrictions on Imports of Tuna: Report of the Panel (DS29/R), 16th June 1994 (available at: http://www.worldtradelaw.net/reports/gattpanels/tunadolphinII.pdf).

Glover, J., 'It makes no difference whether or not I do it', *Proceedings of the Aristotelian Society Supplementary Volume*, Vol. 49, 1975, pp. 171–209.

Goodin, R. E., 'Theories of Compensation', *Oxford Journal of Legal Studies*, Vol. 9, No. 1, 1989, pp. 56–75.

Goodin, R. E., *Green Political Theory* (Cambridge: Polity Press, 1992).

Goodin, R. E., *What's Wrong with Terrorism?* (Cambridge: Polity Press, 2006).

Gordon, P. H. and Meunier, S., 'Globalization and French Cultural Identity', *French Politics, Culture & Society*, Vol. 19, No. 1, 2001, pp. 22–41.

Guardian, The, 'The return of the firing squad? US states reconsider execution methods', *The Guardian*, 28 January 2014 (available at: http://www.theguardian.com/world/2014/jan/28/return-firing-squad-us-states-execution-methods/print).

Harris, J., 'No more excuses. The only defensible option is to go vegetarian', *The Guardian*, 17 February 2013 (available at: http://www.theguardian.com/commentisfree/2013/feb/17/no-more-excuses-go-vegetarian/print).

Hausman, D. M. and McPherson, M. S., *Economic Analysis, Moral Philosophy, and Public Policy: Second Edition* (New York: Cambridge University Press, 2006).

Hicks, D. A. and Williamson, T. (eds.), *Leadership and Global Justice* (Basingstoke: Palgrave Macmillan, 2012).

Howse, R., 'The Turtles Panel: Another Environmental Disaster in Geneva', *Journal of World Trade*, Vol. 32, No. 5, 1998, pp. 73–100.

Howse, R. and Regan, D., 'The Product/Process Distinction—An Illusory Basis for Disciplining "Unilateralism" in Trade Policy', *European Journal of International Law*, Vol. 11, No. 2, 2000, pp. 249–89.

Howse, R. et al., 'Sealing the Deal: The WTO's Appellate Body Report in EC—Seal Products', *American Society of International Law*, Vol. 18, No. 12, 2014.

Hudec, R. E., 'Broadening the Scope of Remedies in WTO Dispute Settlement', in Weiss, F. and Wiers, J. (eds.), (2000).

Hughes, P., 'Recognizing Substantive Equality as a Foundational Constitutional Principle', *Dalhousie Law Journal*, Vol. 22, No. 5, 1999, pp. 1–29.

Irwin, D. A., *Against the Tide: An Intellectual History of Free Trade* (Princeton, NJ: Princeton University Press, 1996).

Irwin, D. A., *Free Trade Under Fire: Third Edition* (Princeton, NJ: Princeton University Press, 2009).

Irwin, D. A. and James, A., *Fairness in Practice: A Social Contract for a Global Economy* (Oxford: Oxford University Press, 2012).

Irwin, D. A., 'A Theory of Fairness in Trade', *Moral Philosophy and Politics*, Vol. 1, No. 2, 2014, pp. 177–200.

Kapstein, E., *Economic Justice in an Unfair World: Toward a Level Playing Field* (Princeton, NJ: Princeton University Press, 2006).

Keck, A. and Low, P., 'Special and Differential Treatment in the WTO: Why, When, and How?', in Evenett, S. and Hoekman, B. M. (eds.), (2006).

Keohane, R., 'Reciprocity in International Relations', in Keohane, R. (ed.), (1989).

Keohane, R. (ed.), *International Institutions and State Power: Essays in International Relations Theory* (Boulder, CO: Westview Press, 1989).

Kleen, P. and Page, S., 'Special and Differential Treatment of Developing Countries in the World Trade Organization', *Global Development Studies*, No. 2, 2005.

Krueger, J., 'The Basel Convention and the International Trade in Hazardous Wastes', in Stokke, O. S. and Thommessen, O. B. (eds.), (2002).

Krugman, P., 'In Praise of Cheap Labor: Bad Jobs at Bad Wages Are Better Than No Jobs at All', in Krugman, P. (ed.), (1998).

Krugman, P. (ed.), *The Accidental Theorist And Other Dispatches from the Dismal Science* (New York: Norton & Company, 1998).

Kurjanska, M. and Risse, M., 'Fairness in Trade II: Export Subsidies and the Fair Trade Movement', *Politics, Philosophy & Economics*, Vol. 7, No. 1, 2008, pp. 29–56.

Leary, V. A., 'Workers' Rights and International Trade: The Social Clause (GATT, ILO, NAFTA, U.S. Laws)', in Bhagwati, J. and Hudec, R. E. (eds.), (1996b).

Leebron, D. W., 'Lying Down with Procrustes: An Analysis of Harmonization Claims', in Bhagwati, J. and Hudec, R. E. (eds.), (1996a).

Lichtenbaum, P., '"Special Treatment" vs. "Equal Participation:" Striking a Balance in the Doha Negotiations', *The American University International Law Review*, Vol. 17, No. 5, 2002, pp. 1003–43.

Lim, C. L., 'The Conventional Morality of Trade', in Carmody, C. et al. (eds.), (2012).

Maggi, G., 'The Role of Multilateral Institutions in International Trade Cooperation', *The American Economic Review*, Vol. 89, No. 1, 1999, pp. 190–214.

Mann, M., 'Globalization and September 11', *New Left Review* 12, November–December 2001, pp. 51–72.

Marx, K., 'The Sale of Labour Power', in McLellan, D. (ed.), (2000).

Marx, K. and Engels, F., *The Communist Manifesto*, in McLellan, D. (ed.), (2000).

Mbirimi, I. et al. (eds.), *From Doha to Cancun: Delivering a Development Round* (London: Commonwealth Secretariat, 2003).

McDonald, P. J., 'Peace through Trade or Free Trade?', *Journal of Conflict Resolution*, Vol. 48, No. 4, 2004, pp. 547–72.

McLellan, D. (ed.), *Karl Marx Selected Writings: Revised Edition* (New York: Oxford University Press, 2000).

McMahan, J., 'Humanitarian Intervention, Consent, and Proportionality', in N. Ann Davis, Richard Keshen, and Jeff McMahan (eds.), (2010).

Meunier, S., 'The French Exception', *Foreign Affairs*, July/August, 2000, pp. 104–16.

Michalopoulos, C., 'Developing Country Strategies for the Millennium Round', *Journal of World Trade*, Vol. 33, No. 5, 1999, pp. 1–30.

Mill, J. S., 'A Few Words on Non-Intervention', in Robson, J. M. (ed.), (1984).

Moellendorf, D., 'The World Trade Organization and Egalitarian Justice', *Metaphilosophy*, Vol. 36, No. 1, 2005, pp. 145–62.

Moon, G., 'Trade and Equality: A Relationship to Discover', *Journal of International Economic Law*, Vol. 12, No. 3, 2009, pp. 617–42.

Nagel, T., 'The Problem of Global Justice', *Philosophy & Public Affairs*, Vol. 33, No. 2, 2005, pp. 113–47.

Nanda, V. P., 'Preemptive and Preventive Use of Force, Collective Security, and Human Security', *Denver Journal of International Law and Policy*, Vol. 33, 2004, pp. 7–15.

Norton, B., 'Commodity, Amenity, and Morality: The Limits of Quantification in Valuing Biodiversity', in Edward O. Wilson (ed.), *Biodiversity* (Washington, DC: National Academy Press, 1988).

Nozick, R., *Anarchy, State, and Utopia* (New York: Basic Books, 1974).

Nunn, N., 'The Importance of History for Economic Development', *Annual Review of Economics*, Vol. 1, 2009, pp. 65–92.

Parr, T., 'How to Identify Disadvantage: Taking the Envy Test Seriously' (Political Studies).

Parrish, R. R. et al., 'Depleted uranium contamination by inhalation exposure and its detection after ∼ 20 years: Implications for human health assessment', *Science of the Total Environment*, Vol. 390, No. 1, 2008, pp. 58–68.

PETA, 'China's Shocking Fur Trade' (available at: http://action.peta.org.uk/ea-campaign/ clientcampaign.do?ea.client.id=5&ea.campaign.id=1537).

Pevnick, R., 'Political Coercion and the Scope of Distributive Justice', *Political Studies*, Vol. 56, No. 2, 2008, pp. 399–413.

Pogge, T., *Realizing Rawls* (Ithaca, NY: Cornell University Press, 1989).

Pogge, T., *World Poverty and Human Rights: Second Edition* (Malden, MA: Polity Press, 2008).

Pogge, T., 'Are We Violating the Human Rights of the World's Poor?', *Yale Human Rights and Development Law Journal*, Vol. 14, No. 2, 2011, pp. 1–33.

Prowda, J. B., 'U.S. Dominance in the "Marketplace of Culture" and the French "Cultural Exception"', *New York University Journal of International Law and Politics*, Vol. 29, 1996–7, 193–210.

Rawls, J., *Political Liberalism* (New York: Columbia University Press, 1993).

Rawls, J., *A Theory of Justice: Revised Edition* (Cambridge, Mass: Harvard University Press, 1999).

Rawls, J., *The Law of Peoples* (Cambridge Mass: Harvard University Press, 1999).

Rawls, J., *Justice as Fairness: A Restatement* (Cambridge, Mass: Harvard University Press, 2001).

Rayfuse, R., 'Biological Resources', in Bodansky, D. et al. (eds.), (2007).

Read, R., 'Dispute Settlement, Compensation and Retaliation Under the WTO', in Kerr and Gaisford (eds.), *Handbook on International Trade Policy* (Northampton, MA: Edward Elgar Publishing, 2007).

Regan, T., *The Case for Animal Rights* (Berkley and Los Angeles, CA: University of California Press, 1983).

Risse, M., 'What to Say about the State', *Social Theory and Practice*, Vol. 32, No. 4, 2006, pp. 671–98.

Risse, M., 'Fairness in trade I: obligations from trading and the pauper-labor argument', *Politics, Philosophy & Economics*, Vol. 6, No. 3, 2007, pp. 355–77.

Risse, M., *On Global Justice* (Princeton, NJ: Princeton University Press, 2012).

Risse, M. and Wollner, G., 'Critical notice of Aaron James, Fairness in Practice: A Social Contract for a Global Economy', *Canadian Journal of Philosophy*, Vol. 43, No. 3, 2013, pp. 382–401.

Risse, M. and Wollner, G., 'Three Images of Trade: On the Place of Trade in a Theory of Global Justice', *Moral Philosophy and Politics*, Vol. 1, No. 2, 2014, pp. 201–25.

Robson, J. M. (ed.), *The Collected Works of John Stuart Mill, Volume XXI: Essays on Equality, Law, and Education* (London: Routledge and Kegan Paul, 1984).

Rodrik, D., 'The Global Governance of Trade As If Development Really Mattered', background paper to the United Nations Development Programme's Project on Trade and Sustainable Human Development, 2001.

Rodrik, D., *The Globalization Paradox: Why Global Markets, States, and Democracy Can't Coexist* (Oxford: Oxford University Press, 2011).

Sanchez, R., 'International Trade in Hazardous Wastes: A Global Problem with Uneven Consequences for the Third World', *The Journal of Environmental Development*, Vol. 3, No. 1, 1994, pp. 139–52.

Sandel, M. J., 'What Money Can't Buy: The Moral Limits of Markets', *The Tanner Lectures on Human Values*, 1998, pp. 87–122.

Sangiovanni, A., 'Global Justice, Reciprocity, and the State', *Philosophy & Public Affairs*, Vol. 35, No. 1, 2007, pp. 3–39.

Sangiovanni, A., 'The Irrelevance of Coercion, Imposition, and Framing to Distributive Justice', *Philosophy & Public Affairs*, Vol. 40, No. 2, 2012, pp. 79–110.

Satz, D., *Why Some Things Should Not Be for Sale: The Moral Limits of Markets* (Oxford: Oxford University Press, 2010).

Shaffner, J. E., *An Introduction to Animals and the Law* (Basingstoke: Palgrave Macmillan, 2011).

Schoenbaum, T. J., 'Free International Trade and Protection of the Environment: Irreconcilable Conflict?', *The American Journal of International Law*, Vol. 86, 1992, pp. 700–27.

Shue, H., 'Exporting Hazards', *Ethics*, Vol. 91, No. 4, 1981, pp. 579–606.

Shue, H., *Basic Rights: Subsistence, Affluence, and US Foreign Policy: Second Edition* (Princeton, NJ: Princeton University Press, 1996).

Sing, J. B. and Lakhan, V. C., 'Business Ethics and the International Trade in Hazardous Wastes', *Journal of Business Ethics*, Vol. 8, 1989, pp. 889–99.

Singer, P., *Animal Liberation*, Second Edition (London: Random House, 1990).

Smith, C. S., 'A welcome U-turn from Vince Cable on execution drug', *The Guardian*, 29 November 2010 (available at: http://www.theguardian.com/commentisfree/cifamerica/2010/nov/29/capital-punishment-vincentcable/print).

Snape, W. J. and Lefkovitz, N. B., 'Searching for GATT's Environmental *Miranda*: Are "Process Standards" Getting "Due Process"?' *Cornell International Law Journal*, Vol. 27, 1994, pp. 777–815.

Stevens, C., 'Special and Differential Treatment', in Mbirimi, I. et al. (eds.), (2003).

Stiglitz, J. E. and Charlton, A., *Fair Trade for All: How Trade can Promote Development* (Oxford: Oxford University Press, 2005).

Stohl, R. and Grillot, S., *The International Arms Trade* (Cambridge, Polity Press: 2009).

Stokke, O. S. and Thommessen, O. B. (eds.), *Yearbook of International Co-operation on Environment and Development 2001/2002* (London: Earthscan Publications, 2002).

Stolper, W. F. and Samuelson, P. A., 'Protection and Real Wages', *Review of Economic Studies*, No. 9, 1941, pp. 58–73.

Tadros, V., 'Duress and Duty', in Bazargan, S. and Rickless, S. C. (eds.), (2017).

Tan, K.-C., *Justice without Borders: Cosmopolitanism, Nationalism, and Patriotism* (Cambridge: Cambridge University Press, 2004).

Tesón, F. R., 'Why Free Trade is Required by Justice', *Social Philosophy and Policy*, Vol. 29, No. 1, 2012, pp. 126–53.

Thomson, J. J., *The Realm of Rights* (Cambridge, Mass: Harvard University Press, 1990).

Trebilcock, M. J. and Howse, R., *The Regulation of International Trade 3rd Edition* (New York: Routledge, 2005).

UNEP, *Basel Convention on the Control of Transboundary Movements of Hazardous Wastes and Their Disposal*, 1998 (available at: http://www.basel.int/Portals/4/Basel%20Convention/docs/text/BaselConventionText-e.pdf).

US Department of State, *Country Reports on Human Rights Practices: Uzbekistan, 2006* (6 March 2007) (available at: http://www.state.gov/j/drl/rls/hrrpt/2006/78848.htm).

Valentini, L., *Justice in a Globalized World: A Normative Framework* (New York: Oxford University Press, 2011).

Wade, R. H., 'What Strategies are Viable for Poor Countries Today? The World Trade Organization and the Shrinking of "Development Space"', *Review of International Political Economy*, Vol. 10, No. 4, 2003, pp. 621–44.

Waldron, J., *Torture, Terror, and Trade-Offs: Philosophy for the White House* (Oxford: Oxford University Press, 2010).

Walton, A., 'The Common Arguments for Fair Trade', *Political Studies*, Vol. 61, No. 3, 2013, pp. 691–706.

Walzer, M., *Just and Unjust Wars* (New York: Basic Books, 1977).

Walzer, M., *Spheres of Justice* (New York: Basic Books, 1983).

Weiss, F. and Wiers, J. (eds.), *Improving WTO Dispute Settlement Procedures* (Folkestone: Cameron May Publishers, 2000).

Wenar, L., 'Property Rights and the Resource Curse', *Philosophy & Public Affairs*, Vol. 36, No. 1, 2008, pp. 2–32.

Wertheimer, A., 'Two questions about Surrogacy and Exploitation', *Philosophy and Public Affairs*, Vol. 21, No. 3, 1992, pp. 211–39.

Williams, B., 'A Critique of Utilitarianism', in J. J. C. Smart and Bernard Williams, *Utilitarianism: For and Against* (Cambridge: Cambridge University Press, 1973).

Williams, J. D., 'Trashing Developing Nations: The Global Hazardous Waste Trade', *Buffalo Law Review*, Vol. 39, 1991, pp. 275–80.

Wilkinson, R. and Pickett, K., *The Spirit Level: Why More Equal Societies Almost Always Do Better* (London: Penguin Books, 2009).

Wilson, E. O., *The Diversity of Life* (London: Penguin Books, 1992).

Wise, S. S. et al., 'Particulate Depleted Uranium Is Cytotoxic and Clastogenic to Human Lung Cells', *Chemical Research in Toxicology*, Vol. 20, No. 5, 2007, pp. 815–20.

Wollner, G., 'Equality and the Significance of Coercion', *Journal Of Social Philosophy*, Vol. 42, No. 4, 2011, pp. 363–81.

Woods, N., 'Trade, Regionalism, and the Threat to Multilateralism', in Woods (ed.) *The Political Economy of Globalization* (London: MacMillan Press, 2000).

WTO, 'Bananas: Discussions Continue on a Long Standing Issue' (available at: http://www.wto.org/english/thewto_e/minist_e/min05_e/brief_e/brief22_e.htm).

Index: *Trade Justice*

Milton Keynes UK
Ingram Content Group UK Ltd.
UKHW020229050923
428074UK00004B/212